The Wildlife Damage Inspection Handbook

A Guide to identifying vertebrate damage to structures, landscapes, and livestock

3rd edition (corrected)

Stephen M. Vantassel

Wildlife Control Consultant
Lincoln, Nebraska
2012(2018)

This edition has been adapted and updated from *The Wildlife Damage Inspection Handbook, Revised Edition,* by Stephen Vantassel with Tom Olander. Springfield, Mass., Wildlife Damage Control, 2001.

"Evaluating Evidence to Identify Ground-Nest Predators in West Texas," by Fidel Hernandez, Dale Rollins, and Ruben Cantu, from *Wildlife Society Bulletin* 1997, 25(4):826–831, copyright © 1997 The Wildlife Society; used by permission.

"Field Key to Guard Hair of Middle Western Furbearers," by Howard J. Stains, from *The Journal of Wildlife Management,* Vol. 22, No. 1 (Jan., 1958), pp. 95-97, copyright © 1958 The Wildlife Society; used by permission.

"Bones of Contention No More," by Richard Wolniewicz, from *Massachusetts Wildlife Magazine* No. 2, 2001, copyright © 2001 Richard Wolniewicz; used by permission.

"Procedures for Evaluating Predation on Livestock and Wildlife," by Dale A. Wade and James E. Bowns, published by Texas Agricultural Extension Service, Texas Agricultural Experiment Station, Texas A&M University System, and U.S. Fish and Wildlife Service, U.S. Department of the Interior, 1982; used by permission.

Design and composition, using Segoe UI types, by Paul Royster.

ISBN 978-0-9668582-5-9

ISBN-10: 0966858255

If you are reading this page without first having read the DISCLAIMER, then STOP and go back and read the **DISCLAIMER**. By continuing to read here you admit to reading the DISCLAIMER and agree to being bound by its terms and disclaimers.

Chapter 1 **Getting Started**

Wildlife damage inspection is a complex area. The information that follows is designed to focus ONLY on the fundamentals. This is not a book about running your business. It is a technical guide to educate readers about the process and interpretation of sign left by vertebrate animals in human-impacted environments. More information could have been added but would have cluttered the text with minutia only useful in extremely marginal situations.

STEP 1. Know the wildlife species in your service area.

Before initiating any inspection, develop a list of the wildlife species in your area. Focus on wildlife implicated in conflicts with humans, as the bulk of your work will include them. After all, who ever heard of a house being infested by salamanders? Note, I did not say to ignore learning about other animals. Many times you will be asked to identify "issues" that stem from species not typically implicated for causing property damage. The key is to begin with the most common species so as to avoid being overwhelmed by the number of species that you may encounter. Wildlife damage management work is too time-consuming to bother with that kind of miscellaneous information early in your business career.

Once your list of wildlife species is compiled, check for potential gaps by consulting your state's fish and wildlife agency. Although the geographic ranges (where a species can be found) can change, generally speaking, state wildlife biologists have at least a basic working knowledge of the resident species in their respective states. The Extension service in your state's land-grant university is another excellent source of information. To locate your local University Extension service, simply contact your state-funded University or visit http://www.extension.org.

Avoid adopting the attitude of, "I will only learn about species that the state allows me to control." Customers expect you to be a professional. If that doesn't motivate you to learn as much about your field as possible, consider the time you may waste trying to capture an animal that you have no authority or need to control, or you need additional permits, because you misidentified damage.

Your knowledge of a wide variety of species will, however, help to exclude them as possible suspects. Furthermore, just because it is prohibited to control the species

does not mean that you cannot use non-lethal control techniques such as exclusion and repellents, as prohibitions against control of protected species usually apply only to lethal control. Nevertheless, always, check federal, state, and local laws before implementing any control measures on a species not specifically listed on your wildlife control permit.

Don't forget domestic animals, like cats, dogs, and livestock. I once received an inquiry from a landowner seeking help to identify a scat similar to that shown in Figure 1. He was perplexed. Though an experienced hunter, he could not determine what left the scat. I, with the help of a colleague, identified the scat as cattle. He responded saying a young calf did wander into his property from a nearby ranch. Case solved.

In the same manner, neither should you ignore learning about exotic (non-native) species. Although the vast majority of your work will involve controlling the damage caused by native species, there will be times when the culprit is not native. On occasion, ferrets, exotic snakes, wolf-hybrids, emus, llamas, and other pet or commercial species get loose or are liberated by their owners. These situations, though rare, are occurring with increasing regularity around the country, particularly in the southern tier states. Nutria, now found in the Pacific Northwest and northeastern states is an excellent example.

Our point is not to be obsessed with learning about unusual or exotic species, but to be mindful that they may be the culprit in certain circumstances. Medicine has an old saying, "When you hear hoof beats, don't

Fig. 1. Cattle droppings can appear in unusual places.

think zebras." However, sometimes in animal damage control, the hoof beats will be zebras.

STEP 2. Assemble your inspection equipment.

The problem with equipment is that it is like money; you never have enough. Resist the urge to buy a lot of neat gadgets. While certain gadgets have their place, most are unnecessary except for the most unique situations. Typically, gadgets are little more than bling used to impress clients because the tools add an air of "professionalism." What follows is a review of the most essential items required for inspection work. Later sections will touch on tools that will be helpful for more difficult cases.

Lights. The most important item (not including personal protection equipment [PPE]) for good inspections is light. Animals have a tendency to live in dark out-of-the-way areas, so proper lighting is essential. We suggest using two different rechargeable lights for inspection work. One light is for spotlighting critical areas. This light needs to emit a minimum of 500,000 beam candles/candela of illumination (not mean spherical candela which measures total light output). You need this much concentrated light in order to inspect dark soffits and eaves on sunny days.

We have used the Nite-Tracker™ spotlight (Fig. 2). It shined like the sun. The weaknesses of the spotlight includes short battery life (lasted only 15 to 20 minutes when fully charged), and cumbersome size. Extend battery-life by using it only when ready to look at something. As for the problem of bulk, you just have to suffer through it. Although the Nite-Tracker™ is no longer available, there are a variety of rechargeable spotlights that fill the need. The following came recommended by CandlePowerForums, a bulletin board site filled with flashlight aficionados whose knowledge of flashlights is impressive. They suggest Sunforce 25 Mill Candlepower HID Rechargeable Spotlight and the Titanium Innovations Mega Illuminator 35W HID Spotlight 3200+ lumens. Check various hunting or hardware stores or websites for models and prices. Additional research can be done by searching YouTube.com.

The second light is for general lighting needs such as in crawl spaces or closets (Fig. 3). Flashlights easily fill this need. Purchase a flashlight that is both durable, convenient, and provides at least 800 lumens (measurement of light output) across a wide enough angle for your needs. Newer flashlights are using advanced LED bulb technology allowing for excellent illumination at a fraction of the power use of traditional bulbs. Flashlights with the capability to widen and narrow the beam can be very helpful.

Flashlights that allow hands-free use (e.g. headlamps) are especially valuable, particularly when crawling in attics. Warning, always carry two sources of light whenever

Fig. 2. Although battery life was short and the unit bulky, the Nite-Tracker spotlight was powerful. (No longer manufactured.)

Fig. 3. Flashlight by Bluestone Lighting.

entering an attic or a crawl space. You never want to be without a back-up light if your primary light fails. I do not suggest buying expensive spotlights and flashlights. Inspectors need to balance quality against risk of loss due to misplacing lights at job sites and dropping lights off of roofs. Don't buy lights that you can't afford to lose. Flashlights are an essential inspection tool, so we strongly suggest that you find those suited to your preferences.

What about ultraviolet (UV) lights? Most pest management professionals (PMP) don't use them or only use them sparingly because as one said, "Mouse droppings are easier to find and identify." Corrigan contends that UV lights still have value because rats often don't leave droppings where they can be found easily.

UV lights need adequate power. Powitz and Balsamo Jr. liked the battery-operated Blak-Ray 26P Series Rechargeable Ultraviolet Lamp manufactured by UVP. Inc. They particularly liked using the UVL model with its "two long-wave 365-nanometer wavelength UV self-filtering tubes." Corrigan recommends UV lamps with 730-80uW/cm^2 at a 6 in (15 cm) viewing distance. Obtain more powerful lamps if you want to observe at distances greater than 8 inches (20 cm).

A less expensive option is the Bluecolt® MicroliteUV™. Its lower power will require you to get a little closer to the inspection area, but its compact size makes it convenient choice.

Since urine from a variety of mammals fluoresces as well as many other materials (e.g. bathroom cleaners), several techniques are helpful to reduce false positives.

1. Rodent urine usually falls in a linear pattern of droplets. Heavily contaminated areas will show lines of urine. Splashes signify a non-rodent source such as a cleaning fluid or human urine.

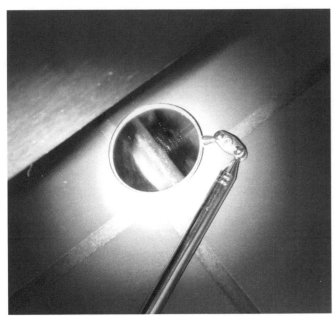

Fig. 4. You can shine light into to mirror to illuminate the area under investigation.

Fig. 5. Canon PowerShot A85 with a flexible tabletop style portable tripod.

2. Wet rodent urine fluoresces bluish-white. Dried urine fluoresces yellow-white and becomes duller over time. Do note that rice fluoresces.
3. Rodent hairs fluoresce bluish-white.
4. False positives also can be reduced by considering context.
5. Alternative tests are required to confirm the presence of mammalian urine. A test strip impregnated with phosphate-buffered urease and Bromthymol Blue is available. These strips could detect as little as 0.005 milliliter of urine. Unfortunately, these strips have limited shelf-life and are difficult if not impossible to obtain.

Corrigan, however, argues that UV lights are not to confirm the presence of rodent urine. Rather, the lights should help inspectors identify active travel areas and openings used by rodents. I would suggest that UV lights are needed only for highly sensitive accounts or when you are having intense difficulty in establishing control over the rodent population.

Mirror. A telescoping reflection mirror would be my next choice for your inspection kit (Fig. 4). Mirrors allow you to see around corners into eaves or above dampers. It is worth its weight in gold and for minimal cost. There are two different kinds of mirrors, glass and steel. Glass mirrors have the advantage of excellent reflective ability and clear reflections. The downside lies in their susceptibility to break. The other option, stainless steel plates, eliminate the breakage problem but the reflection is lacks the clarity of true mirrors. But be warned, metal mirrors can be damaged by rust and scratches. Whichever tool you choose, the trick with these mirrors is to learn how to use your flashlight to illuminate the area

you are looking at with the mirror. Believe it or not, they perform both tasks. They reflect the light of your flashlight on the area, which then allows you to see it by reflection. Tom Olander uses the sun as the light source with his mirror. As he says, "Nothing illuminates better than the sun". These mirrors can be purchased from chimney supply, hardware, auto supply stores, and building inspection companies.

Camera. A digital camera helps document your inspection (good for legal protection and sales pitches) for your client (Fig. 5). Suitable brands include Canon® or Nikon®. Read the camera's user manual. Familiarize yourself with the camera BEFORE using it in the field. Always set your camera to take photos at the highest resolution. Just because the camera says it takes 5 megapixel images doesn't mean the camera is at that maximum setting. Make sure you are getting the largest images possible. I have written articles on taking better photos with your camera in *Wildlife Control Technology* magazine, but you can get the tips for free by visiting http://wildlifecontrolconsultant.com.

I recommend a digital camera with the following features:
1. Three to 5 megapixel images with built in lens cover so you don't have to worry about losing it in the field.
2. 4× optical zoom. A higher number is better. Ignore digital zoom because the images are computer enhanced and become too pixilated for print use.
3. Small enough to fit in your pocket. The key is portability. If it is too big, you won't bring it with you.
4. Macro-lens function. The macro function allows you to take close up shots (less than 6 in [15 cm] away) with good clarity.

5. Ordinary batteries. If your batteries run out you can obtain replacements at the corner store.

6. Neck lanyard to reduce the risk of you dropping it.

The Canon PowerShot A85 or newer models, with portable Weifeng 020 Budget Mini Tripod attached, makes an excellent camera choice (Fig. 5). The portable tripod helps steady the camera for the long-exposure times needed in low-light conditions.

Multi-Tool. If you don't want to carry a lot of stuff around, and who does, I would suggest picking up a Leatherman® Super Tool. It has a variety of tools that are easy to carry. It even has markings on the side in metric and inches so it can be used as a ruler as well.

Binoculars. One must-have item is a good pair of binoculars. Don't go out and buy the best because they will get banged up in your truck in no time. I bought a pair of Bushnell® binoculars at Costco. I think the price was under $50. The binoculars were 8-power with a 22° field of view. I don't know how I worked without them for so long. Just remember a few points. The more powerful the binoculars, the more light that is lost during magnification. If you are looking at a dark area it will become darker through the binoculars. The more expensive brands use higher quality glass so the light loss is less. Choose a pair that fits your needs but remember to ask yourself: "Can I afford to lose it?"

Ladders. Finally, no inspection can be done without a proper ladder(s). The size of your ladder depends on the size of the buildings in your area. When running Wildlife Removal Service Inc., I used a 32-foot ladder, a 24-foot

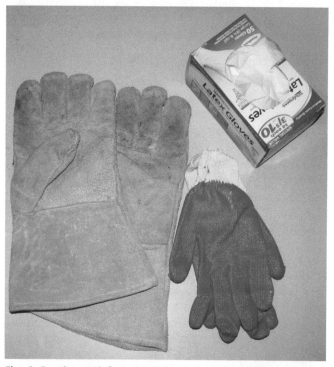

Fig. 6. Starting at left and moving clockwise, welding gauntlet gloves, latex gloves, and rubber-coated cotton gloves.

ladder, and an 8-foot stepladder. I strongly suggest that ladders larger than 32 feet be handled by 2-person teams. Fiberglass ladders provide some protection against electrocution but are substantially heavier than aluminum. Thankfully, electrocutions, from getting too close to power lines, have been rare. But I know that too many WCOs have taken too many chances. When in doubt, contact the power company to place shielding over the electric line if you need to get within 6 ft (1.8 m). Power companies are happy to help.

Whatever sizes you need, purchase quality ladders that are rated for your weight and the weight of items you intend to carry while climbing. Make sure you can handle the ladder because if it is too heavy, I can assure you that you will not want to move it around. When that happens, you are out of business. One caution I want to leave you with is ladder safety. A number of colleagues have fallen off of ladders, some fatally. Take your time and use proper safety precautions when using ladders. Consult the Resources section for additional help in being safe.

Step 3. Assemble your personal protection equipment.

Gloves. Durable leather gloves are the next critical item for inspectors (Fig. 6). Inspections require entry into areas full of ways to injure your hands as well as expose you to potentially dangerous substances. For example, you may find yourself crawling through dust that turns out to be feces. When that happens you will be glad you wore gloves. Several different kinds of leather gloves are on the market. None of them are suitable for every situation. You will need to select gloves to match the kind of work you plan to do.

A 2009 article by Patricia W. Freeman and Cliff A. Lemen entitled, "Puncture-Resistance of Gloves for Handling Bats," published in the *Journal of Wildlife Management* 73:1251-1254 (2009), included a comparison of 18 leather gloves, 2 cotton gloves, and 2 plastic-coated synthetic fiber gloves for their protection against bat bites. Since bats lack the jaw strength to inflict crushing injuries, the authors studied the ability of different kinds of gloves to stop punctures from the fine teeth of bats. They discovered that non-animal skin gloves provided little puncture protection, though the plastic-coated variety provided more than the pure cotton. Of the leather gloves with similar thickness, split leather (cow) provided the best protection against puncture followed by pig, elk, deer, goat, and top grain in descending order. The authors were careful to note that leather thickness varied greatly even with the same glove. They advised people to check out the split-leather gloves for continuity of thickness (and fit) before purchase. Ironically, they also observed that some of the least expensive gloves actually scored the best. What they did note was for balancing protection with high level of hand-dexterity, deer skin gloves would be the best choice.

Here are some general principles. 1. Gloves that protect against puncture and crush injuries tend to use thick material that interferes with dexterity. 2. Gloves should fit your hands properly. 3. Leather gloves will provide better protection against puncture than cloth gloves.

Some gloves only extend to the wrists. Others, like welder's gloves, extend up the forearm. We have used both. One of the authors generally used welder's gloves when handling traps, animals and crawling in attics and underneath porches because of their padding and the author's large hands. It is a personal choice. Use whatever makes you feel more comfortable but wear something, especially when you are crawling around attics and crawl spaces.

Respirators. We cannot emphasize enough the importance of using respirators. You need to protect yourself from the risks of becoming infected with Hantavirus or *Baylisascaris procyonis* among other diseases, not to mention the insulation dust and other contaminants found in confined spaces. Given the importance of respirators, we strongly encourage readers to expand their understanding of respirators beyond the basic information provided here. You only have 1 set of lungs, so take the time to learn how to protect them.

Air-purifying respirators filter either particulates or fumes and gases. Unless you are performing inspections in industrial settings, fume-gas filtration will be needed only in rare occasions. Respirators are given an APN (assigned protection number) to guide users on the relative protection provided by the respirator. "The APN is the ratio of the ambient concentration of a given contaminant to that inside a respirator face piece"(http://dels-old.nas.edu/ilar_n/ilarjournal/44_1/v4401SARGENT.pdf). Filters also come in different ratings: 95 (95%), 99 (99%), and 100 (99.97%). I would not buy anything lower than 100.

What other infectious agents are health risks for workers who disturb accumulations of bat droppings or bird manure? In addition to *H. capsulatum*, inhalation exposure to *Cryptococcus neoformans* may also be a health risk for workers in environments containing accumulations of bat droppings or bird manure. Inhalation exposures to *Chlamydia psittaci* have occurred occasionally in environments containing the manure of certain birds, and exposure to the rabies virus is possible for workers in bat caves and performing necropsies on rabid animals.

Don't waste your time with white paper face-masks. You need NIOSH-certified masks (Fig. 7). Masks come in 2 basic forms, passive and active. Passive masks require your lung power to move the air through the filter. Consult with your physician about whether there is any medical reason that would deem you medically unfit to wear a passive respirator. People with poor lung function

Fig. 7. Author wearing a half-mask, passive respirator.

should be especially careful, as passive respirators will add further strain on your breathing, especially as the filter becomes clogged.

If you are medically cleared, you should get fit-tested. The procedure for undergoing fit-testing can be found at http://osha.gov. Once fit-tested, follow the manufacturer's instructions for wearing the mask to the letter. Get in the habit of checking the fit of the mask with the positive and negative pressure checks as described in the product manufacturer's literature. Improper fit is a leading cause of decreased protection. Protecting yourself from dusts, insulation fibers, and potential airborne diseases must be your highest priority. Even though they are uncomfortable to wear in the summer heat, don't stop wearing it. If you aren't healthy, you can't work.

Active respirators have blowers to push air through the filter, which allows normal breathing. They are more expensive and more cumbersome due to the increased equipment needed to power them. However, they provide significantly more protection over the passive filters, partly because the positive air pressure prevents unfiltered air from entering around the face-mask connection.

Self-contained breathing apparatus, where you are breathing air from a scuba tank rather than relying on filtering air from the contaminated area in which you are working, provides the highest level of protection.

For more information on respirators and their proper use as well as guidelines for choosing the right respirator for the conditions you will encounter, visit the Centers for Disease Control and search for the NIOSH (National Institute of Occupational Safety and Health) NPPTL National Personal Protection Testing Laboratory section. You can learn more about proper use of respirators by contacting your state's pest control licensing board or by searching land-grant university extension publications. They can tell you about trainings, such as respirator fit-tests that will show you on proper respirator care and use. One further note, if the filters become wet, replace them. Some WCOs are now using full-face respirators. Their reasoning lies in the greater safety in terms of eye protection and better seal around the mask, as the mouth-nose mask frequently is unable to keep a good seal. No matter what design you choose, make sure you get proper instructions and be clean shaven.

Optional but useful

Fiber Optic Scopes. These tools can be very useful for investigating behind obstructions, under decks, in walls, and voids. Drilling a small hole (usually >1 in (2.5 cm)) is easier to repair than a large hole. They tend to be expensive, but can pay for themselves rather quickly if your business volume is high enough. Look for scopes that
1. are bright enough to illuminate the crevice,
2. have good optics,
3. have attachments that allow you to record your findings, and
4. have a view screen rather than an eye-piece.

The late Kirk LaPierre at the last wildlife academy in 2007 (Indiana), provided a list of suggested inspection equipment.
1. Reciprocating saw. He suggested it be electric rather than battery, however, battery-powered would be more convenient. Just be sure to carry an extra battery.
2. Highly portable flashlight, such as an LED flashlight that can be carried on a lanyard,
3. Ladder levelers,
4. Parabolic microphone for listening for animals, and
5. Wireless baby camera. These can be attached to poles and used to investigate hard to reach areas. Some even come with infrared lights to allow for night vision.

Other Tools. Other tools you might want to include would be a good pair of tweezers, a magnifying glass, and a measuring tape. Tweezers are useful for picking up feces or breaking feces apart to see what they contain. However, be careful when breaking up fecal material. Diseases can be contracted by inhaling the aerosolized material, so don't place your face too close to the feces when you are breaking them up and be sure to consider prevailing wind. Better yet, wear your NIOSH filter mask!! A magnifying glass is used to enlarge an object you want to observe. Get as strong a magnifying glass

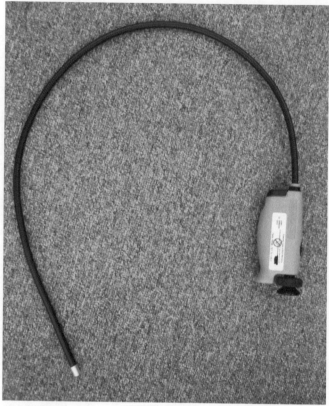

Fig. 8. Fiber optic scopes can be quite useful for inspecting voids. Be sure to test a scope before purchasing.

as you can without breaking your budget. Eight-times strength is a minimum. The measuring tape will help you measure the size of various holes.

Resources

Thanks to Kirk LaPierre (d. 2010) for his input and Tim L. Hiller, a Wildlife Research Scientist from Salem, OR for his review.

Bryant, R. H. (Doc). http://www.theledlight.com/lumens.html for his explanation on lumens, candlepower, etc.

Corrigan, B. 2000. Update in Using Black Lights. *Pest Control Technology,* (Jan): 79-81.

Corrigan, B. 2000. Update in Using Black Lights, Part II. *Pest Control Technology,* (Aug): 90.

Houska, M. 2011. Caught on Camera. *NebraskaLand Magazine,* (Aug-Sept): 28-31.

http://www.pinnacleflashlights.com/blog/2009/04/30/lumens-vs-candlepower-sorting-through-advertising-gimmicks/ accessed June 19, 2010.

National Wildlife Control Operators Association Trade association offers training in safety designed for the issues that regularly confront nuisance wildlife control operators in the field.

Occupational Safety and Health Administration. OSHA.gov. This government site contains a wealth of work-safety information.

Powitz, R. W. and J. J. Balsamo, Jr. 1998. A Practical Ultraviolet Inspection Light for the Detection of Rodent Urine Contamination: The Blak-Ray UVL-26P. *Journal of Environmental Health,* vol. 60. np.

Chapter 2 **Risks: Physical, Biological, & Legal**

As hinted about in Chapter 1, all inspectors face the risk of physical injury and disease. To review: **physical risks** include falls, cuts, scrapes, bites, scratches, bumping head, and vehicle accidents, while **biological risks** include histoplasmosis, rabies, *Baylisascaris procyonis*, other zoonotic diseases, and even includes infections that can be contracted from interacting with the public and customers. But WCOs also face legal risks. All combined form what I call the "Risk Triad" (Fig. 1).

Evaluating Risk

The level of risk one is exposed to is influenced by several factors including: frequency of exposure, duration of exposure, and severity of consequences. Safety is determined by personal protection equipment and your behavior.

Physical Safety

In this section, I want to touch on issues that can arise during the inspection process that you must keep in mind to protect yourself from injury and death.

Roofs, Batten-Style. Mike Page in Florida cautions WCOs about the risks of walking on slate or clay tile roofs. He explains that some of these roofs employ battens rather than a true sub-roof. Batten-style roofs have gaps so if you step on the wrong spot, your foot will go through the tile and into the attic. Look at the roof from the attic before deciding to walk on the roof.

Drop Offs. I have experienced this threat personally. You are walking around a building paying close attention to the roof and eaves. The problem is you aren't paying attention to where you are walking. I almost stepped off an embankment like this one (Fig. 2).

Criminal Assault. Charles Holt of Ohio mentions the risk of being a victim of criminal assault. He is quite correct to note that WCOs drive to addresses almost without question. While impossible to protect yourself from an ambush attack (as demonstrated by the September 2010 murder of Chris Taylor who was delivering pizza in Omaha, NE), it would be prudent to be careful. If you feel uncomfortable around a client, it could be your instincts are telling you something. Holt suggests that you make sure someone always knows where you are going. In addition, remember that your equipment, such as flashlight or multi-purpose tool could be used to save your life.

Biological Risks

Animal Attacks. One of the risks in inspecting areas for wildlife is that you may in fact directly encounter them. While most animals avoid humans by either fleeing or hiding, sometimes animals attack. Don't forget to consider the threat posed by dogs.

Fig. 1. The risk triad.

Fig. 2. Stepping backwards to view the entire roof, could result in a very bad fall off this embankment.

Fig. 3. Wasp investigating crack by this doorbell.

Fig. 4. The saying goes, "If leaves be 3, let it be." Poison ivy can occur in plant, shrub, and vine forms.

Fig. 6. Poison sumac. Photo courtesy of www.poison-ivy.org.

Fig. 5. Poison oak (red) with oak (green). Photo courtesy of www.poison-ivy.org.

Insects, for example, may attack. Bees such as hornets and wasps are probably the most noticed examples. Hornets and wasps tend to build nests on structures in areas with protection from rain (Fig. 2). Hornets can also build nests in the ground.

Brown recluse spiders and their tendency to hide in attics and crawl spaces make them a potential threat as well.

Plants. Watch out for poison ivy (Fig. 4), oak (Fig. 5) and sumac (Fig. 6). The primary symptom is a rash caused by the skin reacting to the oil in the plant. If exposed, wash exposed skin with soap and water immediately being careful not to spread the oils to other parts of the body. Different people have different reactions and that sensitivity to the oil can change as you age.

Diseases. Infectious diseases fall into various classes: viral, rickettsial, bacterial, protozoal, fungal, helminth, and prion. I will deal only with the major diseases confronting WCOs.

Viral Diseases

Rabies

Infectious agent. Rabies is a viral disease that infects the central nervous systems of mammals and humans.

Hosts. Any mammal can contract the disease. Species most commonly associated with rabies include bats, raccoons, skunks, coyotes, and foxes.

Transmission. Bites and contact with infected saliva on open wounds are the most common modes of transmission. Inhalation also is possible, such as bat-inhabited caves. . The rabies virus can remain infectious in a carcass until decomposition is well advanced.

Symptoms. The initial symptoms of rabies mimic other viral infections, including fever, headache, and malaise. Site of the bite may itch. Neurological disorders appear as disease progresses.

Treatment. Preventative vaccine or post exposure shots. Vaccine recipients may still require additional shots after a bite. Once clinical symptoms of rabies have appeared, death is likely. Therefore, it is important to receive medical diagnosis and treatments quickly if exposure was possible.

Prevention. Avoid being bitten or exposure to infected brain or nervous system tissues.

Rickettsial Diseases

Rocky Mountain Spotted Fever
Infectious agent. *Rickettsia rickettsii*
Reservoir. Rodents.
Transmission. A tick bite, including the American dog tick (*Dermacentor variabilis*), Rocky Mountain wood tick (*Dermacentor andersoni*), and brown dog tick (*Rhipicephalus sanguineus*).
Symptoms. Fever, headache, abdominal pain, vomiting, and muscle pain. A rash also may develop, but is often absent for the first few days, and in some patients, never develops.
Treatment. Antibiotics
Prevention. Avoid tick habitat, wear light clothes, use tick repellents, tuck pants into socks, inspect for ticks.

Bacterial Diseases

Lyme Disease
Infectious agent. A spirochete bacterium called *Borrelia burgdorferi*.
Reservoir. Many organisms but the white-footed mouse (*Peromyscus leucopus*) is a key reservoir.
Transmission. Deer tick bites, particularly those at the nymph stage.
Symptoms. Bull's-eye-shaped rashes, ~5 in (12.7 cm) in diameter occur in most infections (Fig. 7). Flu-like symptoms common in early stages of disease.
Treatment. Antibiotics are effective provided they are administered soon enough.
Prevention. Avoid tick habitat, wear light clothes, use tick repellents, tuck pants into socks, inspect for ticks.
Note: There is a new disease called STARI (Southern Tick Associated Rash Illness). STARI presents symptoms similar to those of Lyme disease but it is not caused by the Lyme disease bacterium. The lone star tick (*Amblyomma americanum*) is a vector for STARI and can be found as far north as Maine and west as Texas and Nebraska.

Plague
Infectious agent. *Yersinia pestis*.
Host. Ground squirrels and the fleas that reside on them.
Transmission. Fleas. They will leave their dead host and search for new hosts.
Symptoms. High fever 103 to 106°F (39 to 41°C), headache, nausea, changes in heart rate and altered consciousness.
Treatment. Antibiotics.
Prevention. Treat rodent burrows with insecticide. Wear gloves and other protective equipment when handling ground squirrels.

Salmonelliosis
Infectious agent. Bacterium called *Salmonella*
Source. Contaminated surfaces, food, water.
Transmission. Ingestion
Symptoms. Most persons infected with *Salmonella* develop diarrhea, fever, and abdominal cramps 12 to 72 hours after infection.
Treatment. Most people recover on their own.
Prevention. Keep hands away from mouth and wash hands thoroughly before eating. Cook foods thoroughly.

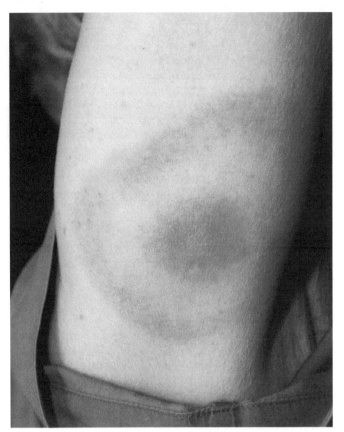

Fig. 7. Bull's-eye rash that occurs with 80% of Lyme disease infections. Photo by James Gathany of the CDC.

Fig. 8. Lone star tick in questing position looking for a host. Photo by James Gathany of the CDC.

Chlamydia psittaci

Infectious agent. Bacterium *C. psittaci.*

Host. While *C. psittaci* has been isolated from approximately 130 avian species, most human infections result from inhalation of aerosolized urine, respiratory secretions, or dried droppings of infected psittacine (parrot-type) birds, such as cockatiels, parakeets, parrots, and macaws; avian chlamydiosis is diagnosed less frequently in canaries and finches. Among caged, nonpsittacine birds, infection with *C. psittaci* occurs most frequently in pigeons, doves, mynah birds. Psittacosis in humans occasionally has been associated with exposures to infected pigeons, turkeys, chickens, ducks, pheasants, and geese, or their droppings.

Transmission. Inhalation of disturbed contaminated birds, and their droppings. Bird bites and even brief passing contact can result in infections.

Symptoms. Symptoms usually appear within 5 to 19 days. The severity of disease experienced by an infected person can range from asymptomatic to severe systemic disease with pneumonia; death occurs in less than 1% of properly treated patients.

Treatment. Antibiotics.

Prevention. Avoid bird droppings or wear protective equipment including protective clothing, gloves, eyewear, and a respirator (N95 or higher rating). Mist detergent water over carcasses and fecal contaminated areas to reduce aerosolization of bacteria.

Protozoal Diseases

Baylisascaris procyonis

Infectious agent. Roundworm called *Baylisascaris procyonis.*

Reservoir. Raccoons are the definitive reservoir.

Transmission. Worm eggs are shed in the feces. Infection occurs through ingestion of incubated eggs.

Symptoms. Infection in eyes—sensitivity to light, inflammation of the eye, and blindness. Visceral symptoms depend on the organ(s) affected.

Treatment. Laser treatment to kill worms in eyes. Antithelminthics.

Prevention. Avoid exposure to raccoon feces.

Fungal Diseases

Cryptococcosis

Infectious agent. Fungal organism called *C. neoformans*

Source. Grows in accumulated and dry droppings of chickens, sparrows, starlings, and other birds, and bat droppings.

Transmission. Believed to be inhalation of spores. Incidence of infection has increased due to the rise of immune-compromised people (e.g. AIDS patients.)

Symptoms. Pneumonia-like illness, with shortness of breath, coughing and fever. Skin lesions may also occur. Another common form of cryptococcosis is central nervous system infection, such as meningoencephalitis. Symptoms may include fever, headache, or a change in mental status.

Treatment. Various medications are available.

Prevention. Avoid areas contaminated with bird droppings.

Histoplasmosis

Infectious agent. *Histoplasma capsulatum*

Host. Bird and bat droppings. Typically bird droppings must have accumulated over 2 to 3 years. Assume bat droppings contain the fungus.

Transmission. Inhalation of spores.

Symptoms. Flu-like symptoms and dry cough typically develop in 10 days after exposure.

Treatment. Mild infections usually resolve themselves. Severe infections can lead to lung damage (Fig. 9). The fungus can disseminate into other bodily organs. Anti-fungal treatments and antibiotics for secondary infections.

Prevention. Avoiding areas contaminated by bird or bat droppings unless wearing protective equipment. Full-face mask is recommended.

Common Sense Behavior. Diseases are contracted through various means. The ones below are the most important and common facing WCOs. WCOs can contract diseases through:

- Inhalation (breathing),
- Injection (bites, including insect bites),
- Ingestion (eating or drinking), and
- Absorption (scratches in skin, contact with mucosa).

Given these 4 routes for infection, it is easy to consider how to protect yourself by employing barriers and sanitary practices to increase the difficulty for infectious material to access you via these routes. In short, wear your protective clothing (see Chapter 1).

The second step is personal hygiene. Washing your hands, said one veterinarian, will protect you from many risks. Since handwashing is difficult in the field, carry and use waterless hand sanitizers. They should have at least 60% alcohol to be effective. Sanitizers with cloth may be even more effective as the scrubbing action will help to remove organic material that holds germs.

Changing your clothes and taking a shower before hugging your children can reduce the risk of exposing your family to zoonotics. Inspect yourself for ticks and any bites.

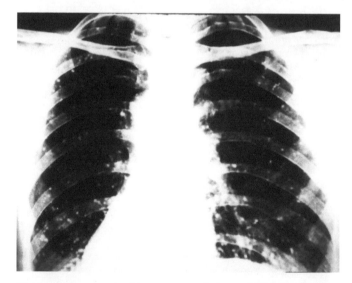

Fig. 9. White spots in this x-ray reveal signs of histoplasmosis infection. Photo by Dr. Lucille K. Georg of the CDC.

Fig. 10. A first-aid kit plays an important role in keeping you healthy.

U.S. Department of Agriculture
Animal and Plant Health Inspection Service
Medical Alert Card

This employee may be working cooperatively or in a volunteer status for other agencies, as a contractor in concert with USDA APHIS surveillance programs, or USDA APHIS emergency programs. The medical information provided on the reverse of this card is to aid in their diagnosis and treatment of potential illness incurred while in the performance of those assignments. The employee bearing this card must provide appropriate identification and this card to aid in diagnosis and treatment.

The bearer of this card is advised to make available appropriate identification and status of coverage for medical/workers' compensation insurance at the time of seeking aid.

APHIS FORM 260a (DEC 2007)   **See Reverse Side**

ATTENTION MEDICAL PERSONNEL

This employee is likely to be exposed to pesticides and certain zoonotic diseases which are not routinely considered in the differential diagnosis of febrile illnesses. APHIS requests that you consider pesticide poisoning and the following diseases in case of serious illness in this individual:

Highly Pathogenic Avian Influenza, Anthrax, Monkeypox, Q Fever, Hantavirus, Plague, Rocky Mountain Spotted Fever, Leptospirosis, Tularemia, Lyme Disease, Brucellosis, Typhus, Arbovirus Encephalitis (Eastern, Western, St. Louis, California), **Giardiasis, Histoplasmosis, Psittacosis, Spirochaetal Relapsing Fever, Bovine Tuberculosis, and West Nile Virus.**

APHIS FORM 260a (Reverse)

Fig. 11. This medical alert card is carried by USDA-Wildlife Services personnel.

Carry a first-aid kit (Fig. 10) so you can quickly treat minor cuts and scrapes with appropriate antiseptic ointments and cover them with a bandage. Remember, your skin is your first line of defense against a number of infectious agents.

Finally, monitor your own health. Most zoonotic infections manifest themselves through fever and body aches within 2 to 3 weeks of exposure. Just because you think it is human flu doesn't mean it isn't something else. Tell your doctor, each and every time you meet, that you work with wildlife. I would recommend carrying a card (Fig. 11) to remind you and medical personnel of the common diseases you can encounter. If you don't, your physician might not think of zoonotic infections.

Be prudent, not paranoid. Remember that many people have hunted and trapped animals for centuries with no ill effects. Even if mistakes are made, the odds of an infection occurring are remote. Professionals however, strive to reduce risks whenever possible.

Legal Risks

Legal risks are the last element of the risk triangle that must be accounted for. Whenever fee-based services are provided, one enters into contractual relations with a client. Contracts imply responsibility and with responsibility comes the legal (and moral) obligation to per-

form work according to accepted standards. Of course, this begs the question, "What is the accepted standard for wildlife damage inspection?" Unfortunately, I am not aware of any such standard at the time of this writing. I expect there will be a standard soon as the industry matures and lawyers discover us as a new revenue opportunity. While it is fun to beat up on lawyers, the fact is many lawsuits frequently occur because of shoddy workmanship. The key to preventing lawsuits is always to maintain the highest ethical standards both in your business practices and in the quality of your service.

If a mature woman can sue McDonalds over a spilled cup of hot coffee and win, how much more vulnerable are you for missing something important in your inspection?

To reduce your liability, consider the following strategies.

First, utilize legal protections for businesses. Incorporate or create a limited liability corporation for your business. Consult your attorney or accountant on which type best meets your needs.

Second, obtain liability insurance. Consult with your insurance agency to ensure you have the right protection. Don't forget your vehicle needs to be included too.

Third, do quality work. This means you must not only do a quality job (no cutting corners), but you must document your activities as well. As they say in the medical field, "If it isn't written down, it didn't happen."

Fourth, report your findings to your client. Failure to inform your client of potential risks (e.g. fecal deposits, lint clogged dryer vents [Fig. 12]) may lead to legal liability on your part. Documentation also protects you.

Remember these key points for documentation:

- Take photos of key areas on the property before and during your inspection. If you are performing control or mitigation, be sure to take photos following your activities.
- Take detailed notes.
- Carry government-created fact sheets on rabies, raccoon roundworm, and others that can be left with clients.
- Direct clients to other sources of information by noting them on your paperwork.

References

I would like to acknowledge the following for information contained in this chapter, namely Chris Anchor, Charles Holt, Mike Page, A All Animal Control, and CDC.gov. Thanks to Tim Hiller, a Wildlife Research Scientist, from Salem, OR for his careful review.

CDC. 1998. Compendium of Measures To Control Chlamydia psittaci Infection Among Humans (Psittacosis) and Pet Birds (Avian Chlamydiosis), 1998. *Morbidity and Mortality Weekly Report,* 47:No.RR-10(July 10):1-19.

Davidson, W. R. editor. 2006. *Field Manual of Wildlife Diseases in the Southeastern United States.* Third edition. Athens, GA: Southeastern Cooperative Wildlife Disease Cooperative.

Liebeck v. McDonald's Restaurants, P.T.S., Inc., No. D-202 CV-93-02419, 1995 WL 360309 (Bernalillo County, N.M. Dist. Ct. August 18, 1994), docket entry from nmcourts.com accessed on December 16, 2011 from Wikipedia.

Metzger, M. 2001. Public Health: Wild Rodents + Fleas=Risky Business. *Pest Control Magazine,* (Feb):28-31.

Mora, Jacki. 2011. http://www.kmtv.com/news/local/135252693.html. (Dec 8) visited January 5, 2012.

National Association of State Public Health Veterinarians. 2010. Compendium of Measures to Control *Chlamydophila psittaci* Infection Among Humans (Psittacosis) and Pet Birds (Avian Chlamydiosis), 2010. National Association of State Public Health Veterinarians. Pp.1-17.

Fig. 12. Fires caused by igniting dryer lint is a major source of home fires in the U.S.

Chapter 3 **Phone Inspections**

When your customer calls, it is necessary for you to gather information that will assist you in being prepared to respond to their particular situation. Don't talk with customers while driving (Fig. 1).

Like a reporter, you need to get as accurate a perspective on the story as possible. Keep the client focused on the present. I have found that customers like to begin talking about their first encounter with wildlife 5 years ago. Coach the client to talk only about the present situation, preferably within the last 30 days. Remember, your client often will be in distress. Don't be surprised if the client overstates the problem. A small problem to you will be a huge problem in the mind of your client. Never forget, reality is whatever you perceive it to be, so don't get into arguments with your clients. Let them vent a little. Nevertheless, keep your client focused, especially on events during the past 30 days.

The first rule in animal damage inspections, as mentioned earlier, is to know what species exist in your part of the country. Obviously, an animal that doesn't live in your region couldn't cause the damage.

Information Needed from Clients

The client should provide you with the following information:

I. General Information

The general location of the problem: structural (such as an attic, basement) or non-structural (such as a garden, lawn, trees, livestock, and pets).

II. Questions for Structural Problems

When did the client first notice the problem and is the problem noted on a consistent basis, i.e., do they hear noises regularly? If so when? At night or during the day?

What kind of noises are being heard? Cracking, scratching, grinding, growling, thumping, screeching, etc.?

What species of animals have they seen on their property? Have their neighbors noticed anything?

Do they have any pets or bird feeders?

Have they seen anything unusual lately, such as their dog's food being scattered about or missing, items missing or damaged?

Have they noticed any signs, such as tracks, scat, middens, damage from chewing, etc.? Have they saved or photographed any of this evidence?

Has there been any construction or landscape changes in their area during the past several months? (e.g. new construction, tree removals, sewer work etc.)?

How have they responded to the problem so far? This question is critical because it could help you rule out

Fig. 1. The author doing something stupid; driving while on the phone.

certain species and also warn you about the possibility of an educated animal.

III. Questions for Non-Structural Damage

When did the client first notice the problem and is the problem noted on a consistent basis, i.e., trash night? At night or during the day?

What plants or animals have been affected? Have they noticed any evidence, such as tracks, scat, middens, damage from chewing, etc.? Have they saved or photographed any of the evidence?

What species of animals have they seen on their property? Have their neighbors noticed anything?

Has there been any construction or landscape changes in their area during the past several months? (e.g. new construction, tree removals, sewer work etc.)?

How have they responded to the problem so far? This question is critical because it could help you rule out certain species and also warn you about the possibility of an educated animal.

With answers to these questions in hand, you are now ready to make an appointment and inspect the property.

When you make your inspection appointments avoid scheduling them when it is raining or snowing. This optimizes your inspection because you will have improved visibility. Also avoid inspections when there are strong contrasting shadows. A high sun casts heavy shadows making it difficult to evaluate dark spaces. Inspecting in daylight hours will not only help you see the outside of the house but the light will help illuminate holes in the attic when inspecting there. Before ending the call, ask the client to remove any barriers to crawl spaces and attic hatchways before you arrive. Having this done before your arrival will assist you in making the best of your time inspecting.

Finally, handling clients on the phone requires finesse. You cannot diagnose a problem over the phone every time, nor should you provide free advice, unless of course you recognize that the problem is non-animal related or for similar reasons. Also, there may be an occasional client that, based on the initial phone conversation, will not be one that you should work with. Clients with aggressive personalities or with extreme concerns about costs may best be avoided.

Caution

Some phone calls require immediate action in order to protect the client from tragic consequences. We cannot provide a comprehensive list of examples as there are too many to consider. However, some situations merit special attention.

An example of one situation is when the client is calling about a bat in the living space of the home then you must inform the client about the risk for rabies exposure. Assume that a bat exposure has occurred if any of the following scenarios has happened:

- client awakened to find a bat flying in the room, or
- client found a bat in a room with an unattended child (8 years old or less) whether sleeping or not, or
- client found a bat in a room with someone who was mentally unable to assess whether he or she was bitten by a bat.

If any one of these conditions has occurred or if your client suspects that a bat exposure has taken place (pets included), you must convince the client to not allow the bat to leave the building. The bat must be captured, without damaging its head, and then tested for rabies. This means no tennis rackets to stun it ! Details on cap-

ture techniques can be obtained at http://icwdm.org. Remember, rabies is carried in the saliva and nerve tissues of its victim. If your pet has bitten the bat or has been bitten you won't know where the saliva of that bat might be on your client's pet. If your client has handled the pet without proper protection, I would suggest that you refer your client to a qualified infectious disease specialist. While the likelihood of rabies transfer is low, legal prudence would suggest that you have someone else take responsibility. Taking extra precautions now will save you a world of regret later.

Another situation that should cause you to immediately warn your client is airborne risks. Say a client called asking about droppings they found while tearing down a wall or other structure. Since most people fail to wear proper personal protection during home remodeling projects, you need to warn your client that he or she (or others involved) may have been exposed to the fungal spores of histoplasmosis or other airborne infectious agents. This doesn't even delve into the issues that insulation or other materials may have regarding health risks.

There are many more similar situations. My point is that you need to warn your clients regardless if you get the job. Be sure to document your conversation.

Problem of Exotics

I want to mention again, the problem of exotic animals. Regrettably, people are obtaining and releasing exotic pets (like snakes, lizards etc.) and these can cause conflicts, so you must always keep them in the back of your mind. This advice is particularly important for those of you residing in warmer climates because warmer temperatures increase the chances that exotics could survive the winter. One exotic animal you should start thinking about is the ferret. As they become more popular as pets, we will start seeing more escapees and owners who eventually abandon them. You will have to start learning more about this animal (and others) and keep it in mind when inspecting property damage.

Resources

Thanks to Tim L. Hiller for his editorial comments.

Corrigan, B. 2000. Home Ranges are Site Specific. *Pest Control Technology* (Oct):141.

Hiller, T. L. Wildlife Research Scientist. Salem, OR.

Chapter 4 **On-Site Inspections**

Inspections can be a frustrating exercise. Crawling around attics, closets, and roofs is not only dirty but can be dangerous as well. Yet, these activities must be done in order to resolve a wildlife conflict properly and efficiently. This chapter will help guide you through the inspection process. It will help systematize your inspections so that you can reduce the variables and narrow the possible causes of the problem. Don't worry if you can't remember all the steps listed. I have included two reproducible inspection sheets (one for structures, and one for landscapes) at the end of the chapter that you can use on jobs.

Readers should understand that this chapter is a survey. Additional inspection tips can be gained from the species chapters. Remember, inspection is a lifelong experience in learning. Failure to allow the animals to teach you will result in many inspection mistakes.

STEP 1: Consider the Habitat. Before entering the driveway, observe the neighborhood and get a good broad look at the house you will be inspecting (Fig. 1). Get a feel for the neighborhood buildings and habitat available there. Are the buildings old or new? Are they well maintained? Do you see poor landscaping, poor trash collection, wooded lots? Think about the three resources all animals need to cause damage to human interests:

1. **Food/Water**—streams, sprinklers, standing water, bird feeders, trash cans, fruit trees etc. Printing a photo of your service area using Google Earth can help you locate habitat reservoirs for wildlife which can be helpful particularly in handling transient damage.
2. **Shelter**—buildings, woodpiles, debris piles, wooded areas,
3. **Access**—trees (within 6 ft [1.8 m] of roofline), wires, vines, downspouts, etc.

For our purposes, access is the most critical as most urban areas have plenty of food/water and shelter available already for a wide variety of wildlife. When you drive up to the house try to take in a big picture view of the building (Fig. 1).

A quick overview frequently can provide you with some insight about how well the structure was maintained. Gutters are amongst my favorite places to look (Fig. 2). Plugged gutters lead to water backups and water leads to softened wood. Squirrels like to sit on the gutter and chew through the fascia board that has been softened by water.

STEP 2: Deal with the Owner. Upon arrival, introduce yourself to the owner. Avoid entering the house immediately upon arrival. Confirm information with owner regarding the complaint(s) at the door. I suggest

Fig. 1. Evaluate the site from a distance.

starting your inspection from the outside as it is easier to find entry-points and damage sign from the outside of the house than on the inside. Potential holes are more exposed to the outside and the hole (which will be dark) will often be in contrasting color to the house. I rarely used a ladder during my inspections. About 90% of the time, all I needed to see could be observed from the ground. (Another 2 to 3% will be discovered from the attic).

Some WCOs may not like customers walking with them. However, if clients are not paranoid, I like to have them accompany me so that I can point out problems that must be addressed. Listen for clues in what your client tells you. Rarely do you get the full story the first time. Feel free to ask the same question stated a different way. Ask open ended questions sprinkled with yes/no questions. Phrase your questions in such a way that doesn't try to lead the client.

Fig. 2. A quick look at the gutters can reveal how well the building was maintained.

Figs.3 a,b. Note how additional light on the right image shows the gap in the ridge vent that was exploited by bats.

Step 3. Inspect systematically.

You will need to develop a system for inspection. I suggest starting high and working down. Whatever you decide, follow the same procedure as your circle the structure. Don't deviate from it. Make it second nature.

Take out your 500,000 or greater, candlepower spotlight to illuminate dark areas. You need spotlights to inspect dark holes around vents, eaves, dormers, and crawlspaces. Spots that remain dark after illumination are holes (Figs. 3a,b).

Roof

Different roofs have different issues.

Asphalt shingled roofs (a.k.a. composition roofs) are the easiest to inspect because the shingles should lay flat making any holes readily apparent. Sometimes squirrels damage composition roofs removing seeds trapped in the shingles. Look for jagged lines randomly distributed along the edges of the tile.

Wood roofs are troublesome due to their tendency to warp, crack, and grow slippery moss. Squirrels may gnaw on some of the shingles. Look for scratch marks and jagged edges randomly distributed.

Tile roofs are the most troublesome. They are not only more difficult to climb but also frequently lack clay closures at the ends to prevent animal entry (Fig. 4).

All Roofs.

Check for continuity, uniformity, and integrity. Pay attention to parts of the roof that look different, particularly sections proximal to tree branches and wires that are highways for wildlife. Look for feces. Raccoons often will defecate before entering the house (Fig. 5).

Snow fall provides an excellent opportunity to look for wildlife movement (Fig. 6).

Pay special attention at the corners, gables (Fig. 7a), eaves, ridge vents (Fig. 7b), and any place where 2 boards or surfaces meet.

Over the years, moisture and heat cause the boards to expand and contract. Ultimately a gap forms between them. These are the places where squirrels like to enter. Don't be surprised if these problems occur at the portion of the house most exposed to sunlight (which is typically the southern exposure) as these locations will sustain the greatest temperature differences.

The fascia board (Fig. 8) behind the gutters is another area you want to investigate.

You can often see behind the gutter by standing directly beneath the gutter and looking for anything unusual between the gutter and the fascia board. Don't neglect to look at the ground as insulation and woodchips may be present, providing further clues of damage activity.

Fig. 4 The tile near the gutter are open to animal entry.

Fig. 5. Raccoon droppings in foreground. Plastic bag over mushroom vent showed whether the vent was continuing to be used.

Fig. 6. Note the squirrel trail in the snow.

Fig. 7a. Demonstration gable with arrow pointing to where animals typically enter.

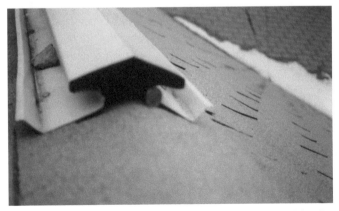

Fig. 7b. End of a ridge vent. Note the head of the nail in the lower right of the vent.

Vents. Vents require close inspection because they can look fine from a distance. Look for louvers that are bent or askew. Check the integrity of the mosquito netting or other screening (Fig. 8b) if possible. If you can't inspect the screen, you will need to do so from the inside.

Walls and Foundations

As you look at the eaves, don't neglect the lower sections of the house. Animals, like red squirrels, chipmunks and mice, can enter at ground level. Pipes (Fig. 9), dryer vents, broken windows, and cracked foundations can permit small creatures into the house.

Look carefully for gaps or any holes ¼ inch or larger. On brick houses, don't forget to look at the weep vents (Fig. 9b).

Gaps in structures frequently occur where 2 different materials meet (e.g. brick and metal (Fig. 10a), concrete and metal (Fig. 10b). Inspect for signs of wear around these holes which would signify use.

Fig. 8a. Note the gap on the fascia.

Fig. 8b. Louvers are intact but a close look shows damaged screen.

Fig. 9a. Note the gap around the electrical line on the right.

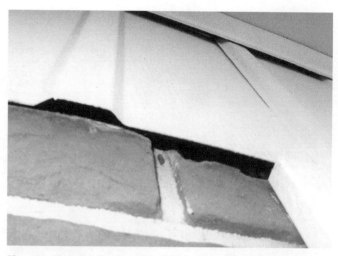

Fig. 10a. The gap between the brick and siding is large enough to permit the entry of mice.

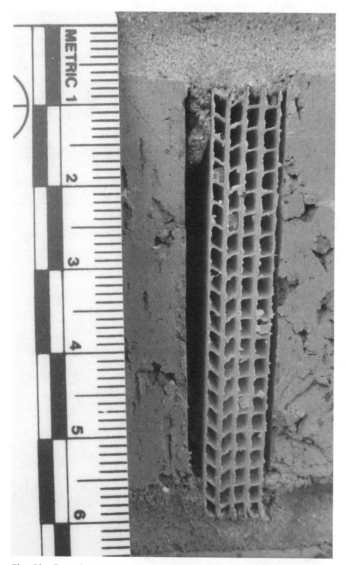

Fig. 10b. Gap between the metal door siding and concrete foundation.

Fig. 9b. Gaps in weep vents can allow entry to snakes and mice.

Fig. 10c. Arrow points to brown smudging caused by bats.

Dirty smudge marks will often appear as the body oils of the creature rub off on the building (Fig. 10c). Whitewash is a classic sign of bird activity (Fig. 10d).

Fig. 10d. White stains show bird activity.

Fig. 12. Red fox fell into the window well and couldn't escape.

Fig. 13. Gap under garage door.

Investigate the corners of the house. Squirrels and raccoons can climb up gutters. Prints will look like brown smears and scratches will be deep and pronounced (Fig. 11).

Squirrels, on the other hand, will leave no prints and the scratches will be very fine. If tree branches overhang or abut the roof, don't be surprised if there are no signs of tracks. Always consider the routes an animal might use to access a home.

Investigate all window wells. They entrap many animals (Fig. 12). Don't' forget that a window well may be hidden by a deck.

Doors

Doors of all types should be inspected as well. Many times hatchways and garage doors don't close tightly (Fig. 13).

Bait stations

Inspect every bait station you encounter. Collect and carry the various keys needed to open them. Before opening, look them over. Is there debris on or around the station? Do you see dust suggesting it has not been maintained

Fig. 11. Black smudges on this downspout caused by a climbing raccoon.

recently? Open carefully. Is the bait fresh or have mice or insects taken up residence? The presence of the stations suggests mice/rats (depending on the size of the station) were a problem at the location and could be again.

Now that the outside is done, proceed to look at the inside

Inspect the inside of the house as systematically as you would the outside. Generally speaking, the most important area of the house to inspect will be the attic and various crawl spaces. If those places don't give you any clues then you should proceed to investigate the basement. I don't like crawling around attics. It is messy, dangerous, and more often than not a useless exercise. However, since you don't know in advance when attics will reveal something, you must check them. From the inside, you can better inspect the screening on the vents. Sometimes it looks intact from the outside but the inside reveals that it has been pulled away from the edge or chewed through (Fig. 14).

Turn your flashlight off and look for light entering the attic. If you see areas where the light is entering make sure it's not due to a ridge vent or soffit vents. Modern houses have a lot more vents than older ones. Be sure to note all vents before you enter the attic. Mushroom vents are difficult to inspect from the outside because the mesh isn't in plain view. Use your mirror to inspect the integrity of the mesh, if not from the outside, then when you are in the attic.

As you enter the attic, you must always be concerned about safety. Falling through the floor is a real possibility. Make sure you walk on the crossbeams and not on the insulation which fills the space between them. If insulation obscures the beams you can get an idea of where they are by looking at the trusses or by moving the insulation. If it is too dangerous to crawl around the attic then at least try to get a good look at it from the ladder on which you are standing.

Pay careful attention to the insulation. You would be surprised how much it can tell you. I like to look for quarter-size holes in it. If I find that, then I know I am dealing with mice. Blown and fiberglass insulation will also reveal trails. Mouse trails can be very faint. The insulation will look like someone rolled a small rubber ball over it (Fig. 15).

Obviously trails made by squirrels or raccoon will be very pronounced. If you see the paper backing of fiberglass insulation without the fiberglass, then you know a squirrel has been stripping the insulation for a nest. As always, keep an eye out for feces. While mice feces are usually under the insulation, there are exceptions. I would also encourage you again, as I did earlier, to wear a high quality filtration mask. I suspect that insulation fibers and your lungs don't get along well. Sure it's hot in the summer (be careful of hyperthermia), but the protection is worth it. Finally, if possible, I like to stand up in the attic so I can follow the roofline down to the soffit area. It is these soffit areas that squirrels in my area like to live. Standing is usually the only way to see the soffit area because it lies below the level of the attic floor.

Noises

I cannot overemphasize the importance of careful inspection when the complaint is noise. Understand the following. First, inspection is the art of reducing options. Customers underestimate the amount of noise that even small animals can cause. If you find places where mice can enter, have the owner or yourself fill these openings and trap for mice. Small holes can be filled with steel wool (preferably stainless X-cluder™), Copper Stuff-it®, caulking or appropriate sealant. Just be sure you have ruled out bats or bees when sealing small holes $3/8$-inch or less. If they still hear noise then it might be something else.

Second, consider duration. Animals need food and water. Rarely can they remain active (and causing noise) for more than 3 days without access to food or water. The

Fig. 14. Arrows point to 2 holes created by red squirrels in the screening.

Fig. 15. Trails in the blown insulation from house mice.

upshot is that noises lasting longer than 3 days suggest that the animal is NOT trapped in the wall or elsewhere.

Third, consider patterns. Noises of mechanical origin tend to occur in regular patterns. Natural noises tend to be more random as when wind causes a branch to scrape or bump a house.

Caveat. Science has a saying, "Absence of evidence is not evidence of absence." Clients can only hear noises when they are around to hear them. Don't be surprised when they tell you that they hear the noises in the morning and early evening as these is the times people leave for and arrive from work.

Consider the following cases. One client told me she thought an animal was caught in the wall. Knowing that animals are rarely trapped in a wall (they may live there but they aren't trapped*), I asked why they thought this. She said, she kept hearing a squealing/grinding type noise. I asked, "For how long?" She answered, "About 3 months." If I had paid more attention to the client's timeline, I would have looked harder for a mechanical cause rather than cutting holes in the wall. What helped to throw me off was the lack of a pattern to the sound. The client said the noise was rather random. As I began to cut my second hole (on the other side of the stud), we started to hear the noise again. I started to unplug appliances. Sure enough, the noise emanated from the stove's clock which seemed to be on its last legs.

At another job, the client complained of noises above his cedar walk-in closet. Finding a squirrel-sized hole leading from the garage, I set squirrel traps. After several days of empty trap, I began to wonder about my trapping abilities. After several more days of frustration, the client finally decided to cut into the ceiling above the cedar closet. He informed me that they discovered a huge carpenter ant nest. So what he was actually hearing was the chewing of thousands of carpenter ants.

Several other sources of noise should be noted. Vinyl sided houses can make noise as the siding expands and contracts with changes in temperature. Of course, don't forget the most common misidentified noise of a smoke detector chirping a low battery signal.

Keep an open mind, but trust your instincts too.

Odors

Most of this chapter has centered on visual signs. I would be remiss if I didn't advise you about using your sense of smell in your inspections. I don't want to give you a false impression. Smells will constitute a very small part of your inspection work. However, I want you to be sure to pay attention to your nose. You will find that house mice, gray squirrels, flying squirrels, bats, and raccoon have a

distinctive odor, just like skunks. Pay attention and you will soon be confronted with a time where you can diagnose the problem just by taking a deep breath. I just wish I could put odors in the book.

Mystery odors. Sometimes, clients complain of odors, such as dead animal smells, rotten flesh smells, etc., and want you to locate the source. To locate bad odors, ask the client to close all the doors in the home overnight. Schedule your appointment for early morning. Have the client accompany you throughout the house opening each door. The goal is to find the room or rooms where the odor is the strongest. Consider that vents may be bringing the odor from elsewhere. Investigate each room where the odor is the strongest. Check carefully before cutting into walls. This recommendation is important especially in kitchens where food may fall behind appliances. I have found rotting food (the odor's source) once beside an appliance and once inside a microwave. Decaying rodents killed by toxicants is another common source of odor.

Remember, for something to be smelled, there must be a source, transmission, and a smeller. Remove any element and the odor can't be perceived. When the carcass dries out, the odor typically diminishes.

Chimneys

Chimneys are a special concern. Generally, I don't check them unless the customer is complaining of noises in or around the chimney. Here are some rules of thumb regarding noises emanating from a chimney:
   a. scratching, think squirrel,
   b. fluttering, think bird,
   c. chirping, think raccoon,
   d. grinding noise, think chimney swift (especially if the chimney is not lined with tile.)
Inspection consists of looking in the flue from the top and the bottom. Ask your client how many fireplaces he has. Each fireplace and furnace will have its own flue. Don't confuse chimneys with flues (Fig. 16).

A chimney can have more than one flue so just because one flue is capped doesn't mean that all the flues are capped (Fig. 17a). A flue that looks capped doesn't mean that the cap screen is still intact (Fig. 17b).

Make sure you ask if there are any fireplaces in the basement. People tend to forget how many fireplaces they have if they don't use them. Always inspect a chimney from the top first (Fig. 19).

You don't want to be surprised by an animal when you open the damper (Fig. 20a).

When inspecting from the top of the chimney look for spider webs in flue. Holes like bullet holes through the flue suggest it was hit by lightning. The presence of spider webs will tell you that nothing has gone down this chimney for a while. Also keep an eye out for footprints caused by the smearing of soot. Even though raccoons

---

* Mike Page of Florida disagrees and contends that many times juvenile animals, such as red squirrels, birds, gray squirrels, raccoons, and mice can and do get caught between studs. This is especially likely if the studs have been milled to a fine, smooth finish which makes climbing for these animals more difficult.

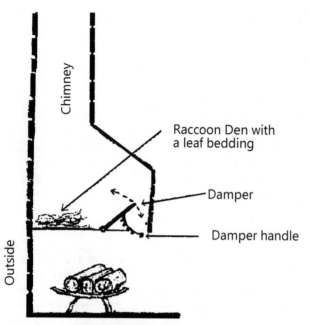

Fig. 16. Diagram of chimney.

Fig. 19. Look down the flue. Note how this one lacks any sign of animal presence.

Fig. 17a. Note the chimney has two flues but only the right one is capped.

Fig. 20a. Gray squirrel peeking over the top of the slightly opened fireplace damper.

Fig. 17b. The left flue looks capped but the arrow points to the bent screen.

rarely enter active furnace flues, it has been known to happen with clean burning gas furnaces. So pay attention. Occasionally, you will even find bits of fur caught in the cracks of rough flue tile.

Investigate furnaces, particularly in older homes (Modern natural gas furnaces draw fresh air directly from the outside preventing animal entry through that route). Squirrels enter basements through old exhausts (Fig. 20b) the fresh air intakes (Fig. 20c).

Check ash clean outs next. While many chimneys don't have them, they may provide clues for what is in the chimney (Fig. 21).

Before opening dampers, wear personal protective equipment (gloves, goggles, and respirator are minimum). Since old fireplaces are full of soot etc., I prime the flue with a propane torch. This way the draft is going up when I crack the damper. I like using propane because it doesn't create smoke and the flame can be turned out immediately. You won't burn the animals if you keep the flame away from the damper. Always open the damper slowly and no more than an inch at first. Shine your flashlight into the crack and look for any paws and fur as you listen for noises.

Fig. 20b. The pie plate (now ajar) was pushed open by a squirrel.

Fig. 20c. Pole shows how an animal, like a squirrel, may enter a basement through the gas furnace's fresh air intake.

A colleague emphasizes a close look at the chimney. He has noted two problems with chimneys. First, chimneys pull away from the building creating a gap that bats in particular love to exploit. Second, the slate part of the chimney often slides away from the building creating a gap that squirrels reportedly love to use. Some have even seen gray squirrels chew an opening if the slate is loose.

Metal Chimneys

Metal chimneys require special attention. These chimneys are double or triple walled to insulate the heat from the inner flue from heating the structure and causing a fire. Older versions look like they are screened (Figs. 18a,b) but the screening only protects the innermost flue (the one that connects to the damper). Animals, usually birds, can fall into the gap between the inner and outer rings. Clients will complain of noise emanating from the fireplace, but when you open the damper nothing comes out. Unless you are willing to tear out the encasement, you will not be able to reach the trapped animal.

Fig. 18a. Metal chimney flue.

Fig. 18b. (bottom): these are double-walled metal flues. Sure the inside flue is screened but notice that the exterior tube is not. Many birds and squirrels do fall in between the two pipes.

Fig. 21. Feathers and debris left by chimney swifts.

Concluding Remarks

Even if the job seems simple, I would still strongly suggest that you inspect the property carefully. Sometimes the customer has multiple problems or you may find a way to solve the problem faster than the one you originally decided upon.

Frequently, identification of the problem species is difficult. Many signs, especially for the smaller animals, overlap each another. The difference between a novice and a professional lays in the ability to:

A. find the sign, and

B. piece them together to make a diagnosis.

Sometimes a definite determination is not possible, however you should be able to significantly narrow the possibilities.

Resources

Thanks to Kirk LaPierre (d. 2010) and Mike Page for information they provided.

Corrigan, B. 2000. Foreseeing Serious Pest Problems. *Pest Control Technology* (Apr):91.

Haag Education. 2006. Composition Roofs Damage Assessment: Field Guide. Irving, TX: Haag Engineering Co.

Haag Engineering Co. 2007. Tile Roofs Damage Assessment: Field Guide. Irving, TX: Haag Engineering Co.

Haag Engineering Co. 2009. Wood Roofs Damage Assessment: Field Guide. Irving, TX: Haag Engineering Co.

McRae, B. 1996. The Art and Science of Spotting Game. *American Hunter,* (April):39-41,61.

How to Observe

One fact that any animal damage controller needs to know is how the eye works. Without going into a long biology lesson, let it be said that the only way to really look at something is to pay close attention to it. We can only clearly focus on what we are specifically looking at. You don't want to inspect with peripheral vision. Use your peripheral vision for hunting, not for inspection. Try this experiment. Take a newspaper and lay it out in front of you. Look at the pictures. Now really look at them. Look at them closely. When you begin to see the dots that make up the pictures then you now know how you need to closely observe. When performing your inspections make sure to pay close attention to the various and typical animal entries. You don't have to be close to an object, although it helps, to inspect it properly. You just need to look at it part by part and use the narrow part (also called the bi-focal vision) of your focused vision. Only with the narrow vision can you properly determine if there is any animal sign present or not. I would strongly encourage you to get a copy of Bill McRae's article cited in the resources.

Inspection Checklist/Service Quote
Wildlife Control Consultant
Visit our web page http://www.wildlifecontrolconsultant.com

Date_____ Tel. _____

Name_____

Address_____

WCC endeavors to provide a thorough inspection. However, we do not claim to have found every problem with your property. Diligent monitoring on your part is still important. If you have any questions, call before you act.

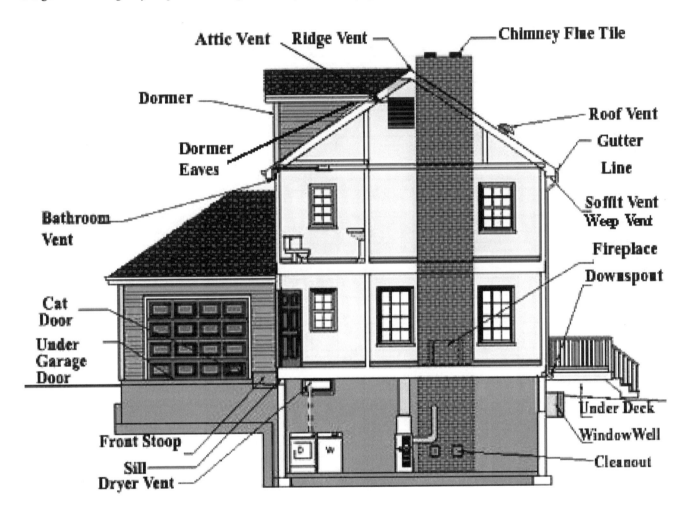

Concerns: Carcasses Histoplasmosis *Bayliscaris procyonis* Rabies Hanta-virus Check/Install Smoke & CO detectors, Note: list is not intended to be complete. Please consult with health professional, if you have further concerns. A risk may be present even if a disease is not circled.

Species Suspected: Mice Voles Moles Rats Bats Chipmunks Red Squirrels Flying Squirrels Birds Gray Squirrels Opossums Skunks Raccoons Woodchucks. Other_____

Further Recommendations:_____
_____
_____

Customer _____   Inspector _____

Inspection Report
Wildlife Control Consultant
Visit our web page http://www.wildlifecontrolconsultant.com

Date_____ Tel. _____

Name_____

Address_____

WCC endeavors to provide a thorough inspection. However, we do not claim to have found every problem with your property. Diligent monitoring on your part is still important. If you have any questions, call before you act.

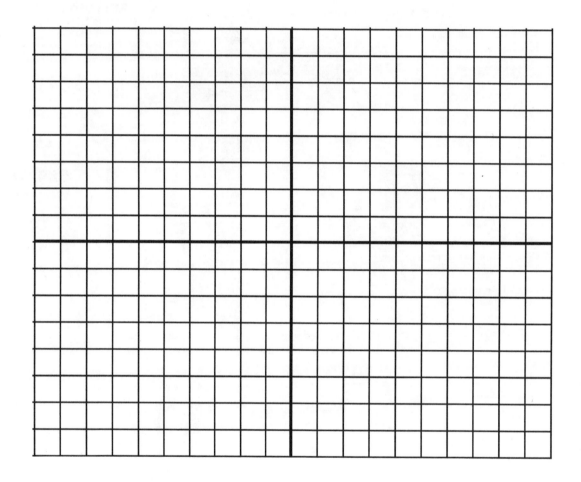

Concerns: Carcasses Histoplasmosis *Bayliscaris procyonis* Rabies Hanta-virus Check/Install Smoke & CO detectors, Note: list is not intended to be complete. Please consult with health professional, if you have further concerns. A risk may be present even if a disease is not circled.

Species Suspected: Mice Voles Moles Rats Bats Chipmunks Red Squirrels Flying Squirrels Birds Gray Squirrels Opossums Skunks Raccoons Woodchucks. Other_____

Further Recommendations:_____
_____
_____

Customer _____   Inspector _____

Chapter 5 **Difficult Jobs**

No matter how good you are, situations will arise where you won't have any idea about the cause of the problem. This can truly be a frustrating situation. Some clients just don't respond well to any admission of ignorance. They will expect you to know what is causing the noise and the damage. Despite their irritation don't lie. If you don't know what the cause is, admit it. Other times, you have a pretty good idea of the problem's cause but you don't know where or how the animals are entering the property or structure.

Tactics for All Difficult Jobs

Just because you don't know doesn't mean you leave clients in the lurch. Several techniques are available to help you identify the cause of the problem. Techniques are ordered from least expensive to the greatest. First, when you find holes that you have some doubts about, fill them or cover them with newspaper. Newspaper has the advantage of being chewed through easily by rodents. In this way, they chew the newspaper rather than the building. If the paper hasn't moved in two to three days of good weather, then you know the hole is no longer being used and can be closed off. Feel free to wait longer if you have doubts. Don't use this technique if you think the culprit is bats, bees, or birds. They may have difficulty getting out.

Second, rule out possible suspects. You may not know what may be causing the problem but you can know what is not causing the problem. Sometimes clients are anxious about a specific species. For example, some clients will feel better when the culprit isn't rats. Help put your clients at ease by telling them what the problem isn't.

Fig. 1. Glue board with German cockroaches in various stages of development.

Third, don't be afraid to ask clients to participate in the solution. Have clients to start paying more attention to their house. Suggest they look at the building when they drive in and out of the driveway. Have them ask neighbors about any animal activity around their home. Have them perform a bat watch if bats are a concern. The bottom line is, if they want the problem solved, you will need their help to solve it.

Traps

As noted above, you may not know what the problem is but you know what it isn't. In these cases, you can set a trap for the size of the animal you believe is causing the problem. Traps have the advantage of quieting clients and giving you an opportunity to make some money. I don't like to set traps unless I know there is an animal around to catch. However, sometimes you just don't have that choice. Choose a trap and bait that can catch a variety of animals. I like to use a squirrel trap, baited with peanut butter on bread. If the peanut butter is gone one day and the bread is gone the next, then you have mice. I am sure you can decide what the animal is by what happens with the trap and bait.

Glueboards

Another technique is to place some glue boards in areas where noise is being heard (Fig. 1). Obviously if the noise is in the walls, you won't be able to put the glue boards there. You do want, however, to place them as close as possible. I recommend using rat-size glue boards. I used glue boards with a stiff paper backing, as they can be stapled down easily. Always anchor glue boards, in case an animal bigger than a mouse gets caught and tries to drag the board away. I don't like glue boards for two reasons. First, they seem to be rather cruel. Second, their effectiveness is questionable because they will educate rodents if they encounter a board and escape. Nevertheless, glue boards have their uses, even if as a last resort. I thought one client had mice. I set a glue board and caught a flying squirrel. Glue boards also catch insects which may provide tips on possible causes as well.

Track Traps

Like the name suggests, track trap are designed to catch the animal's footprint in a manner clear enough to permit identification (Fig. 2). Track traps can be used in baited or blind "sets".

Track traps come in various designs. Some animal damage controllers like to use flour. The softness of the

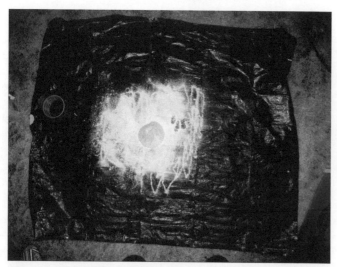

Fig. 2. Baby powder spread on a black plastic bag surrounds a container of peanut butter. Use duct tape or other suitable material to keep the bag in place.

Fig. 3. Norway rat tracks. Photo by Tom Olander.

Fig. 4. Orange and blue Strait-line® chalk under UV light.

a 6-year-old child was very interested in my investigation. Something struck me as odd about the family dynamics so I got this feeling that maybe the child was the source of the feces. I asked his older brother. He said it was possible. The mother didn't want to hear about it. So I opened a box of sardines, put them in the middle of the floor and encircled the sardines with ring of flour. I told them to call if the flour or sardines were disturbed. They never did. The moral here is that sometimes you work to mollify your clients.

Biologists use sooted aluminum sheets with white paper or contact paper to capture tracks. The aluminum sheets are sooted with acetylene torches. Details on how to create them can be found in the USFS document in the resources section.

Fluorescent Track Traps

One WCO recommended using orange Strait-line® chalk by Irwin®, particularly around bait stations (Fig. 4). The chalk is picked up by the animal's feet and carried around. Since the chalk fluoresces, a black light makes it easy to identify where it went. Biologists have used fluorescing powder to track rodents and even amphibians.

RodoTrack puts the tracking powder inside a triangular box filled with cottony fill. Mice investigate the hole, perhaps grab some fill, contact the powder, which then helps you determine their travel movements.

Trail Cameras

Trail cameras can be very helpful effective in identifying culprits in unusual damage situations (Fig. 5). Practice with your cameras before you use them. They can be fussy and not work properly at the worst possible times. Use multiple cameras positioned at different angles to protect against failure and missed shots. Otherwise, pay for quality trail cameras, such as Reconyx.

flour allows it to take a track very easily. The disadvantage of flour is that it can attract insects. Talc, as in some baby powders, won't create an insect problem. Tom Olander and Kirk La Pierre have both used flour and/or baby powder to check animal activity. Note the scratches in the powder where the squirrel climbed out onto the powder covered sheet with bait in the middle on the following page.

Kirk used a spritzer bottle with lure, plastic sheeting, baby powder and bait, in the photo the bait is peanuts which would work well for squirrels. Notice the rat tracks in the powder (Fig. 3).

I have only used this method once in my career (If I knew the technique worked this well, I may have used it more often). A family called with a complaint about a raccoon in their basement. They showed me a few piles of feces on the floor. I investigated around and couldn't find any hole that would allow a raccoon into the basement. There also was no damage to boxes, etc. that should appear if a raccoon was present. I did notice that

There are a plethora of trail cameras on the market so consider ones that have the following features:

   a. memory card that is the same as your digital camera,

   b. long battery life,

   c. sensitive motion settings to trigger when mice come along,

   d. fast shutter speed, and

   e. infrared illumination, preferably one that projects no visible light. Visible light increases the chances of it getting stolen.

Illusory Parisitosis

Illusory parisitosis refers to a condition where a client complains of a pest that does not exist. Typically, pest control companies are confronted with clients reporting mysterious "bug bites" and insects that have powers that approach the magical. Fortunately, this condition is rarer for vertebrate pests because microscopes aren't needed to view them as they are with some insects.

Nevertheless, you must keep in mind the possibility that the "animal" you are looking for may not exist. Warning signs that the problem you are confronting is illusory, includes:

   a. inconsistent client testimony and testimony that changes as you keep ruling out possibilities,

   b. client statements that all the other pest professionals didn't find anything,

   c. client testimony does not match the evidence,

   d. client says he/she has collected evidence but it is unavailable when you look,

   e. client reports that she/he is the only person in the family who notices the problem, and

   f. client has gone to incredible lengths to "treat" the problem which never seems to get resolved.

But before concluding the problem is illusory, consider the following:

   a. rule out all vertebrates, including exotic species,

   b. consider the possibility of insects,

   c. consider mechanical causes, particularly when noises are involved,

   d. assess if environmental elements may be involved, (e.g. wind, rain, sewage pipes, etc.), and

   e. consult with another technician. Sometimes fresh eyes see what you may have missed.

The bottom line is you should not conclude the problem is a phantom without being forced to that position. Be sure to document your findings and REFER the client to the proper professional, such as dermatologist, entomologist, or medical doctor. Failure to refer is a leading cause of lawsuits. While you may believe the client needs professional counseling, use discretion before making such a recommendation. It may be a better idea to have clients tell their medical professional to contact you if he/she needs more background before providing treatment.

Fig. 5. Trail cameras can be helpful in identifying mysterious wildlife activity.

Resources

Borski, A. A. 2011. Itches, Illusions, and Phobias in *Handbook of Pest Control: The Behavior, Life History, and Control of Household Pests* edited by A. Mallis et al. Mallis Handbook, LLC. 635-679 pp.

Lemen, C. A. and P. W. Freeman. 1985. Tracking Mammals with Fluorescent Pigments: A New Technique. *Journal of Mammalogy,* 66:1(Feb.):134-136.

Rittenhouse, T. A., T. T. Altnether, and R. D. Semlitsch. 2006. Fluorescent Powder Pigments as a Harmless Tracking Method for Ambystomatids and Ranids. *Herpetological Review,* 37(2):188–191.

Zielinski, W. J. and T. E. Kucera. 1995. *American Marten, Fisher, Lynx, and Wolverine: Survey Methods for Their Detection,* General Technical Report PSW GTR-157. USDA-FS (August).

Chapter 6 **Identification of Damage by Calendar**

An awareness of the timing of wildlife activity can be an important clue in narrowing the list of potential causes of wildlife damage. Unfortunately, national calendars must have broad time ranges (typically a couple of months) because wildlife activity occurs at different times based on latitude.

You, however, can create a calendar for your own area. I suggest carrying a notebook with a page dedicated to each month. As you encounter sign, record your findings in your notebook. Consult with state wildlife biologists to gain their insights. Over time, you will develop a calendar suitable for your latitude and weather conditions.

To help you get started, I have included a calendar designed by Aaron Franco, Multimedia Designer, Dept. of Agronomy & Horticulture, UNL. I think you will agree that the design could be useful for your area and adapted to include structures as well. Calendar, used with permission, found in Streich, A. M., Timmerman, A. D., Kalisch, J. A., Vantassel, S. M., Baxendale, F. P., &

Hygnstrom, S. E. 2011. *Landscape Diagnostic Guide for Problems Affecting Woody Ornamentals and Herbaceous Perennials* (Vol. EC1260). Lincoln: University of Nebraska-Lincoln, p. 188.

Consult resources for additional materials.

Resources

Braband, L. and J. Shultz. 2002. A typical year for WCOs working in New York State. Cornell Cooperative Extension, Wildlife Damage Management Program in cooperation with the NYS Integrated Pest Management Program. For more copies of this chart, please contact the NYS Department of Environmental Conservation.

Hafer, D. J., S. E. Hygnstrom, R. J. Johnson, and D. M. Ferraro. The Nature and Timing of Wildlife Damage Events in Nebraska: A Five-Year Review of Requests to Three Extension Wildlife Personnel. *11th Great Plains Wildlife Damage Control Workshop Proceedings. April 26-29, 1993*, Kansas City, MO: Kansas State University. 109-110.

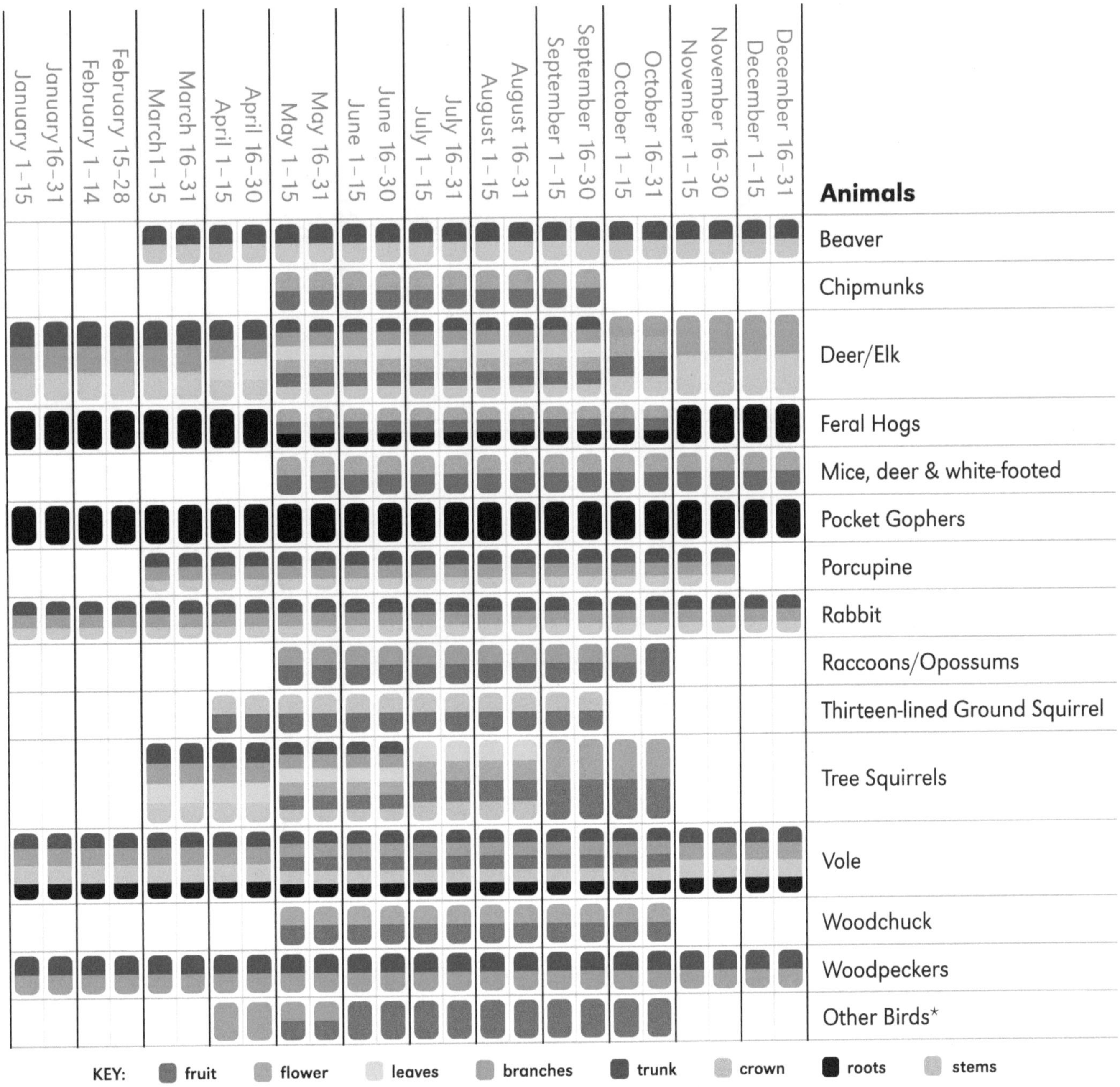

Column headers (half-month periods), left to right:

- January 1-15
- January 16-31
- February 1-14
- February 15-28
- March 1-15
- March 16-31
- April 1-15
- April 16-30
- May 1-15
- May 16-31
- June 1-15
- June 16-30
- July 1-15
- July 16-31
- August 1-15
- August 16-31
- September 1-15
- September 16-30
- October 1-15
- October 16-31
- November 1-15
- November 16-30
- December 1-15
- December 16-31

Animals

- Beaver
- Chipmunks
- Deer/Elk
- Feral Hogs
- Mice, deer & white-footed
- Pocket Gophers
- Porcupine
- Rabbit
- Raccoons/Opossums
- Thirteen-lined Ground Squirrel
- Tree Squirrels
- Vole
- Woodchuck
- Woodpeckers
- Other Birds*

KEY: fruit | flower | leaves | branches | trunk | crown | roots | stems

*Blue jays, crows, grackles, blackbirds, house sparrows, robins, starlings, turkeys

Chapter 7 Identification of Landscape & Garden Damage

Turf and landscaping are susceptible to damage from a variety of wildlife species. Knowing the cause of the damage is the first step in managing it. Damage to turf is more difficult to assess than animal damage to structures because the variety of suspects is increased substantially and the evidence is often not clear cut. Nevertheless, employment of several tactics will help reduce the variables and at least enable you to rule out suspects if not positively identify the guilty culprit. This chapter will provide a list of clues to assist you in identifying the species causing damage to turf, landscape, and gardens.

Turf and Landscape Damage

As always, consider the time the damage takes place (day/night) as well as the species present in your area to help further narrow down your list of suspects.

Damage to turf and landscaping occurs in four different zones:

- Above Eye-Level Zone (above 6 ft [1.8 m]),
- Above Grass Zone (between 6 ft [1.8 m] and the grass),
- Grass Zone, and
- Below Grass Zone (subterranean).

Damage Above Eye-Level Zone

It's an awkward title, but I needed something catchy to refer to damage to plants and gardens that occurred above 6 ft (1.8 m). Damage at this height typically is caused by only a few species, woodpeckers (Fig. 1), porcupines, and squirrels.

Damage Above the Grass-Zone

This zone refers to damage between 6 ft (1.8 m) and the grass level. Trees and shrubs frequently are eaten by rabbits and deer. Look carefully at the damaged branches. Torn and frayed branches signal the presence of deer (Fig. 2.) Branches that sustain a clean 45° angle cut signify rabbit activity (Fig. 3a). The height of the damage often can be helpful as deer can forage at greater heights than rabbits. Rabbit damage to shrubs can be identified through the gnaw marks which will be ¼ in (6.4 mm) wide up to 20 in (51 cm) off the ground depending on snow level (Fig. 3b). If woodchucks, also known as groundhogs, reside in your area, consider them as possible culprits if you sustain damage to plants, especially non-woody ones. Chances are you will see them feeding or sunning themselves during daylight hours.

Fig. 1. Tree damaged by a woodpecker.

During winter, when food is scarce, voles and rabbits can gnaw the bark of plants. Smooth barked plants are favored. Voles tend to gnaw bark covered in snow. Rabbits gnaw bark above the snow. Look for sign of voles when noticing some yellowing of branches in shrubs (Fig. 3c). The yellowed branches frequently is caused by vole damage to the branch either above or below the surface of the soil.

Fig. 2. Left. Deer damage to branch. Note frayed appearance compared with rabbit clipping on right.

Fig. 3a. Rabbit cuttings.

Fig. 3c. Yellowing of these branches was due to feeding by voles.

Damage in the Grass-Zone

Damage in this zone normally occurs in six forms, den holes, furrows, towers, bare spots, divots/holes, rings, and mounds. I will not focus on den holes as it is best described in the species area.

Furrows: Voles are the primary cause of furrows (Fig. 4). Voles travel under the grass canopy or in shallow tunnels to avoid predators. Voles will clip the grass, creating trails under a grass canopy. You may also find furrows after the winter snow melt (Fig. 5a). These are caused by voles continuing to forage beneath the snow as they don't hibernate.

Cicada killers nests can damage the ground and raise suspicion of animal activity. Think of this possibility in dry soil and in late summer (Fig. 5b).

Towers: Crawfish create miniature volcano style dirt mounds in wet meadows. Holes tend to be 0.5 to 1.5 in (1.3 to 3.8 cm) in diameter (Fig. 6a). Some can be 1 in (2.5 cm) wide. Burrowing can occur at end of April to early May in Texas.

Fig. 3b. Rabbit gnawing on bark.

Fig. 4. Vole furrows also called a runway.

Fig. 5a. Vole furrows, left after snow melt.

Fig. 5b. Cicada killer nest. Note the groove. Scale is in inches.

Bare spots: Possible suspect, dog urine. Urine contains nitrogen which can dry the grass out, causing it to die. But dogs tends to urinate near posts and prominent areas to mark their territory. Mole runs can cause grass to die above them because their burrowing separates the grass's roots from the surrounding soil. Carefully probe the spot to determine if a subsurface tunnel is present.

Divots: Divots are more difficult to identify. Fortunately, however, there are some general guidelines that will help you narrow the list of suspects. First, pocket gopher mounds and ground squirrel dens may be excavated by hungry badgers (Fig. 7) or fox (Fig. 8). Distinguish between them by size of digging.

Second, holes dug by skunks and squirrels will be solitary, precise and cleanly dug to a depth around an inch (2.5 cm) or less (Fig. 9). This makes sense as these spe-

cies are able to locate their food precisely. Skunks also systematically dig an area free of grubs, returning night after night until the area is essentially grub free.

If you notice broken acorns in the hole, then you can safely assume that squirrels were doing the digging.

Third, ask yourself, "When did the damage take place?" If the lawn was perfect when you left that evening only to find it destroyed the next morning, you know that the culprit is nocturnal. Skunks and raccoons are nocturnal. Squirrels and birds are diurnal.

Fourth, consider the extent of the soil/turf damage. Damage caused by raccoons, armadillos, and feral hogs can be extensive. While it can be difficult to distinguish raccoon from armadillo damage, rolled up sod is a sure sign the culprit is raccoon. Feral hog activity will look like a berserk plow has been let loose.

Fig. 6a. Crawfish hole with mud tower removed.

Fig. 6b. The mud tower has collapsed.

Fig. 7. Badger hole.

Fig. 8. Digging by a red fox at a hole of a 13-lined ground squirrel.

Fig. 9. Skunk diggings.

Fig. 10. Holes created by blackbirds. 1 ft (30.5 cm) ruler for scale.

Also birds, such as crows, blackbirds, and starlings, can cause substantial turf damage, but their activity will usually be witnessed during daylight hours (Fig. 10). Starlings can stick their beak into the soil and then open their jaws to spread the soil. Other birds grab at the soil and lift to search for bugs and worms. In doing so, they will leave behind tufts of grass. Crows can grab larger chunks of sod. In contrast, skunks and squirrels will poke at the soil with claws and push it to the side rather than plucking and lifting.

Rings: When viewing rings, suspect fungi. Fungi cause the grass to grow faster and darker by breaking down organic matter and thereby releasing nutrients that enable the grass to grow faster. Dark green grass surrounding lighter green grass is a key clue (Fig. 11). Mushrooms may or may not be present. The rings tend to be 3 to 8 in (7.6 to 20 cm) in diameter though the one pictured was ~10 ft (3 m) across.

Fig. 11. Fairie ring.

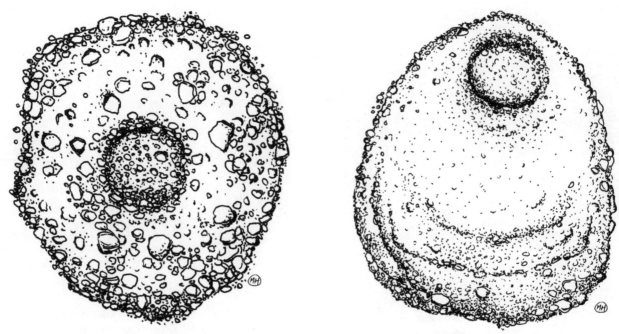

Figs. 12a,b. Top view of mole mound (left) and pocket gopher mound (right). Images by Michael Heller.

Fig. 12c.

Fig. 12d.

Mounds: Identification of mounds is rather straight-forward. From above, moles mounds (also called hills or boils) are round (Fig. 12a) in contrast to the kidney-shaped or oblong shape of the pocket gopher mound (Fig. 12b). From the side, mole mounds are symmetrical, but pocket gopher mounds have more soil on one end (Fig. 12c) than the other (Fig. 12d). Another key difference is that only moles create surface runs that makes the ground feel squishy as you walk on it. Pocket gophers do not.

Mounds less than 3 in (7.5 cm) are likely to be made by worms (Fig. 12e). Soil will be moist to wet and may look like a series of thin tubes of mud.

Pocket gophers, being active year-round, will line the trails through snow with soil. These soil tubes are called "castes" and may be found in the early spring (Fig. 13).

Damage Below the Grass-Zone

For our purposes, only three species are responsible for damage in the below ground zone. Shrews will burrow through mulch looking for insect prey. The mulch will have a ruffled appearance. Moles and pocket gophers live their lives almost completely underground. Their tunneling activity, in search of food, result in mounds of dirt being excavated to the surface.

Fig. 12e. Mound created by a worm. Scale is in cm.

Fig. 13. Pocket gopher castes left over from winter. Photo by Larry Howard.

Fortunately, mole and pocket gopher dirt hills are easily identified as noted above. You should also be aware that moles are insectivores; pocket gophers are vegetarians. Moles damage grass through separating plant roots from the surrounding soil in their quest for insects and earth worms. Gophers damage turf through eating the plant roots. Voles, however, can dig their own tunnels but will also exploit the tunnels made by moles.

Garden Damage Identification

Identification of damage to gardens can be challenging because fruits and vegetables may be removed completely. Additionally, gardeners and farmers are not checking their plants on a daily basis so sign of damage can be removed by weather conditions or confounded by scavengers feeding on the left overs of the guilty party.

What follows are some helpful tips to identify damage to common crops.

Corn

Deer. Telescoping husks signal deer browse damage (Fig. 14). Ears can be scraped the full length. Downed stalks tend to be few (less than 12) and will tend to fall in same direction. Deer rarely feed on corn past the milk stage. They will wait till corn matures. Purple colored stalks in Aug/Sept often indicative of deer.

Raccoons. Most damage concentrated during milk-stage R3. They start inside the field and then move toward the woods. Stalks damaged and fall haphazardly (Fig. 15). They will shuck corn cobs. Cobs will appear dirty and/or muddied.

Rodents. Typically feed on hearts of the kernels (Fig. 16) but can feed on the cob (Fig. 17).

Fig. 14. Telescoping damage signals deer browse.

Fig. 15. Note the stalks knocked over in different directions.

Beaver. Damage to corn occurs near water. Stalks cut at 45° angle typically when stalk is >48 in (>1.2 m) tall prior to tassel. Look for path to water.

Tree Squirrels. Dig up seeds prior and during plant emergence. Soil usually will be dug on one side. Damage normally concentrated along the wooded

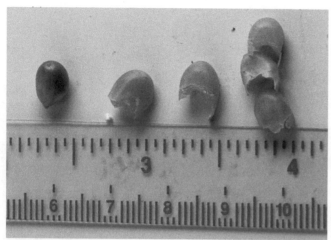

Fig. 16. Left kernel is intact for comparison. Other kernels show the heart removed by fox squirrel.

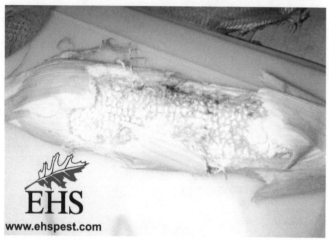

Fig. 17. Mouse damage to corn. Photo by George E. Williams of EHSpest.com

Fig. 18. Pens point to the holes left by a 13-lined ground squirrel digging up the corn seeds. Photo by John Pickle.

Ground Squirrels. Chipmunks and 13-lined ground squirrels (Fig. 18) dig around the entire seedling. Look for den holes. Browsing by woodchucks will be highest near the den.

Birds. Primarily blackbirds and grackles. Corn is damaged as seedling. They dig around the entire seedling and pull from ground. Hole will be shallower than that created by non-birds. Damage will occur

Fig. 19. Corn cobs fed on by birds will have a firecracker look.

throughout the field. Birds can't grab husks, so they have to peck at the seeds. Husk will have a firecracker "exploded" appearance (Fig. 19). During the milk stage, pieces of husk will be pulled back. Note that turkeys don't knock down stalks.

Soybeans

Deer. They feed throughout the growing season. After plant emergence, deer browse to stub. If terminal shoot is clipped, the plant may sprout two (Fig. 20). Look for rough appearance. Later in the plant's development, only the upper leaves are damaged. Damage more intense in the portion of the field closest to cover.

Cottontail rabbit. Damage tends to be minimal. When it occurs it tends to be in the early plant stages. Look for sharp 45° angle cuts.

Woodchuck. Damage concentrated near dens. Begins after emergence. Look for angled cut.

Canada geese. Damage to plants adjacent to water. Most damage occurs after emergence. They yank plants so leaves will look torn.

Turkey. They rarely damage soybeans. They will dust amongst plants. No plants within the dusting area.

Fig. 20 Bean plant whose leader was snipped and responded by growing two others.

Conclusion

Keep a notebook and camera handy to record findings in your area. Identification of wildlife damage to crops will only help your work as a wildlife professional.

The reader should remember that this chapter only provides a starting point for identifying damage caused by wildlife. Animal damage identification is as much an art as it is a science. Readers should continue to learn more about wildlife behavior to improve their knowledge of animal sign.

Resources

Some information provided by Robb Russell of the WildlifeProNetwork.

Backyard Living Magazine. 2009. (Mar):42.
MacGowan, B. et al. *Identification of Wildlife Crop Depredation.* FNR-267. Purdue Univ.

Chapter 8 Scat Identification

Scatology is the study of animal feces. Since all terrestrial and flying animals must excrete solid waste and given that scat generally persists longer than other forms of identification, such as tracks, learning how to identify species by scat is an important inspection skill.

Unfortunately, identifying which species left a scat is confounded by several difficulties.

1. It is expected that different species deposit different looking scats. Similar sized animals, however, from different species (e.g. small coyote and large red fox) can leave behind similar looking scats.
2. By the same token, different sized animals of the same species can deposit different looking scats (e.g. larger animals leave larger scats).
3. The same animal can leave different looking scats, in both form and structure, from one day to the next. For as the animal's diet or health changes, so does the appearance of its scat. If you question this, just consider how much the shape and look of your own scat changes from day to day. The only way to identify scat with 100% certainty is through DNA testing.
4. Finally, the absence of scat should not be taken to mean that the animal is not present. This really applies to outdoor sign. A study in Kansas found that wildlife will eat the feces left by others. Typically, feces may be removed in 2.5 days or less. This ignores, of course, the effect weather has in feces removal, such as heavy rainfall.

Despite these difficulties, visual inspection of scat can provide reasonable, but not certain, confidence concerning what Order or Family (e.g. rodent, lagomorph, carnivore, etc.) of animal left the scat and in many cases, what species was likely to have left it. The key is learning to ask the right questions and paying close attention to the context and setting surrounding the scat. If nothing else, the scat will tell you what animal(s) you are not looking for and that can be as important as knowing what animal you are looking for. Above all, avoid the rush to judgment, consider all the evidence first.

Warning

Before you begin identification of scat, read our safety information (Fig. 1).

Be safe. Droppings can not only soil your clothes and hands, but they also can contain infectious diseases. Avoid handling droppings without proper protection, (e.g. goggles, gloves, nose/mouth dust mask-to prevent accidental ingestion from flying debris). Some diseases may be transmitted by dust which raises the question of whether you should wear a NIOSH rated respirator. I don't want to overstate the risk, but in our litigious world, caution is advisable. If you choose not to wear a respirator, then avoid potentially inhaling debris from the scat (some of which may be microscopic), by keeping your distance and/or wearing a dust mask, by using gloves, forceps when dissecting, and by staying up or perpendicular to the prevailing wind. I do not recommend sniffing the scat as a step in the identification procedure, even though some claim to find odor useful in identification.

Suggested Equipment
- Personal protection equipment
- Nitrile gloves
- Forceps
- Magnifying glass (5× or higher)
- Caliper
- Ruler
- Camera
- Containers to hold scat (sealable bags, plastic containers).

Scat Identification Procedure

Step 1. Safety first. Look, more than touch!! If you have to touch, use a tool and/or properly gloved hands!! **Stay upwind !!** Keep distance.

Step 2a. Consider the macro- and micro-habitat surrounding the scat. The macro-habitat is the nature of the environment in the acres surrounding the scat. Is it urban, suburban, rural, wooded, swampy, dry, grassland, etc.? This step hearkens back to what was mentioned earlier. If the animal doesn't live in your area, don't look for it. Polar bears won't be found in Florida.

The micro-habitat consists of the area within several ft (m) or inches (cm) of the scat's location. Was the scat found among plants, behind boxes, in a crawl space, on the roof? For example, mice tend to avoid walking in the middle of a room where they would be fully exposed to potential predators. Coyote don't climb into attics, so it

Fig. 1. Universal sign for biological hazard.

would be unlikely that a scat found there came from a coyote. Considering the micro-habitat helps you narrow your suspects list down to the animals that would likely travel through this location.

Step 2b. What is above the scat? Could it have dropped from a tree, overhanging plant or roof ledge?

Step 3. Perform a gross visual inspection of the scat. The following tasks will help guide the inspection.
   a. Identify its form and structure (see Table 1).
   b. Determine width and length. Rulers are sufficient for large scats, but a caliper may be needed to measure small scats. As a general rule, the width of the scat is more indicative of the animal's size than the length.
   c. Judge the volume and number of the scat. Large volumes suggest large animals and vice-versa. Does the scat contain one dropping or multiple? Are all these droppings part of one event or can their location designate a latrine?

Step 4. Determine if the scat contains any white. The white portion of a scat, if present, is due to nitrogen-based urine being excreted by the animal with the feces in the intestines. White splashes suggest bird droppings. Scats with a white-cap can be left by reptiles (e.g. snakes or lizards) or birds, such as a turkey.

Step 5. Identify any particles (e.g. hair, insect parts, bone, or food) in the dropping. With appropriate caution and safety equipment, tease apart the scat to see if any particles may be identified. These food remnants will narrow down your list of suspects greatly. Understand, however, that highly refined foods characteristic of human diets may make finding inclusions difficult.

Step 6. Determine when the scat was left, if possible. Soft scats suggest a recent deposit. This step is very difficult because scats dry out at various times due to weather conditions and location. Ask the client if she/he knows when the dropping was left. An answer of at night or during the day can be quite helpful in narrowing potential species.

The categories in Table 1 were adapted from Jim Halfpenny's (1986) table on scat identification, a book I highly recommend. The table is to help train readers to look at scat structure rather than color during the process of analysis. Table 2 provides a rubric to evaluate scat.

Table 1. Scat Structure (all images by Donna Vantassel)

Image	Description	Animal Group	Image	Description	Animal Group
Sphere	Spheres are the most round of all the scats.	Lagomorph and Deer Order	Folded	Cord with folded end.	Weasel Family
Dimple / Nipple	Elongated spheres are longer than they are wide but not to the extent of cords. Elongated spheres tend to be no longer than 1¾ in (moose).	Deer Order	Segmented	Cord-segmented	Felines
Rounded Ends	Elongated Sphere	Rodent Order & Shrews	Non-descript	Scat deposit will exhibit various shapes.	Opossum
Rounded end / Pointed end	Elongated Sphere	Rodent Order & Shrews	Plop		Left by animals that are ill or have eaten a rich diet (e.g. fruit).
Thick cord	Cord	Canines	Toad	Single deposits.	Toads
Flat ends	Cord with flat ends.	Bear & Raccoon Family	White-capped		Bird, Lizard, Snake

Identification Key to Scat

A key to scat adapted from one by Dennis Ferraro, University of Nebraska-Lincoln Extension.

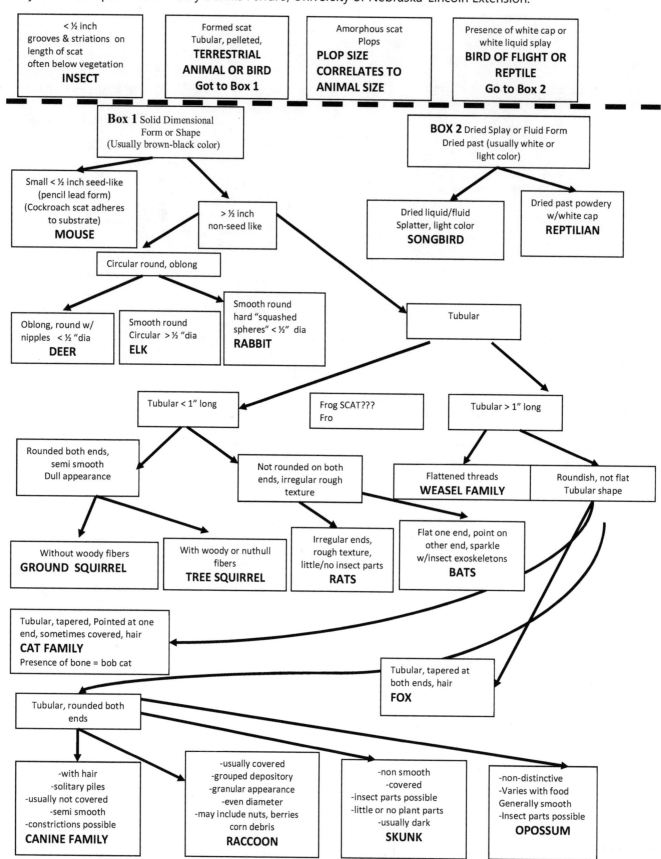

Table 2. Scat observation rubric. (Circle or X out)

Step 1. Be safe								
Step 2. Habitat								
a. Macro	Rural	Suburban	Rural	Woods	Aquatic	Field	Swampy	
b. Micro	Field	Garden	Structure					
Step 3a. Shape	Sphere	Elongate sphere	Thick cord	Segmented cord	Folded cord	Scat with white	Non-descript	Plop
Spheres and cords identify the ends	Nipple-dimple	Pointed	Rounded					
3b.Number	Single	Multiple	Latrine					
3c. Measure the scat	Length		Width					
Step 4. Identify any white	Yes	No						
Step 5. Identify particles	Bone	Insect parts	Hair	Seeds	Crayfish	Fish scales	Nut shell fragments	
Step 6. Determine timing	Day	Night	Soft	Hard				
Suspected Order/Family	Lagomorph Rodent	Rodent/Shrew	Canine	Amphibian	Mustelid	Bird, Reptile	Opossum	Other

Editors' Note: We have adapted the information below from Dr. Jeff Jackson's article in *Wildlife Control Technology* magazine, Dr. Theodore Gravanosky booklet on *Scats*, and Dr. Jim Halfpenny's book on Mammal Tracking.

The purpose of this information to provide specific illustrations of the concepts highlighted discussed in the chapter. Consult the species modules for more information on scat.

Lagomorphs (Rabbits): Rabbit scats are spherical (Fig. 2), few in number, and scattered. They tend to be hard and consist of finely chewed material.

Fig. 2. Cottontail rabbit scat. Scale is mm (top row) and inches (bottom).

Ungulates (Deer): Scats in winter are elongated spheres with bell-shape form (also known as nipple-dimple, Figs. 3a,b). Pellets are found in groups. Droppings may clump when more succulent vegetation eaten.

Fig. 3a. White-tailed deer pellets.

Fig. 3b. Elk pellet.

Fig. 4. Scat of house mouse. Scale in mm.

Rodents: Scats are elongated spheres with smooth ends like a jelly bean like the house mouse scat (Fig. 4). Dropping also may have a point on one end and a rounded end on the other. Rarely will scats be round. Inclusions will be finely chewed and often unidentifiable. Rat scat will look like mouse droppings but ½ to ¾ in (12.7 to 19 mm) long. Look for hair. The presence of hair helps distinguish from insect scat. Muskrat droppings look like rat scat—just plain simple muddy looking ovals a little longer than an inch (2.5 cm). American cockroach: Like mouse droppings but are smaller and showing lengthwise ridges when magnified. They also will lack hair.

Dog Family (Foxes, Domestic Dogs, Coyotes): Scats are thick cords (Fig. 5a)and may be segmented (Fig. 5b), often containing hair from grooming or prey. May consist of a single continuous dropping or be in several sections. One end will likely pointed. Scats located along trails and scent posts. Members of the dog family chew on bones but they usually don't chew them up into cut fragments the way bobcats do. Scat of domestic dogs will tend to be granular due to the grains used in dog food.

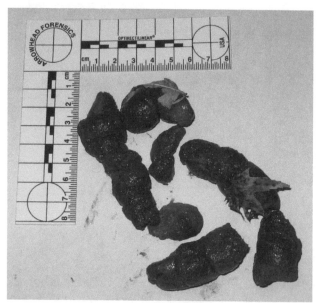

Fig. 5a. Fresh scat of medium-sized Dachshound.

Fig. 5b. Dog dropping from medium-sized bird-hunting dog. Note Pilot G2 Limited pen (6¼ in (15.9 cm) long at left.

Raccoon Family: Scats consist of thick cords and may be found in isolation or in piles (latrines). Ends are blunt and found frequently with seeds, hair, insects, and other undigested material.

Fig. 6. Raccoon scat with seeds.

Felines (House cats and bobcats): Scats of felines are broken cords, pointed at one end and often full of hair due to prey and grooming. Scats may be covered. Bobcat droppings often show chunks and fragments of chewed bone because cats have a well-developed pair of premolars well adapted to slicing bone. They swallow these bone fragments without injury.

Scats Containing White: If droppings are about the size of little fingers and show white material they might be robin (Fig. 7) or turkey droppings. The tom tends to produce a relatively straight or only slightly curved dropping. The hen leaves a smaller curly dropping. Canada goose droppings are similar but they show much less white and are mostly very dark green or black if the geese have been eating grass.

Lizard scats are elongated—½ in (12.7 mm) long dark—with a white spot one end. Look for them on railings, windowsills, or woodpiles.

Snake droppings can contain white (Fig. 8) but rarely are found.

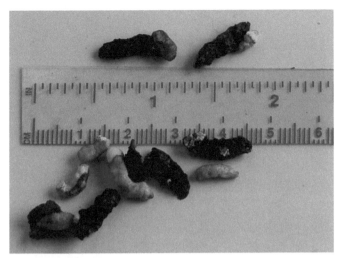

Fig. 7. Suspected robin scat.

Fig. 8. Droppings of the Prairie rattler.

Fig. 9. Droppings of garter snakes who rest underneath the building's siding after feeding on earth worms. Photo by Pam Gabriel.

Identifying Scats by Inclusions

Seeds: If droppings show seeds or fruits such as persimmon seeds, wild cherries, or poke berries then opossum, gray fox or raccoon are likely possibilities. If droppings show pokeberries, think raccoon because they are so adept at picking the berries from the plants. Red stained droppings full of pokeberry seeds lying on logs in a poke thicket are a sure sign of the raccoon in September. Hickory nut shell fragments signify bears as the nuts are quite hard.

Fish/Crayfish: If droppings are full of crayfish parts or fish scales, think raccoon or otter. Raccoon droppings are often on logs along creeks. They may be the diameter of the end of your little finger. Otter droppings are bigger, often chunky or slimy piles full of fish scales and bones. Otter droppings are called "spraints."

Bones: Complete. Large owls regurgitate a pellet of hair and bone fragments. The pellet can appear like mammal dropping (Fig. 10), however, they are light in weight and have no foul odor. Tease them apart and you often will find complete mouse-sized skulls in them.

Insect Parts: Toad—"toadstools" are like rat droppings but with insect exoskeleton fragments inside (Fig. 11). Just soak in water and find them with a magnifying glass. Droppings often found under lights where toads feed on insects attracted to the lights.

Bat dropping will look sparkly from light reflections off the exoskeletons of insects (Fig. 12).

Grass: Grass is difficult to digest so it often can be seen in scats (Fig. 13). Look for a fibrous collection of tan strands (sometimes green).

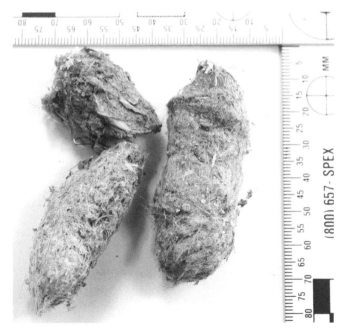

Fig. 10. Pellet of the great-horned owl.

Fig. 11. Toad dropping. Photo by Donna Vantassel.

Fig. 14. Wood borings of *Osmoderma eremicola* (larva stage). They are 0.2 to 0.3 in (5 to 8 mm) long. Photo by Jim Kalisch.

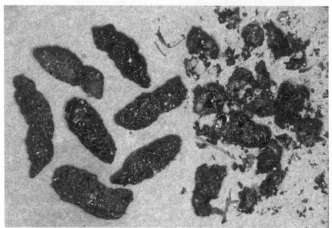

Fig. 12. Bat droppings, whole (left) and crushed (right). Photo by Jim Kalisch.

Fig. 15. Caterpillar droppings. Photo by John Losse of Sedona, AZ.

to black. Often found on decks or picnic tables or patios under overhanging branches or under tomato plants.

Final Thoughts

Scat identification is a challenging exercise. But with practice, you will find it to be a fascinating and rewarding aspect of the inspection process.

Resources

Some information gained from Robert Corrigan.

Granovsky, T. 1995. Scats: A "Who-Did-It?" for PCOs. Granovsky Associates. http://www.granovsky.com

Halfpenny, J. 1986. *A Field Guide to Mammal Tracking in North America*. 2nd ed. Boulder, CO: Johnson Books.

Halfpenny, J. and T. D. Furman. 2010. *Tracking Wolves: The Basics*. Jim Halfpenny.

Jackson. J. 2001. Tips for Turds: Identifying Tiny and Medium Sized Droppings. *Wildlife Control Technology*, 8:2(Mar-April):42-43.

Livingston, T. R., P. S. Gipson, W. B. Ballard, D. M. Sanchez, and P. R. Krausman. 2005. Scat Removal: A Source of Bias in Feces-Related Studies. *Wildlife Society Bulletin* 33:1(Spring):172-178.

Fig. 13. Horse droppings. Note the volume and the strands of tan grass in the dropping.

Caution: Small "scats" should be considered carefully as you might be dealing sign of insect activity (Fig. 14).

Scats with longitudinal grooves or striations signifies insect presence (Fig. 15). For example, caterpillar droppings are tiny, short cylinders 0.4 in (1 cm) length with lengthwise ridges. Color can vary from green to tan

Chapter 9   Hair Identification

You walk along around a house looking for animal sign and you notice a long white hair caught on the wood siding at the top of a 4-in (10 cm) hole under a deck. Skunk, you say to yourself, and then to show off your wilderness prowess, you present it to your client. But have you ever wondered whether your assessment was correct? Wouldn't it be nice to have a strategy or a technique that could help you identify animal hair on a more scientific basis?

Before you get too excited, let me be clear. There is no easy, sure-fire technique to identify animal hairs in the field. Let me explain why. According to Ms. Yates, Senior Forensic Scientist at the National Fish and Wildlife Forensics laboratory, you can't simply identify an animal hair by looking at it and be legally sure (legally as in valid for courtroom evidence) your identification is correct. There are just too many variables. For example, did you know that animal hair color can change from season to season? Second, fur can be different both in color and structure in different parts of an animal's body? Third, fur from the same species can vary in different parts of the country and even in different parts of the same state. Fourth, guard hair changes as the animal matures. Finally, differences exist between guard hairs and the under-fur. All of these factors work against a quick and easy method to identify animal hair, even when you have access to a laboratory.

Nevertheless, Ms. Yates has provided several tips to help narrow the list of possibilities. She provided a 4-step process on how to identify animal fur that will pass muster in the legal sense.

Step 1. Investigate the physical properties of the hair. This process is called the gross morphological assessment step (The Stains article is a fine example of this step, included below) and does not require a microscope. Observe:

    a. the color arrangement (against a gray, white, or blue background),

    b. length (calculated in mm from the basal end to the tip, Fig. 1a,b),

    c. diameter of the fur strand at the widest part,

    d. shaft configuration (wine glass, Fig. 2a, slightly tapered, Fig. 2b, or bulb shaped,),

    e. shaft undulations (Fig. 3, measure from one valley to the next),

    f. shape (does the hair shaft have a regular or irregular curve?), and

    g. color bands (does the hair have sharply differentiated colors? Fig. 4).

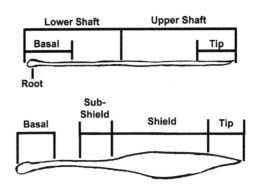

Figs. 1a,b. Labeling for straight (top) and shield-shaped hair (bottom). Images by Donna Vantassel.

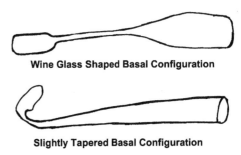

Figs. 2a,b. Wine glass shaped basal configuration (top) and slightly tapered configuration (bottom). Images by Donna Vantassel.

Fig. 3 Undulating hair shaft. Image by Donna Vantassel.

Fig. 4. An example of banding on a shield shaped hair. Image by Donna Vantassel.

The following steps require a microscope.

Step 2. Make a caste of the hair. Hairs often have scales that form specific patterns. For this step, a cuticle and a clear substance, like nail polish, are required. Place the hair in the nail polish and lets it harden. Once dried, the hair follicle is pulled out leaving a caste of the scale structure.

Step 3. Use a bi-focal compound microscope with a power range of 120-400 times with dual stages to allow side by side comparisons between your in-house fur data base and the mystery hair. Mount the hair in a polymer resin like nail polish and look at the internal structure of the hair.

Step. 4. If the previous three steps fail to provide a definitive answer, obtain a cross-section of a follicle. The hair strand needs to be perfectly transected. Ms. Yates says, the dissected piece is difficult to work with as it looks like a dust speck. This piece is then mounted and its structure is investigated.

Howard Stains published an article entitled, "Field Key to Guard Hair of Middle Western Furbearers" in the *Journal of the Wildlife Society* in January 1958, pp. 95-97, where he provides a series of questions to help you identify animal guard hairs. While only covering 17 species, the key is helpful in identifying the guard hairs of animals without having to rely on a microscope. The Wildlife Society has graciously given us permission to reprint this article. It follows this introduction.

Journal of Wildlife Management, Vol. 22, No. 1, January 1958, pp. 95-97

Field Key to Guard Hair of Middle Western Furbearers

Howard J. Stains

Cooperative Wildlife Research and Department of Zoology, Southern Illinois University, Carbondale, Illinois

A number of keys for identifying mammalian lairs have been published. Probably the most recent and refined of such publications is that by Mayer (1952. The hair of California mammals with keys to the dorsal guard hairs of California mammals. *Amer. Midl. Nat.*, 48:480-512) in which earlier papers are summarized. Because laboratory facilities and a microscope are required in order to utilize the above keys, they do not answer entirely the needs of the field biologist. A means of identifying, hairs without a microscope is provided in the key presented in this publication. The key has been tested on Middle Western furbearers in the field and laboratory, with more than 85% of the hairs being identified without difficulty. At least a dozen animals of each species of both freshly killed and museum specimens were examined. In each case, hair was taken from no less than 5 general locations on the specimen, depending upon the variability of the hair on a given animal.

There are 2 principal types of hair on the body of most mammals: the guard hair which is long, coarse, and often pigmented; and the underfur which is short, thin, often wavy, and less pigmented than the guard hair. This key is based upon the guard hairs, as they represent the most common sign left by an animal. Guard hairs can be found on sticks along well-used paths, on barb-wire where the animal passed under or through a fence, near feeding sites, on rocks, roots, bark, sharp surfaces, and splintered wood, or mixed with loose dirt in the bottom of a den entrance.

The effectiveness of the key is lessened when the normal sequence of colors of the guard hair is broken, or when the animals are immature or abnormally colored (albino or melanistic mutants). Because the hairs of domestic animals are so variable in color and size they have not been included.

In addition to the above difficulties, most mammals possess guard hairs that differ from 1 region of the body to another. These differences may be in size, in coloration, or in the combinations of colors to be found from the tip of the hair to the base. Although the key indicates the area of the body where a particular kind of hair can be found, this is not the only region on which this type may occur. On occasions, guard hairs from 2 different animals may appear to the unaided eye to be of the same color and size. By using several hairs from the same animal, the investigator may run through several different branches of the key and thus decrease the chance of error.

The true colors of hairs can be determined best by holding them against a light-blue background; a white, black, or brown background blends with several of the colors found in hairs, and makes use of the key more difficult.

Key to Guard Hairs

1. Tip black 2
   Tip not black 39
2. Only one color, black 3
   More than one color 8
3. Less than one inch long 4
   More than 1 inch long 5
4. Rigid, straight, high in luster . . . . Spotted skunk (belly)
   Soft, curly, dull in color . . . . Bobcat (tail)
5. Less than two inches long 6
   More than two inches long 7
6. Few or many delicate waves at base . . . . Spotted skunk (back)
   Few large waves or straight at base . . . . .Striped skunk (belly)
7. Less than 3 inches long .Striped skunk (back)
   More than 3 inches long .Spotted skunk (tail)
8. Two colors only (from tip, black over white, black over
   brown, or black over tan) 9
   Three or 4 colors 22
9. Colors in 2 to 5 bands 10
   Colors in 8 bands . . . . Fox squirrel (tail)
10. Colors in 2 or 3 bands only 11
    Colors in 4 or 5 bands only 18
11. Colors in 2 bands only 12
    Colors in 3 bands 17
12. Colors from tip: black over brown 13
    Colors from tip: black over white 14
13. Short black tip followed by long band of
    lustrous brown . . . . Beaver (back)
    Black over brown . . . . Bobcat (belly)
14. More than 4 inches long; coarse and with
    little or no wave . . . . Striped skunk (tail)
    Less than 4 inches long 15
15. More white than black, thin and wavy . . . . Opossum (back)
    More black than white, straight from tip to base 16
16. More than 1 inch long . . . . Striped skunk (tail)
    Less than 1 inch long . . . . Badger (front foot)
17. Colors from tip: black-white-black or
    black-brown-black . . . . Woodchuck
    Colors from tip: black-tan-black . . . . .Cottontail (back)
18. Hair colors in 4 band: from tip, black-white-black-white 19
    Two colors in 5 bands: from tip,
    black-white-black-white-black . . . . Woodchuck
19. Black tip less than ½-half inch long; hair
    may have large waves near base 20
    Black tip more than ½-half inch long; hair straight 21
20. In large waves . . . . Coyote (tail)
    Not in large waves . . . . Raccoon (back)
21. Color bands distinct . . . . Gray fox (tail)
    Color bands not distinct, blending . . . . Raccoon (back)
22. Three colors 23
    Four colors: black-white-brown-gray . . . . Raccoon (back)

Received for publication July 26, 1957.

Resources

I would to thank Dave Fellows of the U.S. Geological Survey and Ms. Yates for the information they provided.

If you would like to learn more about identifying animal hair pick up a copy of the following books.

Adorjan, A. S. and G.B. Kolenosky. 1969. *A Manual for the Identification of Hairs of Selected Ontario Mammals.* Research Report (Wildlife) No. 90, Ontario Dept. of Lands and Forests, Toronto.

Appleyard, H. M. and A. B. Wildman. 1969. Fibres of archaeological interest: their examination and identification. In *Science and Archaeology,* edited by D. Brothwell and E. Higgs, pp. 624-633. Bristol: Thames and Hudson.

Appleyard, H. M. 1978. *Guide to the Identification of Animal Fibres.* 2 ed. Wool Industries Research Assn., Leeds.

Brunner, H. and B. Coman. 1974. *The Identification of Mammalian Hairs.* Inkata Press Ltd., Melbourne.

Hair and Fibers Methods Manual. Training manual for RCMP Forensic Hair and Fiber, Central Forensic Laboratory, Ottawa.

Hausman, L. A. 1920. Structural Characteristics of the Hair of Mammals. *American Naturalist,* 54:496-523.

Hicks, J. W. 1977. *Microscopy of Hair, a Practical Guide and Manual.* Issue 2, Federal Bureau of Investigation, Washington, DC.

Moore, T. D., L. E. Spence, and C. E. Dugnolle. 1974. *Identification of the dorsal guard hairs of some mammals of Wyoming.* Wyoming Game and Fish Dept. Bull. No. 14. Laramie, WY: Wyoming Game and Fish Department.

Petraco, N. 1987. A Microscopial Method to Aid in the Identification of Animal Hair. *Microscope,* 35(1):83-92.

Stains, H. J. 1958. Field Key to Guard Hair of Middle Western Furbearers. *Journal of Wildlife Management,* 22(1):95-97.

Teerink, B. J. 1991. *Hair of West-European Mammals: Atlas and Identification Key.* Cambridge: Cambridge University Press.

Walker, D. N. and W. J. Adrian, eds. 2003. *Wildlife Forensic Field Manual.* 3rd ed. Printed by the Association of Midwest Fish and Game Law Enforcement Officers.

Wallis, R. L. 1993. A Key for the Identification of Guard Hairs of Some Ontario Mammals. *Canadian Journal of Zoology,* 71:587-591.

William, A. (ed.) 1996. *The Wildlife Forensic Field Manual.* 2nd ed. Printed by the Association of Midwest Fish and Game Law Enforcement Officers.

Chapter 10 **Bone Identification**

The purpose of this chapter is to provide some basic guidelines to help you quickly narrow done possible suspects. It is not intended to be a comprehensive guide. For that, consult http://digimorph.org/ and the resources at the end of the chapter.

General Bone Identification

Bones are classified into five categories.
Long bones—have a shaft that is closed at both ends by a joint. A femur is a long bone.
Compact bones—bones lacking an identifiable shaft and frequently containing multiple surfaces. Ankle and wrist bones are compact bones.
Flat bones—thin bones that protect vital organs, such as ribs and skull.
Irregular bones—similar to compact bones but have even more complex surfaces and holes for more functions. Vertebrate and pelvis are examples of irregular bones.
Sesamoid bones—bones (small) that occur in tendons designed to provide protective functions. Knee caps are examples of sesamoid bones.

Color: Bones with yellow contain fat. The less yellow the less fat.

Skulls-Flat bones

Skulls are easy, relatively speaking to classify. Skulls of interest to WCOs fall into four categories, mammal, bird, herpetological (amphibians and reptiles), and fish.
Mammal skulls fall into four main categories: carnivore, herbivore, omnivore, and rodent.

Carnivores: Carnivores (Fig. 1) have pronounced incisors for cutting and tearing meat. Incisors are less pronounced as they play only a minor role in the animal's life. Molars and pre-molars are sharp (versus flat for herbivores) to allow the carnivore to tear flesh.

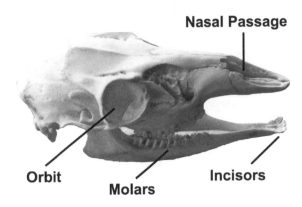

Fig. 2a. Skull of white-tailed deer.

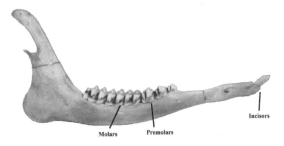

Fig. 2b. Jaw bone of a white-tailed deer. Not the large gap between the incisors and the pre-molars.

Herbivores: Herbivores (Fig. 2a) are plant eaters. Their skulls show pronounced incisors to clip plant material. Molars are wide and flat to allow for the grinding needed to prepare vegetation for digestion. Many herbivores (e.g. ungulates-elk are an exception) will lack upper incisors.
The lower jaw of the deer shows a large gap between the incisors and pre-molars (Fig. 2b).

Omnivores: Omnivores (Fig. 3) consume both vegetation and animal material. Their teeth combine elements of both the carnivore and the herbivore. Rounded molars suggest the animal is primarily a carnivore. Flattened molars suggest diet is primarily herbivore.

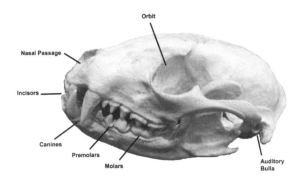

Fig. 1. Skull of a skunk (side view).

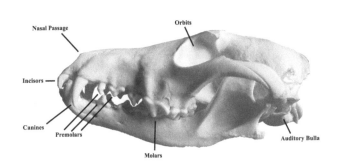

Fig. 3. Coyote skull (side view)

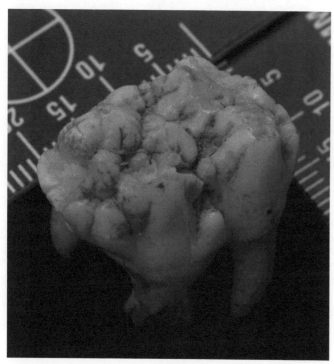

Fig. 4. Molar of domestic pig.

The molar of the domestic pig (Fig. 4) demonstrates the point regarding omnivores. Note how wide the molar is yet, it still has rounding for purposes of cutting. In this way, it can handle meat or plant material.

Rodents: Though rodents can fall within the omnivore category, the uniqueness of their skulls warrants a separate category (Fig. 5a). Rodent skulls, in my opinion, are the easiest of all mammal skulls to identify. Just look for the pronounced incisors followed by a large gap before the molars. Note the pronounced incisors of pocket gopher (Fig. 5b). If you look carefully, you will see how the lips close behind the front teeth. They can do this because of the large gap between the paired incisors and the other teeth. This gap is called the diastema.

Birds: The skulls of birds exhibit great diversity, particularly in the shape of the beak/nose. Fortunately, identifying a skull as from a bird is rather easy. Figures 6a and 6b provide an example of a bird skull and skeleton respectively.

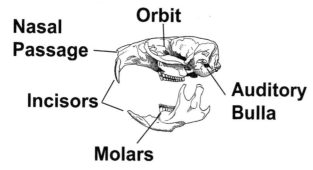

Fig. 5a. Skull of muskrat. Adapted from an image in Stone, W., C. Stone, and W. Everett. 1902. American Animals. p.ix. Image scanned by FromOldBooks.org

Fig. 5b. Incisors of the Plains pocket gopher.

Herpetological Skulls: Amphibians, lizards, and snakes have unique shapes. Just consider the frog skeleton (Fig. 7).

Human vs. Animal Bones: Since WCOs enter crawl spaces and other infrequently traveled areas, it is a good idea to have some ready tips to distinguish human bones from animal. Table 1 contains information adapted from the Arizona State Museum web page.

Strange Bones: Since receiving no less than 2 requests to identify this bone (Fig. 9), I thought I would include in this edition of the handbook.

Bone Gnawing Identification

Carnivores: Use their sharp canines and powerful molars to create grooves (a.k.a. furrows), pits, punctures, radial scars, channels, and chipped back margins in search of the fat and other nutrients in long bones. Lacking epiphyseal ends, long, bones are transformed into tubular shafts with smoothed margins that are polished in appearance due to scooping and licking actions of carnivores while extracting marrow. Studies show that carnivores avoid bones that lack fat and other nutrients desired by canines.

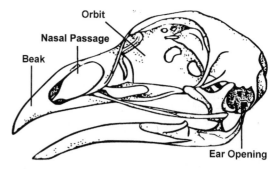

Fig. 6a. Bird skull. Image adapted from C. William Beebe's 1906. *The Bird: Its Form and Function*. Obtained from Wikipedia.

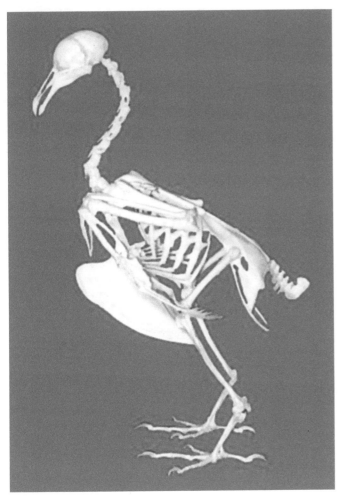

Fig. 6b. Pigeon skeleton. Photo by Uwe Gille. Source: Wikimedia.

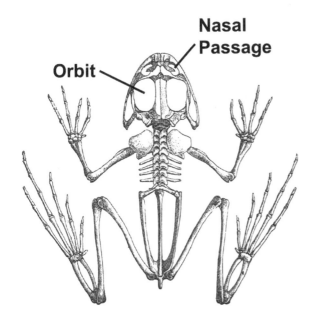

Fig. 7. Skeleton of a frog. Image adapted from Rana, in G. A. Boulenger, *The fauna of British India including Ceylon and Burma. Reptilia and Batrachia,* 1890 (Wikipedia).

Thickness of Bones

Animal   **Human**

Fig. 8. Relative bone thickness between humans and animals.

Table 1. Human vs. Animal Bones

Human Skull	Animal Skull
Large brain area, small face	Small brain area, large face
Brain cap relatively smooth	Pronounced muscle markings, sagittal crest Inferior
Chin present	Chin absent
Orbits at front, above nasal aperture	Orbits at sides, posterior to nasal aperture
Minimal nasal and midface projection	Significant nasal and midface projection
"U"-shaped mandible (no midline separation)	"V"-shaped mandible (separates at midline)

Human Teeth	Animal Teeth
Omnivorous	Carnivorous; Herbivorous; Omnivorous
Incisors larger than other mammals (except for horses)	Incisors smaller

Human Skeleton	Animal Skeleton
Note. Infant bones are frequently mistaken for animal bones.	
Small arms	Strong front limbs
Pelvis broad and short, bowl shaped	Pelvis is long and narrow, blade-shaped
Femur longest bone	Femur similar in length to other bones

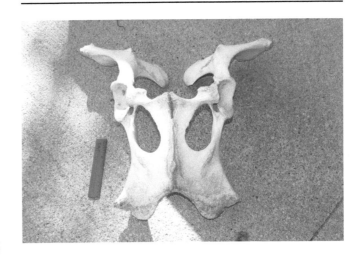

Fig. 9. Pelvis of a young deer.

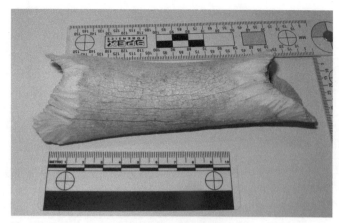

Fig. 10. Bone gnawed on by fox squirrels.

Rodents: Use their paired incisors to create broad, shallow, flat-bottomed grooves on the densest parts of a skeleton as they extract calcium and other minerals from bone and antler (Fig. 10).

Unlike canids, conflicting statements exist regarding the type of bone and region of interest most preferred by rodents. Although often stated to be frequent modifiers of dry, weathered skeletal remains, some have suggested that rodents are involved in modifications to fresh greasy bones.

While generally stated to target locations of the skeleton having thick cortical bone (e.g., long-bone shafts) and a protruding edge, rodents also have been implicated in the modification of trabecular bone.

Rodent Bite force: Body mass and bite force are correlated highly among small rodent (Table 1). The general rule is the larger the animal the greater the bite force.

Table 2. Rodent bite force and body mass

Species	N	Mass (g)	Bite force
Ord's kangaroo rat	11	63	13.98
Plains pocket gopher	5	153	50.61
Microtus ochrogaster	10	34	12.88
Deer mouse	4	21	8.83
White-footed mouse	10	23	10
Fox Squirrel	22	588	72.95
13-lined ground squirrel	4	144	21.05

Remember, animals can only gnaw on what they can obtain purchase with their teeth.

Resources

Beisaw, A.M. ND. Bone Words. http://webspace.webring.com/people/ma/abeisaw/boneid2.html. Visited December 24, 2011.

Elbroch, M. 2006. *Animal Skulls: A Guide to North American Species.* Mechanicsburg, PA: Stackpole Books.

Freeman, P. W. and C. A. Lemen. 2008. A simple morphological predictor of bite force in rodents. *Journal of Zoology,* 275:418-422.

Klippel, W. E. and J. A. Synstelien. 2007. Rodents as Taphonomic Agents: Bone Gnawing by Brown Rats and Gray Squirrels. *J Forensic Sci,* 52:4(July 2007):1556-4029.

Sullivan, L. M. 1999. Wildlife Skull Activities. Tucson, AZ: The University of Arizona Cooperative Extension. AZ1145 (Oct):1-16.

Watson, J. and J. McClelland. *Distinguishing Human from Animal Bone.* Arizona State Museum. http://www.statemuseum.arizona.edu/crservices/human_animal_bone.shtml site visited December 27, 2011.

Bone Identification

Wildlife Control Consultant thanks Richard Wolniewicz, a professional landscaper for the Massachusetts Audubon Society, for granting permission to reprint "Bones of Contention No More," published in the *Massachusetts Wildlife Magazine* No. 2, 2001. His book, *Field Guide to Skulls and Bones of Mammals of the Northeastern United States* (2 volumes) appeared in 2004. It is unfortunately no longer in print, but may be available in digital form from the author.

Bones of Contention No More

by Richard Wolniewicz

Frustrated with the lack of a good reference for identifying the skeletal remains in an owl pellet, the author decided to do it himself, embarking on a "skull and bones" field guide project that eventually expanded to include all the mammals of the Northeast.

It all started innocently enough. There was no bolt of lightning, no divine inspiration, no lifelong dream of creating a field guide to mammal skulls and bones. The fact is, if I hadn't stumbled upon an owl pellet along the trail while I was out hiking one day, this journey probably would never have begun. An owl, if it can, will swallow its prey whole. Its digestive juices aren't strong enough to break down fur and bone, so after a meal an owl regurgitates this material in the form of a pellet. Fur, feathers, claws, scales, bones and any other indigestible material is compressed into a neat little package and ejected several hours after feeding. The pellet—at least if the owl fed on a mammal—is essentially a "fur ball with bones."

The adventure began when I started to pull apart the pellet I had found in an attempt to discover what the owl had been feeding on. The work was somewhat comparable to an archeological dig in which the substrate—in this case the fur encasing and entwined around the bones—must be carefully removed to expose the hard evidence within. Through my careful picking and prising, it soon became clear that there were a number of tiny, dissimilar mammal bones within the pellet. But whose bones were they? How could I identify the original owners of these disarticulated skeletons?

The problem was that I couldn't find any reliable guides or books to help me through the identification process. There were sheets and drawings available from companies that sell owl pellets for educational purposes, but their pellets were often collected in the Pacific Northwest or the Southwest where the small mammal species composition differs considerably from the composition found here in the Northeast. Even the drawings I did manage to turn up were either not to scale or offered little in the way of detail, making it impossible to distinguish between particular bones. I would have had to find a complete skull or jaw in a pellet if I hoped to make an identification (this is sometimes possible, especially in the case of the jaw, but owls are prone to crack into the braincase, often breaking off the back end of their victim's skulls), and even then I could not be guaranteed of correctly identifying the species.

Frustrated with the lack of good reference materials, I decided my best option was to assemble my own collection of known skeletons for direct comparison. To this end I promptly enlisted the help of our neighborhood cat. This grizzled, friendly feline would often leave mice, voles, shrews and other offerings on our back steps, thanking us, I suppose, for the cat treats we'd fed him. Mind you, we did not approve of him decimating the local population of fauna in our neighborhood, and we more than once put a bell on his collar to warn the local inhabitants of his whereabouts, but either the animal took it off or his owners did.

My plan was to retrieve the "cat casualties" and place them in a box where carrion insects would consume the flesh and leave the skeleton behind. The fragrance of death is carried strong and far on the wind, alerting the flesh-eating scavengers to the location of the body. These insects arrive at the scene (of the crime) in sequence, depending on the corpse's specific stage of decomposition. Forensic pathologists know the life cycles of these insects, and use that knowledge to accurately determine the time of death of people found deceased outdoors (and sometimes even indoors).

To keep large scavengers such as raccoons, foxes, and coyotes from carrying off the carcasses, I had to design a "safe house" to hold my specimens while the insects did their work. Using quarter-inch exterior plywood, I constructed a box four inches wide, six inches long and five inches high. I stapled fine screen mesh on the open bottom and drilled a few half-inch holes along the sides. After placing the dead animal in the container, I stapled quarter-inch wire mesh over the open top. The drill holes in the sides and the quarter-inch mesh over the top allowed carrion consuming insects to pass easily in and out of

the box. The fine wire mesh stapled to the bottom prevented any small bones from falling through and possibly being lost.

The first animal I placed in one of these boxes was a white-footed mouse, *Peromyscus leucopus*. After securing the mouse in the box, I put it out into the woods and waited. I didn't have to wait long. It was absolutely astonishing how little time it took for insects to find the body and totally clean the fur and flesh from the bones! Within one week little remained but the skeleton. The "undertaker" insects—mostly fly and beetle larvae—are clearly the piranhas of the terrestrial landscape. I removed the skeleton from the box, placed it in a light solution of bleach and water to whiten the bones and remove any remaining bacteria, and then sun-dried it. I had my first reference specimen!

It was about this time that our family decided to enter the computer age and purchased a PC for the household. Taking advantage of a "package deal," we left the store with monitor, keyboard, CPU, printer, speakers, mouse, scanner, and enough wire to put the Frankenstein monster back on line. I am not, I admit, computer savvy. Even now, four years later, I know what I know simply through necessity, and more often than not, take the long road when executing a task. After many frustrating hours and curses expressed towards this new age, we were finally what we'd call "up and running."

Playing around with the scanner one evening, I placed a bone on it and printed the resulting scan. It was incredible! The image was three-dimensional, finely detailed and—most importantly for my purposes—was the actual size of the bone. I immediately realized how advantageous it would be to scan the same type of bones (femurs, ulnas, etc.) from several similar-sized species together on the same page for comparison and identification purposes. If I could show the bones together, as well as at actual size the images would allow anyone to identify what type of bone they had found, and, through the process of elimination, the species of mammal it represented. The only thing I needed now (other than an enormous amount of time at the scanner) was lots of correctly identified bones so I could scan different views (front back, side) of the bones, as well as any variations in size between male, female and juvenile specimens.

No matter how many neighborhood cats I could recruit, no matter how many road kills I could pick up and stuff into bone boxes, I couldn't imagine how I could possibly assemble a sufficiently large enough collection of bones in a lifetime to produce what I now had in mind: a reasonably thorough reference for identifying the

Given a little warmth and humidity, Nature's invertebrate undertakers can reduce a carcass to bare bones in a matter of days. A month from now, without the quills or a field guide, most outdoorsmen couldn't tell if this was a porcupine or a beaver. (Photo by Bill Byrne)

Major Bones of the Forelimb
The four major bones of the mammal forelimb are the scapula (shoulder-blade), humerus (corresponding to the femur in the hindlimb), ulna, and radius. The right forelimb of a muskrat (lower right) shows the typical articulation of the bones.

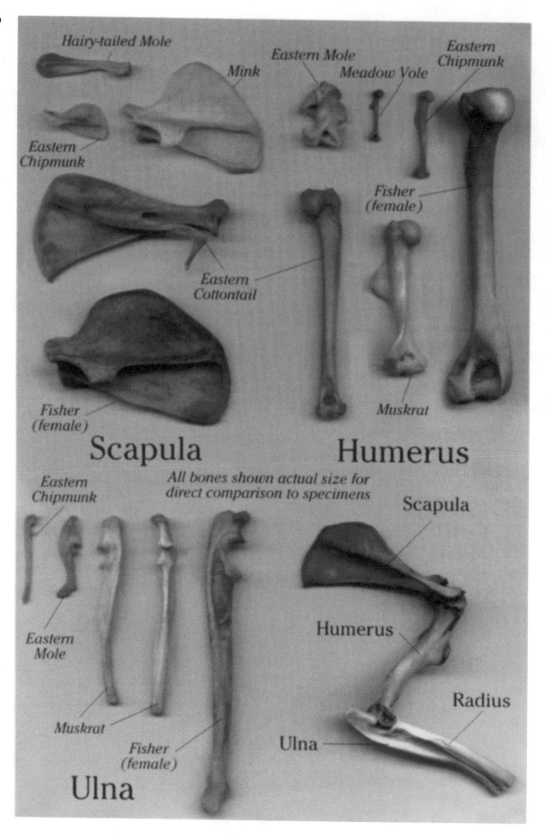

bones of the mammals of the Northeast. So I went in search of a house that had more skeletons in its closets than mine did. I knew a number of colleges and museums would have collections of mammal skeletons, but I had no idea if they'd allow a rank, self-taught naturalist such as myself to utilize them.

Mustering my courage, I put in a call to the Mammal Department at Harvard University. I spoke with the Curatorial Associate, Maria Rutzmoser, who listened patiently as I explained my project. Much to my surprise and delight, she informed me that with just a little paper work and the approval of a department head or two, the way could be opened for me to borrow bones from their collection.

Entering the Osteology (the term used to describe the study of bones) Department for the first time, I was awestruck by how many mammal bones filled every shelf and cabinet, every nook and cranny in the huge building. Lions, tigers and bears, oh my, not to mention primates, marsupials and whales. I was like a kid in a candy store. It was hard to stay focused on just the mammals of the Northeast with so many other incredible specimens at my fingertips.

In order not to make my "bone book" too cumbersome, I decided to include only the skull, mandible (jaw), scapula (shoulder-blade), humerus and ulna (long bones of the forelimb), pelvis (hipbone), and the femur and tibia (long bones of the hindlimb). These bones are the ones most often found in the field and most easily identified, even if they are broken and incomplete. Some of them are also the best specimens for indicating the age and sex of a mammal. (Juvenile animals, being

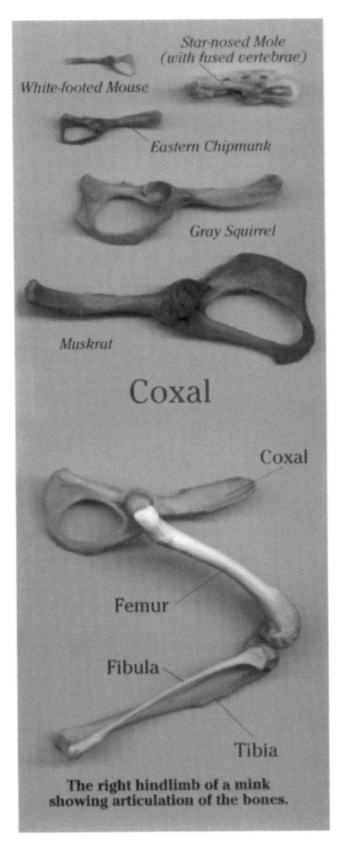

The right hindlimb of a mink showing articulation of the bones.

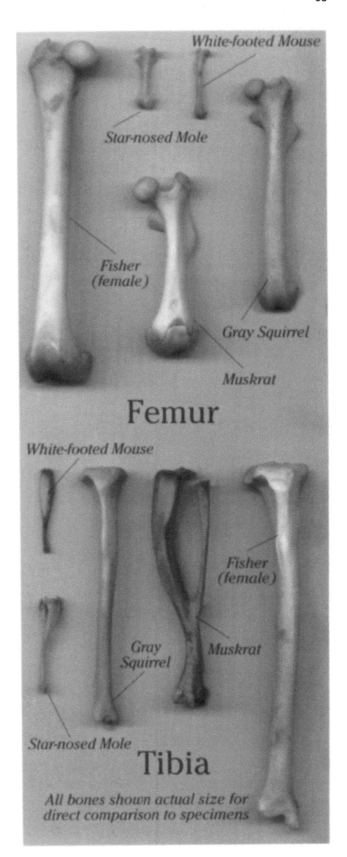

All bones shown actual size for direct comparison to specimens

inexperienced and therefore most likely to make fatal mistakes or fail to find adequate food , typically exhibit the highest mortality rates in most populations, so their bones are apt to be found more frequently than those of adults. I included many juvenile bones in my scans for exactly this reason.)

Major Bones of the Hindlimb
The four major bones of the mammal hindlimb are the coxal (one half of the pelvis), femur (the longest and heaviest bone for many species), tibia, and fibula. Note that the tibia and fibula are fused into a single bone in some species.

Native Rabbit Skulls
Although introduced species can be found on certain islands (and there is always the possibility of stumbling on the remains of an escaped domestic), these three skulls represent our only native lagomorphs and are the ones most commonly encountered. Key identification features are indicated.

It took a lot of time and effort to arrange and scan the bones in a format I felt would be most effective for people to use. I wanted to provide a bone guide that would allow anyone to distinguish between each of the five genera of bats that inhabit the Northeast, as well as the three species of moles that burrow their way into the hearts of so many gardeners. From squirrels to rabbits, raccoons to fishers, bobcats, opossums, deer, moose, bear, and every mammal in between, I wanted my reference book to make it possible for anyone and everyone to accurately identify any resident mammal from just a bone or two. When I had completed enough scanned images I was satisfied with, it was time to begin testing the efficacy of my work.

I began testing the book on two fronts. The first was to bring it to every Audubon sanctuary, every school and nature center—any place I could think of where folks would possibly have a collection of skulls and bones—and have them pull out their

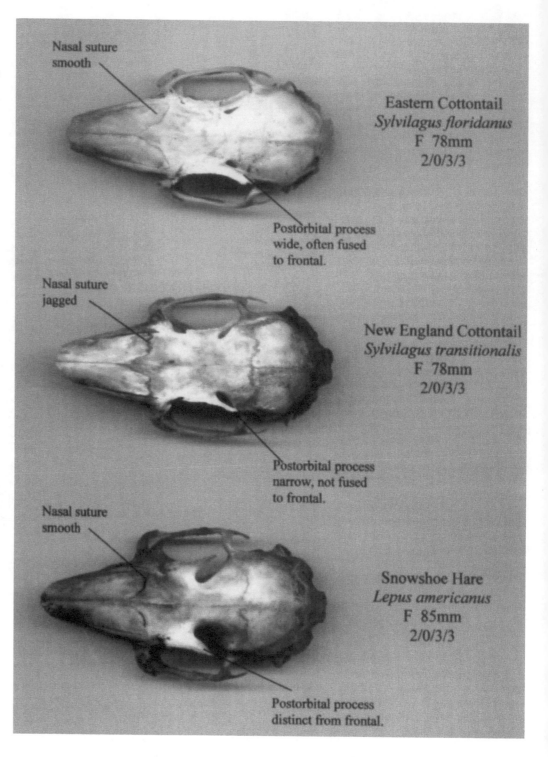

Nasal suture smooth

Eastern Cottontail
Sylvilagus floridanus
F 78mm
2/0/3/3

Postorbital process wide, often fused to frontal.

Nasal suture jagged

New England Cottontail
Sylvilagus transitionalis
F 78mm
2/0/3/3

Postorbital process narrow, not fused to frontal.

Nasal suture smooth

Snowshoe Hare
Lepus americanus
F 85mm
2/0/3/3

Postorbital process distinct from frontal.

specimens and check to see if their identifications were correct. What I found was amazing: the majority of the bones in these local collections were not identified at all, and over 60% of the skulls and bones that *were* labeled, were incorrectly identified! If time permitted, I'd have the resident naturalist, teacher, or curator use the book to identify the bones. Orders for the book—as yet unpublished and incomplete—began coming in at a very gratifying rate.

On the second front I had to find out if my scanned images of the bones were detailed and organized well enough for someone—hopefully anyone—to be able to match an actual

bone with the image, and thus make an accurate identification. So I put together a simple test: I numbered 60 different bones and gave them to people, along with the scanned bone images, and asked them to try to identify all the bones. I had not yet written any key to go with the scans, so those being tested had only the images to use in their identification attempts. I would later use the test results in designing the key guide, basing it in part on how much trouble my test subjects had with certain bones.)

The only thing I told those taking the test was that the scanned images were the *actual size* of the bones. I believe this

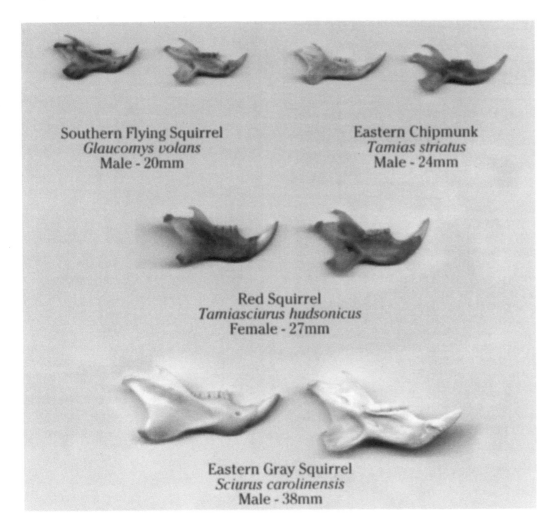

Southern Flying Squirrel
Glaucomys volans
Male - 20mm

Eastern Chipmunk
Tamias striatus
Male - 24mm

Red Squirrel
Tamiasciurus hudsonicus
Female - 27mm

Eastern Gray Squirrel
Sciurus carolinensis
Male - 38mm

Squirrels have a dental formula of 1/0/1/3, meaning each jaw has one incisor, no canine, one premolar, and three molars. Rabbits have a dental formula of 2/0/3/3.

It's been four years since the morning I bent over to pick up that owl pellet along the trail. Since then I have logged thousands of hours on the computer and scanner, examined and manipulated hundreds of skulls and bones, and have filled my head to bursting with obscure knowledge about the skeletal system and the identification of its many parts by species, sex and age. The result, thanks to the help and encouragement of many wonderful people, has led to the creation of what I believe is a unique and useful field guide. I have yet to find a publisher for this guide, but I'm pretty hopeful about the prospects, and even if I don't, the process has been an education in itself and a heck of a lot of fun.

is one the best and most important features of my book, since it allows for direct comparison with any bone specimen. Only a few bones had to be scanned at half or three-quarter size because of their length. Those bones were not included in the test, but I felt reasonably confident that nobody was going to mistake the femur of a moose with that of a mouse! The search for victims began. Any unsuspecting person wandering the halls at work, anyone straying too close to my desk or home, was a potential target. The primary objective was to test people of all ages and from all walks of life. My goal was to produce a user-friendly book, one which could serve not only professionals, but also amateur naturalists, schoolteachers, students, sportsmen, or anyone interested in identifying what a bone is and the mammal to which it belonged. I tested high-school interns from my workplace, co-workers, visitors, mailmen, accountants, twelve-year-olds, eighty-year-olds, teachers, husbands, wives, nieces, nephews, mothers, and fathers. When the pool of victims was exhausted, the scores were tallied.

I was very pleased with the results. Scores ranged from 78% to 100% identification accuracy, with an average of 84%. With these results, I knew that the images were good and that an identification key, supplied with the images, would provide enough additional information to raise the average ID accuracy to nearly 100%. I don't think you can ask much more of any field guide.

Aside from the knowledge I've gained along the way, there's one lesson that has stuck with me throughout this long endeavor: Be careful what you pick up on the trail of life; you never know where it's going to lead you....

Richard Wolniewicz is a professional landscaper and the Property Manager at Massachusetts Audubon's Ipswich River Wildlife Sanctuary in Topsfield, MA. His 2-volume *Field Guide to Skulls and Bones of Mammals of the Northeastern United States* was published in 2004.

Owl Pellet Dissection Guide

One of the most valuable attributes of the author's guide is that it shows the bones at their actual size, allowing for direct matching with a specimen. This spread illustrates the major bones of four types of small mammals commonly found in owl pellets. Once the genus is determined, more specific images will be available to identify the species.

Look for owl pellets under roost trees. Our big owls—great horned and barred—typically choose large, often solitary forest conifers that offer a good view of the ground and provide concealment from crows and other annoyances. Smaller owls like the screech may use dense shrubbery or even hollow apple or shade trees in the midst of suburbia. Note that skulls found in owl pellets are often missing the braincase, a target instinctively favored by raptors.

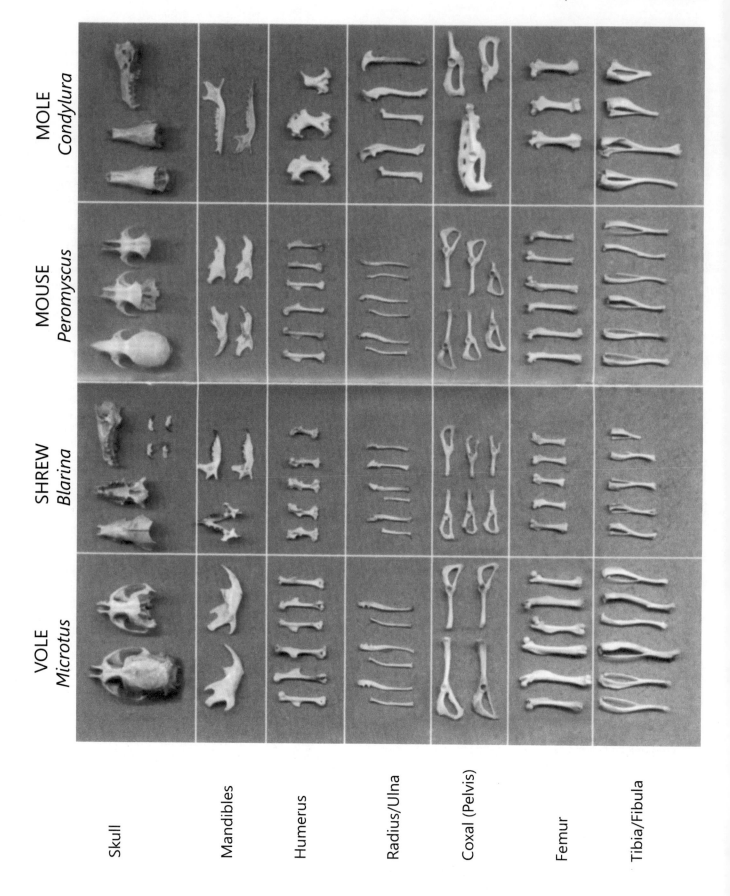

	MOLE *Condylura*	MOUSE *Peromyscus*	SHREW *Blarina*	VOLE *Microtus*
Skull				
Mandibles				
Humerus				
Radius/Ulna				
Coxal (Pelvis)				
Femur				
Tibia/Fibula				

Chapter 11 **Eyeshine**

Eye shine may seem to be a rather esoteric identification technique but you might think differently if you discover eyes peering back at you while you are wedged in a crawl space. According to Rob Strachan, eye shine occurs when light bounces off a group of special cells in the rear of the retina called the *tapetum lucidum*. He adds the color of the reflection (green, blue, orange, or red) is determined by whether the animal is looking directly at the light or at a 90° angle to the light.

Others have noted that the color of the eye's reflection is determined also by the angle at which we view the animal's eyes. In other words, the angle of the light's refraction will modify what "color" we see. In addition, the amount of the *tapetum lucidum* in the particular species affects the amount of reflection as well. For instance, humans lack the *tapetum lucidum* so our eye shine looks red from us seeing the blood cells in the back of our eyes. Of course, we haven't even considered the way humidity, light intensity, curvature of the eye's lens impacts the way we perceive the reflected color.

Just consider Figures 1 to 4 which show the eyeshine of cottontail rabbit, fox squirrel, raccoon, and dog (Dachshund) respectively. Note how the rabbit eye exhibits the color red, orange, and yellow, depending on what part of the eye you consider. The raccoon image (Fig. 3) shows how angle of light can impact the colors of the reflection of the eye. Dog photo (Fig. 4) illustrates the reflection of a dog's eye to camera flash.

Despite the challenges of using eye shine to identify an animal species, I have combined his information along with others into the following tables. I believe

Fig. 2. Eye shine of fox squirrel. Light source was camera flash.

Fig. 3. Eye shine of raccoon. Light source likely a mix of flashlight and camera flash. Photo by Reginald Murray, Oklahoma Wildlife Control, LLC.

Fig. 1. Eye shine of cottontail rabbit.

Fig. 4. Eye shine of a dog to the flash of an iPhone.

that this information coupled with habitat, relative head height (Fig. 5), and distance between the eyes will combine to help eliminate suspects if not identify a specific species.

Color	Species
Red	Alligator (bright reddish-orange to an iridescent pink)
	Barn Owl (dull)
	Black Bear
	Gray Fox (medium)
	Lagomorphs
	Nighthawks (pinkish)
	Opossum (bright red)
	Otter (dull)
	Poorwills (pinkish)
	Porcupine (deep)
	Ring-tailed Cat (red-yellow)
	Screech Owl (dull)
	Seals (dull)
Red or Orange	Fox
	Hares
	Rabbits
	Rodents
Orange	Red fox
Yellow-Amber	Bobcat
	Great-horned Owl (bright yellow)
	Opossum (dull orange)
	Raccoon (eyes close together)
	Red Fox (golden-yellow; eyes widely separated)
	Striped Skunk (deep amber)
Green	Badger
	Black-footed Ferret (blue/green)
	House Cat (cat families; reddish-gold to bright green)
	Cougar (yellow/green)
	Sheep
	White-tailed Deer (dead)
Blue	Dogs (bluish; Irish setters-reddish)
	Pine marten (electric-blue)
	Woodchuck
White/Silver	Badger
	Flamulated Owl (tiny pinpoints adjacent to tree)
	Flying Squirrel
	White-tailed Deer (strong silver-white)
No Eyeshine	Armadillos
	Feral Hogs
	Little brown bats

Fig. 5. Look carefully at the tall pine tree in the middle of the image. The trail camera picked up the eye reflection of an owl perched in the tree.

Resources

I would like to thank George R. Gallagher, Professor of Animal Science of Berry College, Anne Ruggles of Bear Canyon Consulting, LLC., Rick Griffiths, and Jim Halfpenney for their helpful and generous comments and insights. All errors are mine.

Alderman, Craig. 2007. *Ozarks Newstand.* Feb 26. TheOutdoorsman@cpimo.com.

Fenton, M. B. and R. M. R. Barclay. 1980. *Myotis lucifugus.* Mammalian Species No. 142 (Nov. 20):1-8.

Harding, J. 1979. *An Animal Damage Identification Guide for Massachusetts.* Amherst, MA: Cooperative Extension Service, University of Massachusetts, SP-113.

Inbar, M. and R. T. Mayer. 1999. Spatio-Temporal Trends in Armadillo Diurnal Activity and Road-Kills in Central Florida. *Wildlife Society Bulletin,* 27:3 (Autumn):865-872.

Reid, F. A. 2006. *Mammals of North America.* Peterson Field Guides. 4th ed. NY, NY: Houghton Mifflin.

Strachan, R. 1998. *Mammal Detective.* Essex, UK: Whittet Books.

Texas Parks and Wildlife. 2011. Eyeshine. http://www.tpwd.state.tx.us/publications/nonpwdpubs/young_naturalist/animals/eyeshine/, page visited Aug 6, 2011.

Chapter 12 Predator Damage Identification

Predator damage identification is a complex and difficult area of wildlife damage identification. But it can be very important, particularly when a prized bull can be valued in the thousands of dollars (Fig. 1) or a client's favorite pet.

Process for Evaluating a Carcass

Identification of what killed an animal requires deliberate and methodical evaluation of the evidence. Just as the late O. J. Simpson defense attorney Johnny Cochran used to say, "We must avoid a rush to judgment."

Step 1. Get to the scene as soon as possible. Time is perhaps the greatest single challenge to accurate determination of cause of death. The reason is the animal could have died of natural causes and then was scavenged by coyotes and/or other animals. Many times predators have been accused of causing the animal's death when in fact they only fed on an animal that died by other means.

Step 2. Evaluate the scene. Nervous livestock and herds suggest a predator attack. Do the plants and ground appear to be torn up or trampled, suggesting a struggle? Look for blood splatter and trail suggesting dragging. Dead animals only continue to bleed for a few minutes as the heart is no longer beating. Severed arteries of live animals will spray blood each time the heart beats. Are any other animals in the herd injured? Frequently attacks will result in injuries (survivable) of other animals. Look for fresh tracks, scat, and urine marks.

Step 3. Consider the animal's body position. Animals that are lying down with legs beneath them suggest natural death from illness.

Step 4. Evaluate the carcass as is, noting any injuries, signs (sputum at mouth) visible. Determine the approximate age and weight of the animal. Try to rule out possible suspects (e.g. house cats don't attack 1000 lb (453.5 kg) bulls.

Step 5. Skin the carcass. Wear appropriate personal protective equipment (e.g. water-proof gloves, face shield, coveralls, and antiseptics/cleaning agents) and remove the skin. You will be looking for puncture marks (teeth, talons, and claws) as well as bruising and cuts which may not have been visible in step 4.

Blood around wounds suggests the animal's heart was still beating, thus it was alive at the moment of the bite. A word of caution should be noted. Decomposition of the carcass can result in blood spots (hemorrhages) that can be confused with injuries due to trauma. The reason is as the carcass decays, blood vessels rupture leaking into the surrounding tissue. Remember: carcass decay occurs faster on the side which is warmer. Additionally, blood pools at the lowest part of the animal due to gravity.

Step 6. Rule out alternative causes of death, if possible. Consult with owner or livestock manager concerning the health of the animal. Young may be stillborn. Livestock eat poisonous plants or die of disease. Consider weather as animals can die of exposure and lightning too.

Typical Signs of Predation

Only larger animals are mentioned as small and even medium-sized animals are eaten in their entirety.

Black bears
Prey. Sheep, calves, cows, pigs, and sometimes poultry; fawns.
Site of attack. Bites to top of head, neck, back, and ribs. Claw marks usually seen. Bears tend to maul. Attack by ambush and won't chase prey for long distances like coyotes or wolves.
Number in attack. Bears hunt alone. Two small animals may be killed at a time (more if poultry or if prey are small). One animal killed if calf sized or larger. Sometimes animals die due to trampling each other as they run away or pile up against one another.
Feeding behavior. Eats udders. May move prey to cover and return later. May consume animal in one feeding. Skin usually is ignored but turned inside out and licked clean. Bones ignored and often scattered.
Technical sign. Neck may be broken. Upper canines are

Fig. 1. Loss of livestock to predation can be a significant financial loss to owners.

1.7 to 2.5 in (4.3 to 6.4 cm) apart. Scat width greater than 1.25 in (3.175 cm).

Bobcats

Prey. Poultry; fawns and adult deer.

Site of attack. Neck.

Number in attack. They hunt alone. Birds removed one at a time. Will return each evening to kill more even though they can't eat all of the food.

Feeding behavior. Begin at abdomen with internal organs eaten first. Legs and shoulders eaten last probably due to lower fat content. Look for scrapes at cache sites reaching out 1 ft (0.3 m) from carcass.

Technical sign. Track is usually less than 2½ in (6 cm) in length. Upper canines are 0.6 to 1.06 in (1.4 to 2.7 cm) apart.

Cougars

Prey. Sheep, calves, cows, and colts; deer.

Site of attack. Bite marks on back of neck. Look for claw marks on neck, shoulders, flanks as it grasps the prey. Little sign of chase.

Number in attack. Cougars hunt alone. Often kill only one animal at a time.

Feeding behavior. After removing hair from entry point, it begins feeding at the abdomen just behind the ribs, legs, and eats the meat on the neck also. Uses rough tongue to clean bones of meat. Will gorge. Will relocate kill, cover, and cache it for later feeding. Look for paw scrapes at cache sites reaching out 3 ft (1 m) from carcass. Does not eat carrion.

Technical sign. Neck broken from bite. Generally, does not need to re-grip the bite. Avoids eating stomach. Cuts in the meat are clean. Front foot track is 3½ in (9 cm) in width. Claw marks are absent in track. Upper canines are 1.6 to 2.05 in (4.1 to 5.2 cm) apart.

Coyotes

Prey. Lambs, calves, pigs, poultry. Rare, cows (during birthing) and horses; fawns and deer.

Site of attack. Throat is the site for short animals such a lambs (sometimes ewes) and pigs. Small lambs may have a crushed skull and be completely removed from the site. Look for multiple bites as the coyote re-grips. Flanks and legs will show bites on larger animals such as calves.

Number in attack. Usually one animal.

Feeding behavior. Feeding begins at the flanks or anus and continues through internal organs. Coyotes will cache and return to carcass to continue feeding. Won't/can't move large animals. Bird will be taken away completely, unless confined, then multiple birds may be killed.

Technical sign. Upper canines are spaced 1.06 to 1.44 in (2.7 to 3.7 cm) apart. Look for grasses or leaves stained with blood etc. due to muzzle wiping. See wolves for more information.

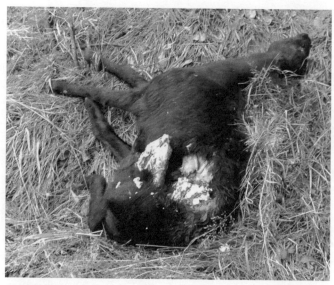

Fig. 2. This goat was killed by dogs. Photo by John Consolini.

Crows, Ravens, & Magpies

Prey. Animals that can't defend themselves; eggs.

Site of attack. Soft-tissue (eyes, nose, anus, neck, and wounds). Birds tend to penetrate eggs along the side rather than the end.

Number in attack. Multiple birds may attack a single animal.

Feeding behavior. Pull on flesh. Look for white feces at sites. Eggs will have a puncture on one side.

Dogs

Prey. Sheep, calves, goats, pigs, and poultry. Less common, cows and horses.

Site of attack. Almost anywhere on smaller species, and flanks of larger (Fig. 2).

Number in attack. Dogs tend to attack in groups. They frequently injure more than 1 animal.

Feeding behavior. Often mutilate the body rather than feed. Attacks are drawn out as they chase the animal(s).

Feral Pigs

Prey. Sheep, calves, and smaller animals.

Site of attack. Death typically occurs by biting and crushing the skull or neck.

Number in attack. Can attack in groups.

Feeding behavior. Depredation to calves and lambs can be difficult to identify because these small animals may be killed and completely consumed, leaving little or no evidence to determine the cause of death. Feeding begins on the underside of the lamb starting at the chest and stomach. After the heart, lungs, liver, stomach, and intestines are removed the predatory pig eats the ends of the ribs, breaks the back, and exposes the muscle surrounding one of the legs. It then consumes the backbone area (approaching from the belly side) to eat the leg muscle tissue. Feeding ends with the brain, eyes, and tongue. Wild pigs tend to step on the carcass while feeding. The presence of scat can help also with identification. Since pigs also feed on carrion, confirmation of predation must occur shortly after the death of the prey.

Eagles

Prey. Lambs and young goats.

Site of attack. Back of animal.

Number in attack. Hunt alone.

Feeding behavior. Prey will be plucked and bones remain unbroken. Don't pluck eyes or pluck the tongue of prey.

Technical sign. Dolbeer et al. says "The front talons normally leave punctures about 1 to 2 inches (2.5 to 5.0 cm) apart in a straight line or small "V" and the wound from the hallux will be 4 to 6 inches (10 to 15 cm) from the middle toe. In contrast, mammalian predators almost always leave 4 punctures or bruises from the canine teeth. Talon punctures are usually deeper than tooth punctures and there is seldom any crushing of tissue between the talon punctures." Head injuries are found infrequently.

Grizzly Bears

Prey. Sheep, calves, cows, and pigs. Rarely, poultry.

Site of attack. Bites to top of neck, back, and ribs. Claw marks may be seen but not as often as with black bears. Bears tend to maul.

Number in attack. Bears hunt alone. Two small animals may be killed at a time (more if prey are small). One animal killed if calf-sized or larger. Sometimes animals die due to trampling each other as they run away or pile up against one another.

Feeding behavior. Eats udders. Often move prey and cover it to return later. May consume animal in 1 feeding. Skin usually is ignored. Bones not eaten and will be scattered.

House Cats

Prey. Australian research shows that on the mainland, cats can kill mammals up to 4.2 lbs (2000 g) and birds up to 2.1 lbs (1000 g), but most kills are on mammals <7.8 oz (220 g) and birds <7.1 oz (200 g). On islands, kills on land mammals can reach 6.6 lbs (3000 g).

Site of attack. Cats frequently pounce on their prey and bite to the neck or chest. Multiple bites may be found for larger animals (rabbits) as the cat tries to subdue it.

Number in attack. Cats are solitary hunters.

Feeding behavior. Can consume round object up to 0.2 in (4.7 mm) in diameter consistently. Will feed on the portions with the most meat. Messy feeding pattern with portions of prey strewn around (Fig. 3).

Technical sign. Upper canines are ½ to $^9/_{16}$ in (1.3 to 1.4 cm) apart. Look for tooth marks on exposed bones.

Fig. 3. Bird killed by a house cat.

Mink

Prey. Poultry and fish.

Site of attack. Bite at base of skull.

Number in attack. Hunts alone. Will kill a number of birds if penned.

Feeding behavior. Head usually eaten as well as chest. Will kill more than it can eat.

Technical sign. Upper canines are $^3/_8$ to ¾ in (1 to 1.9 cm). Rats will bring food to den.

Opossum

Prey. Poultry.

Site of attack. Prey often mauled.

Number in attack. Hunts alone. Will kill a number of birds if penned.

Feeding behavior. Begin feeding at the anus. May consume the entire carcass leaving only a few feathers. Will kill more than it can eat.

Otters

Prey. Fish, crayfish, and snakes.

Site of attack. Unknown.

Number in attack. Single or families.

Feeding behavior. Look for chew marks on fins. Gills and viscera tend to be eaten.

Technical sign. Upper canines are ¾ to 1 in (1.9 to 2.5 cm).

Raccoon

Prey. Poultry and fish.

Site of attack. Bodies will be torn. Head may be missing.

Number in attack. Hunt alone but mothers may be accompanied by young. Multiple animals may be killed per visit.

Feeding behavior. Prey often dragged to area of cover before feeding. Entrails eaten.

Raptors (non-eagle)

Prey. Poultry, rabbits, fish and snakes.

Site of attack. Body with talons reaching into vital organs.

Fig. 4. Red-tailed hawk with a snake. Photo by Aaron Hildreth.

Number in attack. Solitary hunters. Prey, if light enough, disappears (Fig. 4).

Feeding behavior. Head removed close to body (owls). Great-horned owls may kill multiple birds by removing their head but only feed on one. Look for white droppings at attack and feeding sites. Confined fowl that are chased by raptors will often pile up in a corner, resulting in the suffocation of some birds. Reproduction may also be impaired in some fowl if harassment persists.

Technical sign. Look for hemorrhage where talons punctured chest. Dolbeer et. al says "Raptors generally pluck birds, leaving piles of feathers. Plucked feathers with small amounts of tissue clinging to their bases were pulled from a cold bird that had probably died from other causes and was simply scavenged by the raptor. If the base of a plucked feather is smooth and clean, the bird was plucked soon after dying."

Rats
Prey. Birds, such as pigeons, and mollusks.
Site of attack. Birds will be attacked at the neck. Mollusks will be bitten at the end of the shell where it is the most thin.
Number in attack. Usually hunt alone.
Feeding behavior. Due to their tendency to feed in the same location, remnants of prey may be found littering the area. With birds and eggs, only a small part of the item will be eaten. Chicks will be bitten through the chest. May bring food to den.

Red Fox
Prey. Poultry, fowl, rabbits. Rarely, lambs (newborn), and house cats.
Site of attack. Birds taken away from site. Small lambs may be bitten multiple times. Fawns will be strangled.
Number in attack. Hunt alone and target one bird, unless birds are confined.

Feeding behavior. Tend to eat the breast and legs first.
Technical sign. Upper canines of fox are spaced $^{15}/_{16}$ to 1.12 in (2.4 to 2.9 cm) apart.

Skunks
Prey. Poultry and eggs.
Site of attack. Bites at neck and chest. Birds often mauled.
Number in attack. Hunts alone. Mothers may be accompanied with young. Will kill a couple of birds, if penned.
Feeding behavior. Head usually eaten as well as chest. Head may be found to be crushed. Will kill more than it can eat.
Technical sign. Upper canines are spaced $^{7}/_{16}$ to ½ in (1.1 to 1.3 cm) apart.

Weasels
Prey. Poultry.
Site of attack. Bite at base of skull.
Number in attack. Hunts alone. Will kill a number of birds if penned.
Feeding behavior. Head usually eaten as well as chest. Will kill more than it can eat.
Technical sign. Upper canines are spaced $^{3}/_{16}$ to $^{5}/_{16}$ in (5 to 8 mm) apart.

Wolves (gray)
First, ask if wolves exist in your area.
Prey. Elk, moose, sheep, calves, cows, pigs, and horses. Uncommon, poultry.
Site of attack. For sheep and similar sized animals, attacks will be at the throat. Larger animals, flanks, hindquarters, and even tail.
Number in attack. Wolves hunt in packs. Usually one animal is targeted, though two pigs may be killed at a time. But kills will be repeated over successive days.
Feeding behavior. Often begins at hind quarters, continues through internal organs. One wolf can eat 20 lbs (9.1 kg) in a single feeding. Often entire animal may be consumed (except stomach and intestines), including hide and bones. Look for grasses or leaves stained with blood etc. due to muzzle wiping.
Technical sign. Incisors (upper and lower) 1¾ to 2 in (4.4 to 5.1 cm) apart. Skin of animal will be folded up like an accordion. Wolves will mark site with scat and urine. Distinguish coyote from wolf predation by looking for the following:
- Presence of crushing injuries. Tissue damage extensive.
- Tracks 4.72 × 3.94 in (12 × 10 cm) vs 2.4 × 2.4 in (6 × 6 cm) for coyote
- Scat whose diameter is 1 in (2.5 cm) or larger is wolf.

Other Predation Issues

Eggs: For years, biologists have claimed that predators of eggs (nests) could be identified by the way the eggs were damaged. Lariviere (1999) argues that such claims have no foundation in reality. The reasons are many but can be simplified as:

1. many predators break eggs the same way,
2. predators and scavengers will visit nests predated by others,
3. the same predator can damage eggs in different ways, and
4. people forget or overlook the possibility that less common predators may have caused the damage (e.g. mink and various birds).

Nevertheless, I have adapted portions of an article by Fidel Hernandez, Dale Rollins, and Ruben Cantu. (1997) to help you decide for yourself. As always, consider the total context when making your evaluation. I would like to express my thanks to the Wildlife Society for granting permission to reprint this article.

Published in *Wildlife Society Bulletin* 1997, 25(4):826–831. Peer edited.
Copyright © 1997 The Wildlife Society; used by permission.

Evaluating evidence to identify ground-nest predators in west Texas

Fidel Hernandez, Dale Rollins, and Ruben Cantu

Keywords: Bobwhite, *Colinus virginianus*, *Meleagris gallopavo*, nest depredation, remote-sensing techniques, Texas, TrailMaster, wild turkey

Traditionally, biologists have relied on physical evidence (e.g., eggshell fragments, tracks, feces) left at nests to identify nest predators (Major 1991). However, none of these methods provides incontestable reliability (Stoddard 1931, Rearden 1951, Wilcove 1985) because specific identification is open to speculation (Rearden 1951, Yahner and Wright 1985, Angelstam 1986). More objective techniques, such as "trip" cameras, have been developed for identifying nest predators (Martin 1987, Picmann 1988, Reitsma et al. 1990). Unfortunately, this approach also has limitations. For example, it is impractical and expensive to monitor many nests with trip cameras.

We evaluated a technique that integrated direct and indirect observations of depredation behavior. We used trip cameras for positive identification of the nest predator, then complemented this information with a subsequent examination of the physical evidence (i.e., eggshells) at the nest site. Our objectives were to characterize various nest predators' *modus operandi* and to assess the effect of egg size (i.e., small [quail] vs. large [chicken]) on the amount and type of physical evidence at the scene. Our intent was to develop a dichotomous key to various quail- and turkey-nest predators based on indirect physical evidence.

Study area

We monitored simulated nests at 2 sites in west Texas: (a) the Angelo State University Management, Instruction, and Research Center (MIRC) and (b) and the Stone Ranch (SR). The 2 study sites were located about 15 km apart in northern Tom Green County, Texas. Both areas are ecotones of the South-

ern Rolling Plains and the Edwards Plateau ecoregions. Woody vegetation was dominated by mesquite (*Prosopis glandulosa*), with liveoak (*Quercus fusiformis*), pecan (*Cara illinoinensis*), and hackberry (*Celtis reticulata*) common in riparian habitats. Potential nest predators at these sites included raccoons, striped skunks (*Mephitis mephitis*), opossums, badgers (*Eaxidea taxus*), red foxes (*Vulpes vulpes*), gray foxes (*Urocyon cinereoargenteus*), cotton rats (*Sigmodon hispidus*), common ravens (*Corvus corax*), greater roadrunners (*Geococcyx californianus*), and various snakes. Nest predators noticeably absent from these study areas included coyotes (*Canis latrans*), feral hogs (*Sus scrofa*), and common crows.

Methods

Construction of simulated nests

Ten simulated ground nests (5/site) were constructed and monitored from March to July 1995. Simulated nests were established along ranch roads, and no attempt was made to conceal them. Our intent was to place nests so that predators could locate and depredate the nests. Nests were baited with 3 "large" unwashed chicken eggs to simulate turkey nests or 5 bobwhite eggs for quail nests. Once constructed, simulated nests were replenished with fresh eggs daily as needed during morning hours (0700-1200). Nest sites were ≥1 km apart.

Results

Nest predator species composition

Five hundred and eighty-nine depredation events (frames) were photographed during the simulated turkey-nest phase, compared to 190 incidents during the quail-nest phase. Photographs revealed 7 "actual" and 2 "potential" predators. "Actual" indicates predators photographed in the act of depredating a nest. "Potential" indicates predators photographed at undisturbed nests or nests destroyed previously by "actual" predators. Raccoons were the principal nest predators observed, accounting for 80% and 91% of the incidents photographed at simulated turkey and quail nests, respectively.

Other commonly reported nest predators included striped skunks, gray foxes, and bobcats (*Lynx rufus*). Less common or previously unreported nest predators photographed in the act of depredating a nest included turkey vultures (*Cathartes aura*), a wild turkey (*Meleagris gallopavo*), a woodrat (*Neotoma* sp.), and a golden-fronted woodpecker (*Melanerpes aurifrons*). Roadrunners were photographed on 3 occasions, but not observed depredating a nest. We believe the nests lost to turkey vultures were an artifact of the way in which the simulated nests were placed out in the open. We do not believe turkey vultures are predators on actual quail or turkey nests.

Eggshell evidence

We collected and analyzed 130 eggshells. Raccoons accounted for 104 (80.0%) of the eggshells, skunks 14 (10.8%), bobcats 7 (5.4%), and gray foxes 5 (3.8%).

Quail eggshells were found on only 3 of 92 occasions (3.3%), all at the MIRC. Eggshells found on 9 April 1995 could not be linked to a predator because the film recording the incident was developed improperly. A bobcat was responsible for eggshells found at depredated nests on 14 and 17 April 1995.

With the exception of raccoons, only a small sample size of chicken eggshells was obtained for each of the predators described below. Consequently, these descriptions should be

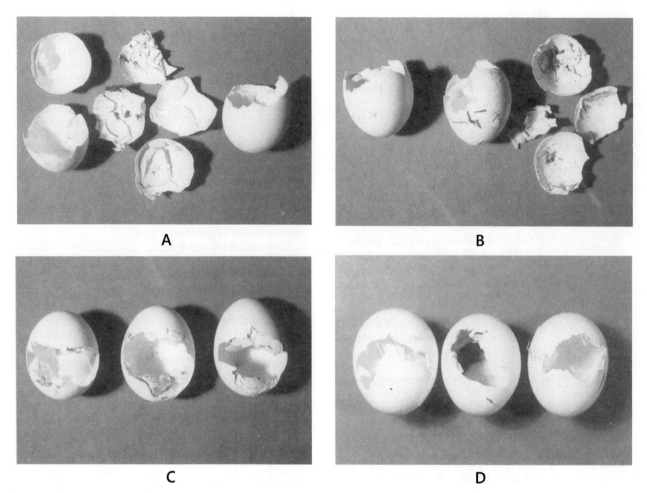

Fig. 2 (A–D). Characteristic eggshell evidence of nest predators in west Texas, including: (A) raccoon, (B) striped skunk, (C) gray fox, and (D) bobcat.

viewed as common eggshell characteristics shared for a particular predator and pertain only to large chicken eggs.

Raccoon. Raccoons tended to leave eggshells (*n* = 104 eggshells) in 1 of 3 different conditions (Fig. 2A)

1. The eggshell was in 2 distinct fragments of approximately equal size, the top and bottom of the egg. Smaller fragments were attached to the main fragments, or scattered about them (55% of eggshells identified).
2. The eggshell was crushed into small, numerous fragments. The top and base of the egg could sometimes be distinguished (39% of eggshells).
3. The eggshell was 1 large fragment with a bite on the side of the egg (6% of eggshells).

TrailMaster photographs revealed that raccoons held eggs upright and typically bit into one end of the egg. Most eggshells were found in the vicinity of the nest (within 5 m).

Skunks. The 14 eggshells examined for skunks could be classified into 3 groups (Fig. 2B):

1. The egg was bitten on 1 end, leaving a fragment that was approximately 75% complete. The eggshell had a small- to medium-size hole with the shell crushed inward (9 of 14 eggshells observed).
2. The eggshell was in the same condition as above, but the bite was not at the very end, but offset to the side of the egg. There was still 1 large fragment approximately 75% complete (3 of 14 eggshells).

3. The eggshell was crushed into several small-medium fragments (2 of 14 eggshells).

Skunks probably cannot easily carry or hold chicken-sized eggs; therefore the eggshells are found near the nest (within 1 m).

Gray fox. Of the 5 eggshells found for gray foxes, all shared the following characteristics (Fig. 2C). The eggshells had a small (<2.5 cm), round opening extending across the middle to lower base of the egg. The eggshell fragment was large and >75% complete. All 5 fragments were found >25 m from the nest. In 1 study (A. Sargeant, Northern Prairie Sci. Cent., unpubl. data) nest predation by red foxes was observed; the foxes grabbed 1 egg at a time and departed immediately to cache it. The process was repeated until all the eggs were cached. Most (450; 99.8%) of 454 eggs eaten by red foxes were buried, and only 1 (0.2%) was eaten at the nest. In our limited sample of gray fox observations, we found that their behavior was similar to that of red foxes.

Bobcat. Seven eggshells were collected from bobcat incidents and had several characteristics in common (Fig. 2D). The eggshells had a small (<1.5 cm), narrow opening in the center of the egg. The eggshell fragment was large and >75% complete. Five of the 7 eggshells were only partially eaten (with some contents still present), and 2 were completely eaten. In 1 instance, only 1 egg was partially eaten, leaving 2 eggs intact. All 7 eggshells were left in place in the nest bowl.

Discussion

Several factors may influence a nest predator's *modus operandi* and the amount and type of evidence found at a depredated nest, e.g., age of the predator (juvenile vs. adult), presence of other predators (conspecifics or different species) and egg size (A. Sargeant, Northern Prairie Sci. Cent., unpubl. data). We believe egg size played an important role in the amount and type of physical evidence found during our study.

The likelihood of eggs being carried away from the nest may increase as egg size decreases. A nest consisting of relatively large eggs (e.g., chicken eggs) affords more eggshell evidence at the nest site. For example, Montevecchi (1976) reported that American crows (*Corvus brachyrhynchos*) were more likely to eat large chicken eggs at the nest site. Small chicken eggs were more likely to be transported away from the nest site before being eaten. Similarly, we found quail eggshell fragments at nest sites on only 3 of 92 occasions (3.3%), but we found chicken eggshells at the nests on 89 of 96 occasions (92.7%). This may be our most significant finding. Snakes usually are suspected at depredated nests whenever no physical evidence can be found (Stoddard 1931, Skutch 1966, Best 1978, Best and Stauffer 1980). Stoddard (1931) speculated that most of the nests labeled as "unknown" and many of the "empties" encountered afield were depredated by snakes. Our results indicate that egg size is directly related to the amount of physical evidence found at depredated nests. Thus, in the past, snakes may have been incorrectly designated as nest predators when no physical evidence was found. It is possible that other nest predators (particularly raccoons in this study) were eating the eggs entirely and leaving no eggshells.

The original intent of the study was to develop a dichotomous key to ground-nest predators of west Texas based on physical evidence. However, we observed considerable intraspecific variability and interspecific similarities in physical evidence left at depredated nests. Other factors also may confound the amount and type of evidence left at a nest. Further, it was difficult to gather sufficient eggshell evidence for predators other than raccoons in our study. For these reasons, we were unable to develop a dichotomous key to ground-nest predators of west Texas. However, the information obtained during our study does not preclude its usefulness in assigning nest predators more objectively, especially for wild turkeys. The technique of incorporating both direct and indirect evidence of depredation events needs to be evaluated in other habitats with different predator communities in order to assess this method's biases.

Literature cited

Angelstam, P. 1986. Predation on ground-nesting birds in relation to predator densities and habitat edge. Oikos 47:365-378.

Best, L. B. 1978. Field sparrow reproductive success and nesting ecology. Auk 95:9-22.

Best, L. B., and D. F. Stauffer. 1980. Factors affecting nesting success in riparian bird communities. Condor 82:149-158.

Conover, M. R. 1985. Using conditioned food aversions to protect blueberries from birds: Comparison of two carbamate repellents. Appl. Anim. Behav. Sci. 13:383-386.

Creighton, P. D., and D. K. Porter. 1974. Nest predation and interference by western meadowlarks. Auk 91:177-178.

Kucera, T. E., and R. H. Barrett. 1993. The TrailMaster camera system for detecting wildlife. Wildl. Soc. Bull. 21:505-508.

Lehmann, V. W. 1984. Bobwhites in the Rio Grande Plain of Texas. Texas A&M Univ. Press, College Station. 371 pp.

Major, R. E. 1991. Identification of nest predators by photography, dummy eggs, and adhesive tape. Auk 108:190-195.

Martin, T. E. 1987. Artificial nest experiments: Effects of nest appearance and type of predator. Condor 89:925-928.

Montevecchi, W. A. 1976. Egg size and the egg predatory behavior of crows. Behaviour 57:307-320.

Picmann, J. 1988. Experimental study of predation on eggs of ground-nesting birds: Effects of habitat and nest distribution. Condor 90:124-131.

Rearden, J. D. 1951. Identification of waterfowl nest predators. J. Wildl. Manage. 15:386-395.

Reitsma, L. R., T. Holmes, and T. W. Sherry. 1990. Effects of removal of red squirrels, *Tamias hudsonicus*, and eastern chipmunk, *Tamias striatus*, on nest predation in a northern hardwood forest: An artificial nest experiment. Oikos 57:375- 380.

Rosene, W. 1969. The bobwhite quail: Its life and management. Rutgers Univ. Press, New Brunswick, NJ. 418 pp.

Skutch, A. F. 1966. A breeding bird census and nesting success in central America. Ibis 108:1-16.

Stoddard, H. L. 1931. The bobwhite quail: Its habits, preservation, and increase. Charles Scribner's Sons, New York, N.Y. 559 pp.

Wilcove, D. S. 1985. Nest predation in forest tracts and the decline of migratory song birds. Ecology 66:1211-1214.

Yahner, R. H., and A. L. Wright. 1985. Depredation on artificial ground nests: Effects of edge and plot age. J. Wildl. Manage. 49:508-513

Yahner, R. H., and C. G. Mahan. 1996. Depredation of artificial ground nests in a managed, forested landscape. Conserv. Biol. 10:285-288.

Fidel Hernandez (left) received his B.S. and M.S. in biology from Angelo State University. As a graduate student at Angelo State University, Fidel researched nest depredation ecology and evaluated conditioned taste aversion as a nonlethal alternative to deter ground-nest predators. He is currently pursuing his Ph.D. in wildlife science at Texas A&M University. His current research focuses on northern bobwhite survival and reproduction relative to pricklypear control in the Rolling Plains of Texas.

Dale Rollins (right) is a professor and extension wildlife specialist with the Texas Agricultural Extension Service (TAEX) headquartered in San Angelo. He received his B.S. in biology from Southwestern Oklahoma State University, his M.S. in wildlife ecology from Oklahoma State University, and his Ph.D. in range management from Texas Tech University. His recent extension emphases involve leadership training for high school youth (i.e., The Bobwhite Brigade) and school curriculum programs addressing predator ecology. Dale currently serves as the president of the Texas Chapter of The Wildlife Society.

Ruben Cantu received his B. S. in range science and wildlife science and M.S. in wildlife science from Texas A&I University (now Texas A&M–Kingsville). He has worked for the Texas Parks and Wildlife Department as a wildlife biologist, providing technical assistance to landowners throughout west Texas. Ruben currently is the Regional Director for Texas Parks and Wildlife Department's Wildlife Region 1, where he oversees 2 wildlife regulatory districts, wildlife management areas, and wildlife research projects in the Trans-Pecos and Pan-handle of Texas.

Address for Fidel Hernandez: Biology Department, Angelo State University, San Angelo, TX 76909, USA.

Current address for Fidel Hernandez: Department of Wildlife and Fisheries Sciences, Texas A&M University, College Station, TX 77840, USA.

Address for Dale Rollins: Texas Agricultural Extension Service, 7887 N. Hwy. 87, San Angelo, TX 76901, USA.

Address for Ruben Cantu: Texas Parks and Wildlife Department, 151 Las Lomas Ct., San Angelo, TX 76901, USA.

The following section is copied from Wildlife Services field assessment tool used in Idaho.

Criteria for Classification of Reported Depredation Incidents

Reported wolf, bear, or lion depredation incidents should be classified as **confirmed, probable, possible/unknown**, or **other**, based on the following criteria. *For MIS reporting purposes, "reported" damage may often include incidents described as **probable, possible/unknown**, and/or **other**, if the cooperator first reported these incidents as predation.*

CONFIRMED – Depredation is **confirmed** in those cases where there is reasonable physical evidence that an animal was actually attacked and/or killed by a predator. The primary confirmation factor would ordinarily be the presence of bite marks and associated subcutaneous hemorrhaging and tissue damage, indicating that the attack occurred while the victim was alive, as opposed to simply feeding on an already dead animal. Spacing between canine tooth punctures, feeding pattern on the car-

cass, fresh tracks, scat, hairs rubbed off on fences or brush, and/or eye witness accounts of the attack may help identify the specific species or individual responsible for the depredation. Predation might also be confirmed in the absence of bite marks and associated hemorrhaging (i.e., if much of the carcass has already been consumed by the predator or scavengers) **if** there is other physical evidence to confirm predation on the live animal. This might include blood spilled or sprayed at a nearby attack site or other evidence of an attack or struggle. There may also be nearby remains of other victims for which there is still sufficient evidence to confirm predation, allowing reasonable inference of confirmed predation on the animal that has been largely consumed.

PROBABLE – Having some evidence to suggest possible predation, but lacking sufficient evidence to clearly confirm predation by a particular species, a kill may be classified as **probable** depending on a number of other factors such as:

(1) Has there been any recently confirmed predation by the suspected depredating species in the same or nearby area?

(2) How recently had the livestock owner or his employees observed the livestock?

(3) Is there evidence (telemetry monitoring data, sightings, howling, fresh tracks, etc.) to suggest that the suspected depredating species may have been in the area when the depredation occurred?

All of these factors, and possibly others, should be considered in the investigator's best professional judgment.

POSSIBLE/UNKNOWN – Lacking sufficient evidence to classify an incident as either confirmed or probable predation, the **possible/unknown** classification is appropriate if it is unclear what the cause of death may have been. The investigator may or may not have much of a carcass remaining for inspection, or the carcass may have deteriorated so as to be of no use. The investigator would want to consider if the area has been frequented by a predator, or if the habitat is one which the predator is likely to use. Possible predation may include cases where counts show that abnormal numbers of livestock are missing or have disappeared above and beyond past experience, and where other known cases of predation have occurred previously in the area.

OTHER – Cause of livestock deaths should be classified as **other** when it is discovered that the cause of death was not likely caused by the animal originally reported to Wildlife Services during a request for assistance. Examples of **other** may include cases where the cause of death is confirmed or is likely due to predation by some other animal or cause determined at the time of the investigation such as red fox instead of coyote or other causes such as, bloat, poisonous plants, stillborn, disease, lightning strike, vehicle collision, etc. If the specific other cause of death can be determined, it should be written in the space provided for Other.

WS FORM 200 (Reverse)

Resources

I would like to thank USDA-Aphis-Wildlife Services officials for their assistance.

Acorn, R. C. and M. J. Dorrance. 1998. *Coyote Predation of Livestock*. Alberta: Alberta Agriculture and Rural Development.

Acorn, R. C. and M. J. Dorrance. 1990, 1998. *Methods of Investigating Predation of Livestock*. Alberta: Alberta Agriculture and Rural Development.

Austin, O. L. 1948. Predation by the Common Rat (*Rattus norvegicus*) in the Cape Cod Colonies of Nesting Terns. *Bird-Banding*, 19:2(Apr):60-65.

Dickman, C. R. 1996. Overview of the Impacts of Feral Cats on Australian Native Fauna: Invasive Species Program. Sydney, NSW: Australian Nature Conservation Agency and University of Sydney. 1-97. http://www.feral.org.au/wp-content/uploads/2010/03/impacts-feral-cats.pdf.

Dolbeer, R. A., N. R. Holler, and D. W. Hawthorne. Identification and Assessment of Wildlife Damage: An Overview. *Prevention and Control of Wildlife Damage*. Editors, S. E. Hygnstrom, R. M. Timm, G. E. Larson. 1994. University of Nebraska-Lincoln. 2 vols.

Elbroch, M. 2001. *Bird Tracks & Sign: A Guide to North American Species*. Mechanicsburg, PA: Stackpole Books.

Elbroch, M. 2003. *Mammal Tracks and Sign: A Guide to North American Species*. Mechanicsburg, PA: Stackpole Books.

Halfpenny, J. C. and T. D. Furman. 2010. *Tracking Wolves: The Basics*. A Naturalist's World.

Hernandez, F., D. Rollins, and R. Cantu. 1997. Evaluating Evidence to Identify Ground-Nest Predators in West Texas. *Wildlife Society Bulletin*, 25:4 (Winter):826-831.

Lariviere, S. 1999. Reasons Why Predators Cannot Be Inferred From Nest Remains. *The Condor* 101:718-721.

Manning, T. 1990. Summer Feeding Habits of River Otter (*Lutra canadensis*) on the Mendocino National Forest. *Northwestern Naturalist*, 71:2 (Autumn):38-42.

Marks, C. A., M. J. Johnston, P. M. Fisher, K. Pontin, and M. J. Shaw. 2006. Differential Particle Size Ingestion: Promoting Target-Specific Baiting of Feral Cats. *The Journal of Wildlife Management*, 70:4 (Aug):1119-1124.

Parisi, V. and G. Gandolfi. 1974. Further Aspects of the Predation by Rats on Various Mollusc Species, *Bolletino di zoologia*, 41:2, 87-106.

Vantassel, S. M., P. D. Curtis, and S. E. Hygnstrom. 2012. Wild Pigs. National Wildlife Control Training Program: Species Accounts. Ithaca, NY: Cornell University and University of Nebraska-Lincoln.

Wiley, R. W. and E. G. Bolen. 1971. Eagle-Livestock Relationships: Livestock Carcass Census and Wound Characteristics. *The Southwestern Naturalist*, 16:2 (Nov. 15):151-169.

Procedures for Evaluating Predation on Livestock and Wildlife

Dale A. Wade and James E. Bowns

Foreword

This bulletin briefly describes the evidence left by a variety of predatory mammals and birds of the United States when preying upon livestock and game animals. Their methods of attacking, killing and/or feeding on prey animals are reviewed, in addition to the type of wounds they cause, their tracks and other evidence they may leave. The bulletin is intended primarily for those who do not have experience with predators and livestock behavior, predation and other causes of livestock losses, as well as other factors which must also be considered in determining the cause of injuries and death. Although predators are responsible for injuries and death of many domestic and game animals, malnutrition, exposure, parasites, poisonous plants and diseases may be more important in many instances. Sound livestock management requires accurate determination of the factors involved in animal losses.

The authors of this bulletin have extensive personal experience in predation and identification of predator damage but are not specialists in animal nutrition and disease. Only brief descriptions of nutrition and disease as causes of animal deaths are given. Where poisonous plants, malnutrition or disease may be responsible for loss, the help of specialists in range management, nutrition and diseases is recommended.

Carnivore predation on other species is a natural event that occurs throughout their range. In some cases, it may provide an essential part of control for some wildlife populations; however, it may be harmful to other wildlife populations and is detrimental to livestock production. In addition to livestock, native and exotic wildlife are lost to predators on both public and private lands, including game ranches and preserves. In determining the cause of these losses, the general criteria used to evaluate predation on livestock may be applied to other species.

Evidence of predation is normally present where large animals are killed but is frequently absent with small animals which may simply disappear without a trace. The presence of predators and predator sign in the area, in addition to hair, feathers and other remains in predator droppings (feces), even when simultaneous with livestock disappearance, are not sufficient evidence to confirm predation. Predators often scavenge animals dead of other causes and livestock can disappear in other ways.

Animal losses are easiest to confirm and evaluate if examination is conducted soon after losses occur. Examination of wounded animals and fresh kills is relatively simple. Carcass decomposition, which is rapid during warm weather, obliterates evidence. Scavenging birds and mammals also can eliminate evidence, frequently in a few hours.

Dale A. Wade, Ph.D., Extension Wildlife Specialist, Texas Agricultural Extension Service, The Tecas A&M University System, San Angelo, Texas.

James E. Bowns, Ph.D., Range Ecologist, with joint appointments by Range Science Department, Utah State University (Logan) and Life Science Department, Southern Utah State College (Cedar City), Utah.

In separating predation from other mortality factors, the following information may be required:
1. Predator species present in the area
2. Habits and signs of each predator species
3. History of depredation problems in the area
4. Normal and abnormal livestock appearance and behavior
5. Common causes of livestock losses other than predators:
    a. Starvation and/or exposure
    b. Internal parasites
    c. Bacterial and viral diseases
    d. Pregnancy disease and other metabolic diseases
    e. "Hardware" disease caused by ingestion of nails, wire or other metal objects which penetrate walls of the digestive tract
    f. Bloat
    g. Suffocation
    h. Poisonous plants and moldy feeds
    i. Other poison sources such as chemicals and lead-based paints, or discarded batteries
    j. Lightning
    k. Snake bite
    l. Theft

In some instances, the causes of death are obvious; however, in many cases they may be obscure. When the cause of livestock loss cannot be readily determined, assistance may be necessary. Veterinarians can identify and treat internal parasites and other diseases which kill livestock. Where poisonous plants cause loss, county Extension agents and range specialists can help identify these plants and devise corrective management procedures. Poisoned animals may require treatment by a veterinarian.

Animal Health

Careful observation of livestock and range conditions can provide information useful in preventing death; thus, indications of ill health in live animals may aid diagnosis when dead animals are found. When the cause of loss is unknown or uncertain, a veterinarian's assistance in diagnosing the cause of death may help prevent further losses. Diagnostic laboratories may help determine the cause of death; these facilities are available in all states. Some animal diseases can be transmitted to humans and proper precautions always should be taken to prevent exposure during carcass and tissue sample examination.

External Appearance of Animal and Carcasses

Although hair or fleece length and density varies with livestock breeds, healthy animals normally have a coat that is glossy from natural oils and is "live" to the touch; their skin is soft and flexible. In contrast, unhealthy animals have dry, dull coats that are harsh to the touch. Extended periods of poor health cause their skin to become dry and less flexible.

Coat condition is more difficult to evaluate in sheep since there is wide variation in fleece length, diameter and density in different breeds. There is also great variation, resulting from diet and nutrition, in the amount of natural oils in the fleece. Range type, vegetation and weather conditions also can cause marked differences in wool color and appearance. For example, extended wet periods, particularly in forested areas, cause fleece darkening. Also, unshorn sheep in late spring and summer may have a ragged appearance from some wool loss, particularly where they range in brush and lose wool on snags.

An alert appearance of the eyes and ears of livestock normally indicates a healthy animal. Sunken eyes and drooping ears indicate poor health. In fresh carcasses of healthy animals, the eyes fill the sockets and are not sunken from dehydration; however, carcasses dehydrate and decompose rapidly in temperatures above freezing.

Normally, livestock feces are relatively firm and dry. Exceptions include young animals receiving large amounts of milk and adult animals on lush, green forage. High quantities of concentrates also will cause soft feces. This should not be confused with diarrhea, an unhealthy condition resulting from excessive quantities of concentrates, certain infectious diseases or diseases caused by internal parasites.

Animals that die from causes other than predation normally die on their side or chest with their legs folded under them. Animals which get on their backs and die of suffocation are one major exception. This occurs most often in sheep attempting to scratch by rolling on their backs. Those with long, dense fleece may be unable to right themselves. In this position, gas cannot escape from the rumen, which distends and compresses the lungs, causing suffocation.

Another common cause of death is gas distention of the rumen (bloat) which may be caused by ingesting excessive amounts of grain or by feeding on alfalfa, clover and certain other plants. Bloat should not be confused with excessive carcass distention caused by gasses formed during decomposition.

Carcasses should be examined for abnormal excretions, particularly pus or blood, from body openings (the eyes, ears, mouth, genitals and anus). Live animals and carcasses should be examined by a veterinarian if such abnormalities exist or are suspected.

The carcass should be examined for skull fractures, broken bones and other wounds. The chest and stomach cavities should be opened to check for internal injuries and hemorrhage

Internal Carcass Appearance

Body Fat

Animals receiving adequate nutrition normally have deposits of white or yellow fat around the kidneys, heart and intestines and in the bone marrow. Animals that are sick or are receiving insufficient feed normally metabolize this fat to meet body needs, leaving a gelatinous red deposit in the bone marrow. Internal fat is metabolized first while fat in the bone marrow is metabolized last during starvation. Breaking the large leg bones permits examination of the bone marrow. Some caution is necessary in evaluating bone marrow fat deposits in healthy young animals making rapid growth. Their bone marrow may be red from extensive red blood cell production to meet body needs and may have little stored fat.

Intestinal Tract

The contents of the stomach and intestines are indicators of health. Normally, healthy ruminants (cattle, sheep, goats and other animals with multiple stomachs) older than weaning age will have a rumen (first compartment) that is one-third to one-half full of food. The rumen is not fully developed at birth, but the abomasum (fourth compartment) is fully functional. The abomasum is the functional stomach in nursing young and should contain milk. A small, empty rumen is normal in nursing young for the first 2 to 3 weeks. A mixture of milk and vegetation in the rumen is normal from then until weaning age when the rumen is fully functional.

Partially digested foods should be present through the rest of the gut and the feces (in the large intestine) should be relatively firm. Exceptions as noted earlier include animals on concentrates and lush green feeds.

When dietary contents such as excessive amounts of grain or poisonous plants are a possible cause of death, the contents of the stomach and intestines should be noted. Samples of the stomach contents should be taken for analysis if poisonous plants or other toxic agents are suspected.

Lungs and Respiratory Tract

Pneumonia is a relatively common cause of animal death and is evident in lung tissue by fluid accumulation and other lesions in the affected areas. Healthy lungs are pink, spongy and lightweight with sharp, well defined edges on the lobes. Infected lung tissue is dark colored, firmer and heavier than healthy lung tissue. Some diseases cause abscesses in lung tissue. These abscesses may be filled with pus and often have a hard outer shell. Incisions through sections of normal and infected lung tissue will demonstrate these differences.

The trachea and bronchi should be opened from above the larynx into the lungs to check for infection and other abnormalities. Animals killed by a bite in the throat frequently have physical injury to the larynx and trachea. Also, these bites frequently cause hemorrhage and foam in the trachea which contribute to death by suffocation.

Animal Age and Health

Very old and very young animals are less likely than healthy adults to survive poor nutrition, adverse weather and exposure, and they are generally more susceptible to disease. Therefore, age and apparent health of animals prior to death should be considered in evaluating losses.

Young animals, particularly newborn pigs, lambs and kids are extremely vulnerable to exposure during cold, wet weather. If they do not receive adequate maternal care and do not nurse within the first few hours they are not likely to survive. Birth weight also is important to survival; newborn young that are small and weak are less likely to survive than healthy, vigorous young of average or larger size.

Diseases of pregnancy and difficult births may cause the death of either or both the mother and fetus. Necropsy (examination and dissection of a body after death) of females in parturition should include attention to pregnancy diseases and to injuries sustained in giving birth, in addition to unusually large fetuses and those in abnormal positions. Post-mortem examination of newborn and very young animals should include attention to the major characteristics of healthy young, such as: 1) Young born alive will have a distinct blood clot at the closed end of the navel (umbilical artery); stillborn young will not have this clot. 2) If young animals breathe after birth, the lungs inflate, become light pink and will float in water (complete lung inflation may require several hours); stillborn young have uninflated, dark, red-purple lungs which do not float. 3) Firm, white fat deposits around the heart and kidneys indicate health; the lack of this fat indicates poor nutrition or starvation. As young healthy animals grow, they also develop fat deposits in tissues around the stomach and intestines (mesenteric fat). 4) Milk is normally present in the stomach and intestines of healthy young. The absence of milk during the first few weeks indicates poor nutrition; however, milk content of the stomach decreases as the diet changes to solid foods and weaning takes place. 5) Digestion of milk produces chyle, a white emulsion of milk fat and lymph.

This is found in the lymphatic vessels which drain the intestinal tract and is present immediately after young animals suckle. 6) The soft membrane on the hooves of newborn animals begins to wear as soon as the young stand and begin walking. Hard, dry soil surfaces cause more rapid wear than soft, wet surfaces.

Missing Livestock

It is not unusual for livestock to disappear from pastures and herds and there are numerous possible causes. Young or small animals such as pigs, calves, lambs and kid goats frequently disappear. However, when no trace of the animals can be found, particularly when they have been well tended and confined to pasture, predation or theft may be the cause.

Livestock and their young normally remain close enough that young animals can nurse several times daily, particularly for the first few weeks after birth. Therefore, a lactating female with engorged udder, searching for her young for prolonged periods may be evidence that the young is missing or dead. This type of maternal behavior is less likely to occur where females have one remaining of two or more offspring. Because they behave differently and have large litters, hogs are less likely to respond in this fashion if several young remain.

Domestic animals are much less wary and nervous than wild species, particularly when they are herded or otherwise handled regularly. Their customary behavior is modified by weather, temperature, availability of feed and other factors. However, the behavior pattern is characteristic for each individual herd under a specific type of management.

Other livestock behavior is useful as indirect evidence of predation. The presence of carnivores which appear to exhibit a threat usually will cause most cows to bawl and attempt to locate their young. Their behavior will be alert, much exaggerated from normal and will include urgent calling, running to find their calves and attempts to chase the carnivores. Sheep and goats respond in a similar manner when alerted but they are much less aggressive than cattle. They do call urgently and attempt to find their young, but some may abandon their search and try to escape to protect themselves.

Almost without exception, the behavior of livestock in herds which are raided repeatedly by predators becomes more alert and defensive. They appear frightened even by common management practices that do not normally disturb them, especially when carnivore hunting behavior involves chasing the herd while making a kill rather than by stalking individual animals. Once established by repeated depredation, this response continues and will recur for days or weeks. With normal management, this unusual behavior will gradually disappear if predation stops. To the person versed in livestock production and familiar with the individual herd, abnormal behavior is readily apparent and indicates a reaction to an unusual disturbance.

Evaluation of Suspected Predator Kills

There is a logical, scientific procedure for evaluating predator kills and feeding to determine the species responsible, but there is no simple series of steps which lead to consistent and accurate determinations. Predators frequently feed on carrion (dead animals) and take other predator kills. Several species may feed on the same carcass. Much experience and intuitive judgment may be essential for successfully identifying the predator species responsible.

A common error made in evaluating predator kills and feeding is the tendency to stereotype these by species. Most predators do follow a general pattern, but individuals vary in food preferences, method of attack and feeding behavior. These behaviors may overlap extensively between individuals of different species; consequently, evidence other than the carcass is frequently essential to make accurate judgments. The following procedure is suggested for determining if a loss has resulted from predators and for identifying the species.

Because humans are susceptible to many diseases carried by animals, always take proper precautions to prevent exposure during examination of all animal carcasses.

1. Examine injured animals for the type and extent of wounds and feeding. If possible, determine whether wounds were made by mammals (canine teeth and/or claws), by birds (talons and/or beaks), or by other causes. Some animals are fed upon without being killed. Coyotes may bite off the tails and feed on the hindquarters of live calves. They may feed on calves and on the genitals and hindquarters of cows giving birth. Black bears and coyotes occasionally feed on the udders of lactating females without killing them. At times, raccoons also feed on young or defenseless livestock without killing them, Similarly, vultures, magpies, ravens and gulls may attack and feed on young or defenseless livestock, peck out their eyes and kill them. Newborn young, females giving birth and other helpless animals are especially vulnerable. Dogs often cause extensive injuries to young and small livestock without killing them, but do not usually feed on them. Some dogs learn to kill efficiently and feed like coyotes normally do. Injuries caused by coyotes sometimes resemble those caused by dogs. This may be a result of inexperience in killing, two or more coyotes attacking the same animal or a heavy fleece which prevents effective attack at the throat. Other factors, such as physical injuries which restrict coyotes from their normal attack, also affect killing behavior of individual coyotes. A high percentage of animals injured in such attacks die later from shock, loss of blood or infections.

Such wounds and feeding patterns confirm predation but injuries do result from other causes such as thorns, nails, barbed wire and vehicles. Venomous snake bites cause injuries which may be difficult to identify without careful examination.

2. Where predation is suspected or confirmed, locate the attack, kill and feeding sites if possible. Avoid tracking over and destroying evidence such as tracks and droppings around these sites and the carcass. Since feeding and other predator sign may be similar, it is often essential to have all available evidence to confirm the cause of death and/or the species responsible.

Many predators move their kills. Small animals are frequently carried away by foxes, bobcats and coyotes. Cougars, bobcats and black bears seem to prefer feeding in a secluded area and they may drag or carry their kills to cover. All three species normally feed in a limited area without scattering carcass remains and they frequently cover carcasses with dirt, grass, leaves or other debris. In contrast, coyotes that feed extensively tend to scatter carcass remains, wool and hair over much larger areas while feeding.

Predator sign is frequently found near kill sites. Trails, fence-lines, creeks, waterholes and dry washes in the vicinity should be checked for tracks and droppings. Crawls through or under net wire fences are quite common and hair is often found on the soil or clinging to wire where predators pass through or under these fences.

3. Examine carcasses for wounds, hemorrhage, bruises, broken bones and feeding. If necessary, the entire carcass should be skinned and opened to identify internal wounds and other factors which help confirm the cause of death. For example, some animals are killed by a single grip at the throat which causes suffocation but leaves little external evidence. Bears and cougars may kill by blows from the front paws that break the neck or back and may cause extensive bruises but these may not be apparent prior to necropsy. Claw marks caused by cougars and bobcats may be much more evident on the flesh side of the skin because of dense hair or wool.

Be careful not to confuse bruises, which are localized and a dark color from clotted blood, with the conditions caused by decomposition. At certain stages, decomposition may resemble extensive bruises. Also, body fluids collect on the lower side of the carcass during decomposition and cause extensive areas of discoloration. Discoloration caused by snakebite may also be obscured by decomposition; careful and complete examination may be necessary to find these wounds.

The position of the carcass may be important. Animals that are killed are rarely found lying in a natural position. Also, scavengers may move or turn a carcass over while feeding. As a result, caution is necessary in attempting to reconstruct the circumstances of death since postmortem changes which developed with the body in one position may cause judgment errors when its position has been changed.

General Characteristics of Predator Kills

The number, size, depth and location of tooth or talon punctures vary. Some animals are killed by a single bite at the throat or neck. Small animals are often killed by a bite over the head, neck, shoulders or back. Since most predators find large animals harder to kill than small prey, they may bite repeatedly while shifting their grip to subdue prey animals.

In contrast, when prey is relatively small compared to the predator, a single bite is often sufficient to kill. As a rule, therefore, where many tooth punctures accompanied by hemorrhage are found, predators smaller than their prey are the most probable cause of death. However, young, inexperienced predators are also likely to inflict multiple injuries by indiscriminate attacks without killing their prey. This is relatively common with foxes, coyotes and dogs and is particularly true of dogs.

Although size and spacing between the canine teeth (responsible for most tooth punctures) are characteristic for each species, tooth punctures in tissue are often difficult to assign to a species since there are close similarities in species of similar size. Also, punctures do not remain clear and distinct because of tissue pliancy and movement. Differences are further obscured by multiple bites and punctures; therefore, additional information may be needed.

Foxes rarely crush the skull or spine on small livestock prey, but such injuries are relatively common on small lambs, goats and pigs killed by coyotes, bobcats and larger carnivores. Cougars and bears are capable of and frequently cause similar massive injuries to adult sheep and goats, calves and other animals of similar size with bites over the head, neck or shoulders. Broken bones are more commonly found when the predator is relatively large compared to its prey.

Most predators tend to attack the head and neck, although eagles may grasp small prey anywhere. Eagles commonly leave talon wounds in the shoulders, ribs and back, and often in the brisket and abdomen of small animals such as lambs and kid goats. They often grasp small prey by the head or neck but the spacing between the talon wounds (1 to 3 inches between front talons, and 4 to 6 inches between the middle front talon and the back talon or hallux), the triangular shape, and the depth of the wounds (up to 2 inches) are different than canine tooth punctures. Compression skull fractures of small prey, such as lambs and kids, may result from the eagle's grip. Internal bleeding is common in animals killed by eagles when their talons have entered the abdominal or thoracic cavities. Frequently, an eagle's talons puncture major internal veins and arteries, particularly the dorsal aorta, causing massive internal hemorrhage.

Bruises and extensive shoulder and back injuries are frequent in bear attacks on adult livestock but should not be confused with bruises caused by other livestock. For example, sheep may be injured by cattle and horses, particularly when livestock concentrates at the same locations. Bears may also claw and bruise the sides and abdomen while holding their prey. Bears may leave claw marks on the head, neck and shoulders, but these are more commonly found on cougar and bobcat kills.

Hemorrhage from arteries and veins differs. Arterial blood is normally bright red while veinous blood is dark. Blood pressure is much higher in arteries than in veins and arterial blood is ejected in rapid spurts, often for several feet, as the heart contracts. In contrast, veinous bleeding is steady and much slower because of low pressure. Blood from wounds or from the nose and mouth of injured animals is thick and will readily clot. It is distinctly different from the thin, reddish fluids resulting from decomposition.

Observation of predators making kills is relatively rare; therefore, when predators are removed, there is the question of whether the individual responsible predators or groups have been removed, or whether those removed were simply scavengers. Evidence that the responsible animals were removed is usually indirect. Occasionally they are observed in the act of killing or may be identified by other information such as unique tracks, killing methods or other definitive factors.

Knowledge that only specific animals live in the area or travel into an area to kill provides some evidence. More commonly, the evidence depends on predation patterns and loss levels that stop or are reduced when predators are removed. Occasionally, a predator is shot while attacking or may be trailed (by tracks or use of dogs) from a kill site to assure its removal. Stomach contents can be examined to determine if the captured predator has fed on a fresh kill. This alone is not sufficient to confirm responsibility for the kill but it suggests involvement.

Carnivore tracks and territorial marks are characteristic for each species, but they may be difficult to find. The characteristics of tracks are most easily seen in mud, dust or snow but often are not clear on other surfaces. Experience is essential for accurate identification of predator tracks, feces and other marks.

Coyotes

Coyotes are the most common and the most serious predator of livestock in the western United States. Westwide, they cause a majority of the predation losses of sheep, goats and cattle. In some states, this is also true for hogs and poultry.

In attacks on adult sheep and goats, coyotes typically bite the throat just behind the jaw and below the ear, although repeated bites made while shifting their hold may obscure the initial tooth punctures. Death commonly results from suffocation and shock; blood loss is usually a secondary cause of death. On small prey, such as young lambs and kids, coyotes may kill by biting the head , neck or back, causing massive tissue and bone damage. Young lambs, kids and pigs may be carried away by coyotes and disappear without a trace. Bloody soil and vegetation, missing animals or females searching for their young may be the only evidence that a problem exists.

Some coyotes kill by attacking the flanks or hindquarters, causing shock and loss of blood. This is quite common on calves, but is less common with sheep and goats. It does seem to occur more often in sheep during winter months, possibly because of the heavy fleece during this period. Death of the calf and severe injuries to the genital organs and hindquarters of cows are characteristic when coyotes attack cows giving birth. This is more common with heifers (young cows having their first calf) than with older cows. It is also quite common in some areas to see calves bobtailed by coyote attacks.

Young coyotes are more likely to kill in a manner not typical of that which is expected, but some coyotes consistently kill in an atypical manner. Coyotes, like other animals, are individuals and each may have unique food habits and behavior depending on circumstances.

Some animals are attacked by coyotes without being killed but die later from injuries and infection. In these cases, sheep and goats are more likely to have throat injuries and cows and calves to have injuries to the hindquarters. Calves frequently are fed upon extensively at the hindquarters before they die. Even with prompt medical treatment, few of these animals survive because massive infections usually develop.

Coyotes normally begin feeding on kills in the flank or just behind the ribs, but there are exceptions. Some seem to choose the viscera (liver, heart, lungs, mesenteric fat, etc.) first and the milk-filled stomach is a preferred item. Feeding on the hindquarters is also common and small animals may be entirely consumed.

Multiple coyote kills are frequent and many of these kills are not fed upon. Coyotes usually leave the hide and most of the skeleton of larger animals relatively intact, but when food is scarce, they may leave only the largest bones. Coyote feeding leaves ragged edges on muscle tissue and tendons, splintered and chewed ribs and other bone;;. Scattered wool, bits of skin and other parts are characteristic where coyotes feed extensively on larger carcasses.

The canine teeth of coyotes vary in size and spacing but on the average coyote (20 to 30 pounds), normal spacing between the upper canine teeth is $1 \frac{1}{8}$ to $1 \frac{3}{8}$ inches and 1 to $1 \frac{1}{4}$ inches between the lower canine teeth. As a result of tissue pliancy and movement and multiple bites, paired punctures made by the canine teeth are often difficult to identify and an accurate estimate of the canine tooth size and spacing may not be possible. Nonetheless, when these can be determined they are a definite aid in confirming the predator species responsible.

If not disturbed at a feeding site, coyotes often rub and roll after feeding, possibly to clean themselves. They may also urinate and defecate soon after feeding and usually scratch with their feet after defecation. These activities leave useful evidence if it can be found.

Some dog tracks may be easily confused with coyote tracks even when the tracks are well defined. The shape of tracks, the length of the stride, the prominence of nail marks and the pattern of travel are important. Coyote tracks tend to be more oval-shaped and compact than those of common dogs. Nail marks are less prominent and the tracks tend to follow a straight line more closely than those of dogs. Except for greyhounds and whippets, most dogs of the same weight as coyotes have a slightly shorter stride. The normal coyote track is about 2 inches wide and 2½ inches long, with the hind track slightly smaller than the front. The average coyote's stride at a trot is 16 to 18 inches and the hind tracks tend to follow directly in line with or on top of front tracks.

Dogs

Domestic dogs can be a serious problem where they are permitted to run at large, particularly near urban areas. True feral dogs and coydogs (coyote-dog hybrids) are also a problem but are far less common.

Domestic dogs do not normally kill for food and their attacks usually lead to indiscriminate mutilation of prey. When they do feed, they tend to leave torn, ragged tissue and splintered bones much like coyotes do.

As a rule, domestic dogs feed very little on their prey. Some individual dogs, including pets, have the instinctive ability to kill effectively, whether or not they feed and some become adept through repeated killing. True feral dogs are more likely to kill for food. Feral dogs and coydogs are also more likely to kill in a manner similar to coyotes, possibly as a result of experience in killing for food.

Both domestic and feral dogs often range in packs and do extensive damage once they begin to attack livestock. Dog packs often harass livestock and persist in chasing injured animals, often for several hours. Careful searching where this occurs often reveals many attack sites with tracks, hair or wool and pieces of skin widely scattered. Fences damaged by livestock attempting to escape, exhaustion, injuries, weight loss, loss of young, and abortion are some common consequences of such attacks. Sheep and goats are especially vulnerable. They may drown in streams or reservoirs while trying to escape, or they may "pile up" and suffocate in fence corners, gullies, and sheds. Many more may be injured or killed in this manner than from dog bites.

Livestock proximity to urban areas, limited enforcement of leash laws and tagging regulations, and estrous female dogs at large are major factors that encourage dog damage problems. Because dogs vary in size and cause diverse injuries, size and spacing between the canine teeth are less useful for confirming the species responsible. Tooth punctures often are not clear where skin and muscle are torn on prey animals.

Dog tracks are also highly variable because of size and weight differences. However, dog tracks are typically more round and show more prominent nail marks than coyote tracks and are larger than fox tracks. In contrast to coyote tracks, a dog's rear tracks normally are slightly to one side of the front tracks. Also, canine tracks made at the same time and location that vary widely in size suggest dog predation, especially near urban areas where stray dogs may range.

Foxes

Although poultry are their more common domestic prey, both red and gray foxes may prey on livestock. This is generally less typical of gray foxes. Usually, foxes kill only young or small animals, particularly lambs and kids. However, in some circumstances, probably because their food is limited, red foxes may kill large lambs and kids, adult sheep and goats and small calves.

Foxes usually attack the throat of lambs and kids but kill some by multiple bites to the neck and back. This may result from young animals being caught while lying down. Foxes do not have the size and strength to hold and immobilize adult sheep and goats easily or to crush the skull and large bones; therefore, repeated bites may be required to subdue prey, even smaller animals. Numerous injuries also may result when young foxes attempt to kill but lack the experience to attack the throat or other vital areas.

Foxes generally prefer the viscera and begin feeding through an entry behind the ribs. However, some seem to prefer the nose and tongue and may consume the head of small prey. It has been noted in some areas that red foxes tend to feed on the carcasses of large prey and carrion on the side nearest the ground. Red foxes also are noted for carrying small carcasses back to their dens to feed their young which may account for some poultry, lambs, and kids that disappear and are never found.

Canine teeth in foxes are smaller and spacing is narrower than in coyotes. In general, these teeth are approximately ½ to ¾ inch apart on gray foxes and $^{11}/_{16}$ to 1 inch apart on red foxes. Foxes rarely cause severe bone damage to livestock other than poultry. This helps to distinguish their kills from those made by coyotes and other larger carnivores.

Fox tracks resemble coyote tracks but are typically smaller and foxes have a shorter stride. Red fox tracks are normally about 1¾ inches wide and 2¼ inches long; gray fox tracks are slightly smaller. A normal red fox's trotting stride is about 13 to 15 inches; a gray fox's stride is about 11 to 13 inches.

Cougars

Cougars attempt to stalk their prey and attack from cover. They frequently kill sheep and goats by biting the top of the neck or head. Broken necks are common in these kills. This differs from the typical coyote bite in the throat and general mutilation caused by dogs. However, cougars also may kill sheep and goats by biting the throat. This may result from prey falling or being knocked down and caught, or it may simply be the method found effective by individual cougars and most convenient on some prey animals. Cougars may kill by grasping the head of prey such as sheep, goats, and deer and pulling the head until the neck is broken. Many of these may not have been bitten but die quickly. Cougars kill calves much like they do sheep and goats. Multiple kills of sheep and goats by cougars are common; cases of a hundred or more animals killed in a single incident have been recorded. As a rule, very few animals, often only one or two in such incidents, are fed upon by the cougar.

Cougars usually kill larger animals, such as deer, elk, horses, and cattle, by leaping on their shoulders or back and biting the neck. Claw marks on the neck, back, and shoulders are characteristic of these kills. The prey animal's neck may be broken by bites or by the animal falling from the attack. There may also be bites in the throat of these larger prey. The size of the canine tooth punctures and the type of bone damage help distinguish cougar kills from those made by coyotes, dogs, and foxes. An adult cougar's upper canine teeth are approximately 1½ to 2¼ inches apart; the lower teeth are approximately $^{3}/_{8}$

to ½ inch closer together. A cougar's teeth are massive compared to those of the average coyote or bobcat.

Except when prey is scarce, cougars do not normally feed on carrion other than their own kills or possibly those taken away from other predators. They usually carry or drag their kills to a secluded area under cover to feed and drag marks are frequently found at fresh kill sites. Cougars generally begin feeding on the viscera (liver, heart, lungs, etc.) through the abdomen or thorax but like other carnivores, individuals differ. Some begin feeding on the neck or shoulder while others prefer the hindquarters. Like other cats, cougars normally leave relatively clean-cut edges when they feed compared to the ragged edges of tissue and bone left by coyotes. They also may break large bones in feeding on domestic and wild animals.

Cougars frequently try to cover their kills with soil, vegetation (leaves, grass, limbs) or snow. They may eviscerate prey and cover the viscera separately from the rest of the carcass. Even where little debris is available, bits of soil, rock, grass, or sticks may be found on the carcass. However, where multiple kills are made at one time, there may be no effort to cover more than one or two of them.

Cougar "scrapes" or "scratches", composed of mounds of soil, grass, leaves, or snow, are probably a means of communication with other cougars. These scrapes are generally 6 to 8 inches high and urine is deposited on the mounds. Male cougars appear to make scrapes as territorial markers around their kills and near trails and deposit urine and feces on them; these markers may be considerably larger than others, up to 2 feet long, 12 inches wide, and 6 to 8 inches high in some cases.

Cougar tracks are relatively round and rarely show any claw marks since the claws are normally retracted. Tracks of large adult males' front feet may be 4 inches or more long and about the same or slightly less in width. The hind tracks are slightly smaller. The rear pads of the feet are distinctively different from those of other carnivores. Typically, there are two lobes in front and three on the rear of the rear pads although there are individual variations. With extensive experience, some hunters can recognize individual cougars by their tracks, even without distinctive features such as missing toes or other deformities.

Bobcats

Bobcat hunting and killing behavior is much like that of cougars because they prefer to stalk their prey and attack from cover. On small prey, such as lambs, kids, and fawns, they bite into the skull or back of the neck and may leave claw marks on the back, sides and shoulders. Bobcats may also kill with a bite in the throat, typically just back of the jaws over the larynx. This could result from catching the prey after it falls, or it may be individual bobcat behavior.

Bobcats normally do not prefer to bite repeatedly in killing prey but tend to secure a lethal hold on the neck or throat and hang on until the prey stops struggling. Frequently, when bobcats secure a grip over the larynx, the animal suffocates rapidly and there is virtually no bleeding from the injury. The adult bobcat's canine teeth are normally about ¾ to 1 inch apart. Generally, an estimate of this spacing is easier to make on bobcat kills than on fox and coyote kills.

As a rule, bobcats do not prey on adult sheep and goats, or on calves, but are known to kill adult deer and antelope. They attack larger prey much like cougars by leaping on the back or shoulders and commonly leave claw marks. On small prey, there may be claw marks on any part of the body, but they are usually concentrated on the neck, shoulders and ribs.

Bobcats generally seem to begin feeding on the viscera by entering behind the ribs, but their feeding patterns vary. They may begin feeding on the neck, shoulders, or hindquarters. Their feeding pattern is relatively neat, typical of the cat family. On small animals, they may consume nearly the entire body, including the head, in a single feeding or they may carry the carcass away. Bobcats prefer to kill their own food but seem to feed somewhat more readily on carrion than cougars do.

Bobcats also may cover carcass remains, and frequently feed several times on a carcass. Being smaller than cougars, bobcats do not reach out as far in raking up debris, normally not much more than 15 inches. This, and much smaller tracks, helps distinguish between bobcat and cougar caches. Bobcats also may cover their urine and feces with a small mound of debris, typically much smaller than those made by cougars.

Like cougar tracks, bobcat tracks are round and lack claw marks but they are much smaller, only 2 to 3 inches in diameter. Also, the rear pad is shaped differently, being relatively straight in front, with a lobe at each side in the rear.

Bears

Grizzly Bears. Grizzly bears are common in parts of Canada and Alaska but occur only in limited areas of the west in the lower 48 United States, primarily in Yellowstone Park and in northwestern Montana. They are omnivores and consume large amounts of vegetation and wild fruits in addition to carrion and prey. They will take nearly any domestic animal species, but cattle and sheep are their most common livestock prey, primarily because these are the most common species available. Grizzly bears are large and powerful and generally have little trouble killing adult livestock. They kill with bites and blows to the head or neck and commonly break bones of the skull, neck or shoulders. They may leave claw marks and tooth punctures on the head, neck and back.

Grizzlies typically drag their kills into cover prior to feeding. They skin out the carcass, leaving skin and skeleton relatively intact. They do not chew and scatter bones like canids do. Commonly, they cover their kills with soil and vegetation and feed repeatedly as long as flesh remains. They readily feed on carrion, and leave extensive sign (matted vegetation, tracks and feces) around a carcass.

Black Bear. Predation by black bears on livestock is most common in spring and summer. Limited food sources in early spring and failures of wild berry and nut crops during summer months are probably major contributing factors. Black bears are also omnivorous and vegetation is a significant part of their diet. They do extensive damage in some areas of the northwestern states by stripping the bark from trees and feeding on the cambium. Black bears raid beeyards for honey and orchards for fruit. They also feed readily on carrion.

Black bears will attack adult cattle and horses but seem to prefer sheep, goats, calves, and pigs. They may break the neck or back of prey with blows from the paws, but normally they kill by biting the neck and shoulders. Claw marks are frequently found on the neck, back, and shoulders of these larger animals. Multiple kills of sheep and goats are relatively common, possibly because they are easy prey. Whether by accident or design, bears have been known to frighten livestock herds over cliffs, causing injuries and death to many animals.

Black bears prefer to feed in seclusion and often drag their prey to cover. They frequently begin feeding on the udder of lactating females, but generally prefer meat to the viscera. Some begin feeding at the neck or shoulders where the initial attack occurs. Where most of the prey is consumed, the skin of large prey is stripped back and turned inside out. The skin and skeleton are usually left largely intact. The carcass is rarely scattered by black bears although this may be done by coyotes or other animals that scavenge the remains. Vegetation around the carcass is usually matted down by black bears and their droppings are frequently found nearby.

Black bears may attempt to cover remains of larger carcasses but seem somewhat less inclined to do so than cougars and grizzly bears. Bear tracks have distinct characteristics. Bears have five toes with a broad, short pad on the front foot and five toes with a triangular pad on the rear foot. The rear foot oversteps the front foot in normal travel.

Hogs

In some areas, domestic or wild hogs (Russian boar, domestic hogs gone wild, and their crosses) prey on poultry and livestock. This occurs more often during drouths or other periods when mast (acorns, etc.) and other foods are scarce. Hogs will also feed readily on carrion but some hogs become highly efficient predators. Hog predation on livestock usually occurs on lambing or calving grounds, perhaps partially because of the prevalence of afterbirth. Occasionally, adult animals giving birth are fed upon and killed by hogs.

Young and small animals are often entirely consumed by hogs and the only evidence may be tracks and blood where feeding occurred. Missing young and their mothers with full udders may indicate such predation, particularly where this is frequent and no other causes for loss can be found.

Hogs feed on carcasses much like bears do although they are not as proficient in skinning them out. They may consume some parts that bears do not, such as the rumen and its contents. Since hogs commonly root up soil and vegetation their presence is usually evident and their tracks are distinctive.

Eagles

Both bald and golden eagles may prey on livestock, but usually golden eagles are responsible. Both species readily accept livestock carrion and carcasses of foxes and coyotes, although some individuals may prefer live prey to carrion. Eagles are efficient predators and they can cause severe losses of young livestock, particularly where concentrations of eagles exist. Generally, they prey on young animals, primarily sheep and goats, although they are capable of killing adults. Golden eagles also take young deer and antelope, as well as some adults.

Eagles have three front toes opposing the hind toe or hallux on each foot. The front talons normally leave wounds 1 to 3 inches apart, with the wound from the hallux 4 to 6 inches from the wound made by the middle front talon. On animals the size of small lambs and kids, fewer than four talon wounds may be found, one made by the hallux and one or two by the opposing talons. Talon punctures are typically deeper than those caused by canine teeth and somewhat triangular or oblong. Crushing between the wounds is not usually found , although compression fractures of the skulls of small animals may occur from an eagle's grip. Bruises from their grip are relatively common on eagle kills.

Eagles seize small lambs and kids anywhere on the head, neck, or body; lambs are frequently grasped from the front or side. Eagles usually kill adult animals and lambs and kids weighing 25 pounds or more by multiple talon stabs into the upper ribs and back. Their feet and talons are well adapted to closing around the backbone, with the talons puncturing large internal arteries, frequently the aorta in front of the kidneys. Massive internal hemorrhage from punctured arteries and/or collapse of the lungs when the thorax (ribcage) is punctured contribute to shock as the major cause of death. Eagles may also simply seize young lambs, kids, or fawns and begin feeding, causing the prey to die from shock and loss of blood as they are eviscerated.

Eagles skin out carcasses, turning the hide inside out, and leave much of the skeleton intact with the lower legs and skull attached to the hide. However, on very young animals, the ribs are often clipped off neatly close to the backbone and eaten, although eagles frequently do not eat the sternum (breast bone). Some eagles clip off and eat the mandible (lower jaw) , nose and ears. Quite often, they remove the palate and floor pan of the skull and eat the brain. They may clean all major hemorrhages off the skin, leaving very little evidence of the cause of death, even though there may be many talon punctures in the skin. Ears, tendons, and other tissues are sheared off cleanly by the eagle's beak.

Larger carcasses heavily fed on by eagles may have the skin turned inside out with the skull, backbone, ribs, and leg bones intact, but with nearly all flesh and viscera missing. However, the rumen is not normally eaten. Eagles may defecate around a carcass, leaving characteristic white streaks of feces on the soil and their tracks may be visible in soft or dusty soil.

Scavenging Birds

Vultures, ravens, crows, magpies, and some gulls commonly scavenge carcasses. In some circumstances, they may attack live animals and kill those that are unable to escape or defend themselves. Initial attacks by these birds are usually at the eyes and nose, navel, and anal area. Typically, they blind the animals by pecking out the eyes even if they do not kill them.

Magpies may attack the anal area and back as well as wound sites on healthy adult livestock under certain conditions. Unhealed brands and other wounds, such as saddle sores on horses, are preferred sites for attack. This is not a common occurrence, except possibly in northern states during severe winters when food for magpies is scarce.

Some hawk species also scavenge carcasses and may attack small animals that are not able to defend themselves. Hawks generally seem to attack and begin feeding in the shoulder or ribs.

Snakes

Venomous snakes, particularly rattlesnakes, occur on nearly all livestock ranges of the southern and western United States and in many other areas; thus, it is inevitable that substantial numbers of livestock are bitten. Because young animals (colts, calves, lambs, and kids) are curious and far less cautious than adults, they are the most common victims of snakebite in livestock. Many of them are bitten on the nose or head as they attempt to investigate snakes.

During summer months, livestock concentrate around streams and ponds for water during the hot, midday hours. This frequently leads to crowding, particularly of sheep, into shady areas during the time snakes must have shade. As a consequence, sheep are frequently bitten on the legs or lower body by being pushed close to snakes. Typical snakebite injuries include swollen, discolored tissue, lethargy, and fever. Animals bitten on the head may have severe swelling of the head and neck. A large percentage of young animals die but some survive, possibly because of greater resistance and/or smaller doses of venom.

Fang punctures and tissue discoloration which follow the major arteries and veins from the bite area are generally evident at necropsy.

Illustrated Field Guide

The following review describes the principles and procedures used to separate predator-caused injuries and mortalities in livestock and wildlife from those resulting from other causes. Proper identification demands recognition and evaluation of all available evidence. Application of these principles will help the investigator determine whether or not predation was involved and frequently what predator species was responsible.

Diseases, parasites, toxic plants and other mortality factors may require diagnoses by veterinarians and pathologists. In some instances, the absence of food or the presence of toxic plant materials in the digestive tract may provide definitive evidence of the cause of death. In others, the presence of parasites and symptoms of disease can be readily diagnosed. Nu-

merous references on these factors are noted in the reference list for those who wish to review these topics.

Knowledge and skill are often necessary to determine the cause of injuries or death. Although direct observation of predation is rare, it is the most specific evidence possible and may also permit identification of the responsible animal. Fresh injuries or kills which exhibit tooth, claw or talon punctures and hemorrhage are also specific evidence of predation. However, it is seldom possible to identify the individual predator responsible and occasionally it is not possible to identify the species from the carcass appearance alone.

In many instances, determination of predation as the cause of death must be made from circumstantial evidence where the carcasses alone do not provide adequate evidence. The history of predation in a specific area, aberrant livestock behavior, young or small livestock that simply disappear, predator sign (including tracks and droppings containing bone fragments or hair of prey species) are factors that provide circumstantial evidence. With sufficient care and evaluation of indirect evidence, it is often possible to rule out or to confirm predation as a cause of death with a reasonable degree of certainty.

Elements Used to Identify Predation

Livestock behavior
Direct evidence
Indirect evidence

Turkey vultures circling above a livestock carcass. Scavenging birds such as vultures, magpies, ravens, crows and eagles can be very helpful in finding animal carcasses even though their feeding may destroy evidence of the cause of death.

It is quite common to find young animals alone for short periods of time while their mothers feed or go to water. Calves, kids or lambs are often found sleeping by themselves during such intervals. Although this lamb was found dead of exposure, it is common to find young livestock sleeping by themselves in a natural position.

This ewe, standing alone with her stillborn lambs, exhibits typical maternal behavior. Livestock commonly remain separated from the herd to care for their young (even stillborn) several hours or days after giving birth and until the young are able to follow. Therefore, animals found away from the herd may or may not be exhibiting abnormal behavior.

A close-up view of this lamb's throat indicates the cause of his illness, a severe injury to the throat which was probably caused by a coyote attack.

Livestock are gregarious and normally are not found alone, particularly young animals. This lamb was found by himself away from the herd and exhibits the gaunt appearance and low head carriage of an animal that is obviously sick.

These two lambs exhibit the typical appearance of stillborn young or of those that have died very shortly after birth. There is no indication that they have made any strong attempt to rise and the fetal membrane is still present on the lamb on the left.

This whitetail fawn carcass exhibits the appearance of an animal that has been fed upon by a carnivore. In this particular case, the fawn was killed and fed upon by a coyote.

The carcass of this ewe, although beginning to decompose, still retains evidence of injuries in the shoulder and neck area. Thus, although the carcass is reaching an advanced stage of decomposition, there is evidence of an abnormal injury which suggests the need for further investigation.

The carcass of this elk calf exhibits injuries typical of predation, in this case, tooth punctures in the throat. This calf was killed and fed upon by coyotes.

This newborn calf also exhibits the appearance of an animal fed upon by a predator. In this case, the calf was killed and fed upon by coyotes.

The carcass of this lamb exhibits injuries which are typical of some kinds of predation. In this case, the lamb was bitten in the skull by a coyote.

This pronghorn antelope exhibits similar injuries, punctures in the throat, typical of predation. In this case, the pronghorn was killed by a coyote.

This carcass exemplifies the need for caution in interpreting evidence. Although the blood on the lamb's nose and shoulder where it has been fed upon suggests that it died of predation, in fact it was fed upon by scavenging birds several hours after death. The apparent bleeding resulted from a deficiency in blood clotting factors.

It is frequently necessary to skin animal carcasses to determine whether injuries have occurred. The lamb on the left was bitten in the throat and killed by coyotes and the lamb on the right died of non-predation causes.

The throat of this whitetail fawn exhibits the injuries typical of predation by several carnivore species, including lacerations in the area of the larynx and rear of the jaw. During necropsy of carcasses, the larynx and trachea should be opened and checked for the presence of foam that indicates that the animal was alive and breathing when the injuries occurred. The fawn was killed by a coyote.

A second view of the same whitetail fawn demonstrates the injuries to the skull caused in this attack by coyotes.

This lamb carcass exhibits injuries typical of predation: scratches, tooth punctures, and hemorrhage. This lamb was killed by a bobcat.

This Angora wether exhibits injuries typical of predation with tooth punctures and hemorrhage in the jaw and throat. In this case, the wether was killed and fed upon by coyotes.

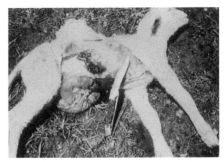

Caution is essential in interpreting injuries. For example, this lamb died of injuries to the liver caused by trampling in a corral.

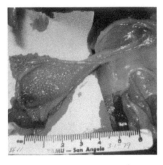

In contrast to the well-filled stomach of the Angora kid, this is the empty stomach of a young lamb fed upon by two red-tailed hawks. Thus, although the lamb was killed by hawks, it would not have survived.

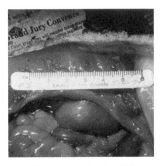

The lack of fat deposits in the kidney area of this lamb, which was dying of starvation when killed by a red fox, indicates that it was at a very low plane of nutrition when it was killed.

During necropsy, the carcass should be examined for evidence of adequate nutrition. This Angora kid's stomach was full of milk, indicating that it was well nourished when it was killed by an eagle.

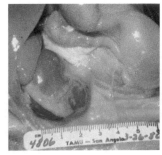

During necropsy the carcass should also be examined for the presence of deposits which indicate the plane of nutrition. Fat deposits in the kidney area of this lamb indicate that it was well nourished.

Evidence of predation may persist for days or weeks after death as long as certain portions of the carcass remain intact. This sheep had been killed by a coyote several days earlier but the tooth punctures and hemorrhage in the skin of the throat area persist and are evidence of predation.

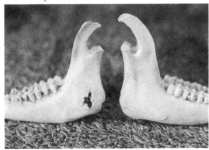

In many instances evidence of predation will persist as long as certain portions of the skeleton are intact. In this instance, the jaw bone on the left is from a goat killed by a coyote attack at the throat. The injuries to the rear of the jaw are typical of this type of kill. The jaw bone on the right is that of a goat that died of non-predation causes.

The site where the fawn was killed by the bobcat does provide graphic evidence of predation through scattered hair and the blood on the snow.

By examining a series of factors, it is sometimes possible to build a strong case for the cause of death even though individual pieces of evidence are insufficient to provide a diagnosis. The cow shown here is a three-year old heifer that had given birth to her first calf some 12 hours earlier. Her udder provides evidence that her calf had nursed.

This is the carcass of her calf about 12 hours after birth. The carcass was almost entirely consumed by coyotes but no external evidence on the carcass was sufficient to determine the cause of death. However, the calf's nose was chapped and peeling, indicating that the calf had nursed, and its skin had been cleaned of placental waste, which suggests good maternal care.

This is the carcass of a mule deer fawn which was fed upon by a bobcat, identified by tracks in the snow. Although some blood is present in the snow around the carcass, it is not sufficient to confirm predation as the cause of death, even though the fawn was partially covered with snow by the cat.

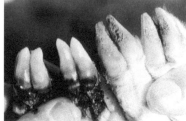

In examining carcasses to determine the cause of death of young animals, one factor is whether the animal has been able to rise and walk. The hooves on the left are those of a young goat that did not walk, since it was dead at birth. Those hooves on the right are those of a lamb that lived and walked for 18 hours after birth.

The coagulated blood indicates that the calf had bled extensively, not a normal circumstance for newborn young. Coyote tracks in the immediate vicinity of the carcass indicate predation.

It is often necessary to search for other evidence such as the tracks and hair which might be left at crossings under or through fences. In this case, a coyote has been using this crawl under a fence.

Skinning out the head and neck of the calf provided additional information.

The calf's hooves indicate that it had been up and walked extensively prior to death.

Numerous small hemorrhages around the calf's jaws and nose are evidence of a difficult birth. Indirect evidence from the carcass and vicinity indicates that the calf was born alive and had walked, nursed and received good maternal care. Warm, dry weather ruled out exposure as the cause of death. Coyote tracks, coagulated blood, and the cow's skidding tracks nearby indicate predation by coyotes.

Coyote tracks and scat shown here by this grass clump are concrete evidence of coyote presence in the area.

These two lambs that were killed by coyotes exhibit the typical appearance of an attack at the throat by coyotes. The lamb at the right exhibits the most typical coyote feeding pattern.

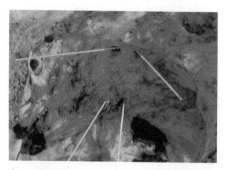

The neck of this lamb exhibits the typical tooth punctures and massive hemorrhage resulting from a coyote attack at the throat. The extensive hemorrhage in this case occurred because the lamb lived for several hours after the attack.

Tooth cuts on the throat and flank of this calf that escaped and survived were made by coyotes.

The Angora goat carcass exhibits the typical coyote attack at the throat as well as coyote feeding in the rib cage and flank.

Matches are inserted into the tooth punctures in the skull and scalp of this young lamb killed by a coyote biting the head.

This calf, still living, was attacked by coyotes which fed extensively on its hindquarters.

This calf carcass exhibits the feeding on the nose which seems to be relatively common with coyotes preying on young calves.

Persistent attacks by coyotes may result in the calf losing its entire tail and the coyotes feeding into the rectal area. This calf attacked by coyotes is one such example.

This Angora nanny exhibits the results of a coyote attack at the rear. This goat was attacked by a young, inexperienced coyote. The attack could have been interpreted as an attack by dogs had it not been for additional evidence including coyote tracks and droppings in the immediate vicinity of the goat.

The calf in the center was attacked by coyotes which bit off part of its tail. Bobtailed calves are frequently seen in areas where coyote predation is a common occurrence.

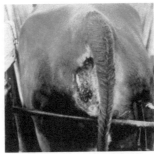

It is also relatively common for coyotes to feed on calves during birth, and they may also feed on the cow. This cow exhibits the results of such attack by coyotes.

This goat was attacked at the rear and fed upon by coyotes. The goat died of shock and loss of blood during the feeding process. This type of attack could be interpreted as typical of dogs, but in fact is also relatively typical of young inexperienced coyotes. In addition, it is less common for dogs to feed on their kills.

These injuries to the nose are a further example of what might be considered non-typical coyote attack behavior. Such attacks frequently lead to the appearance of carcasses such as shown in the next illustration.

The attack and feeding on this lamb's nose would normally be considered typical of dogs; however, this lamb was killed and fed upon by coyotes.

This nanny was attacked and her udder was eaten by a coyote. This is considered an aberrant coyote attack and feeding pattern, one which is far more typical of black bear.

Tracks made by dogs and coyotes of similar size are often easily confused. The tracks at the left were made by a collie dog weighing about 30 pounds while those at the right were made by a male coyote of similar size. Note the difference in the nail marks and the shape of the tracks.

Since it is easy to misinterpret and confuse predator sign made by species which are similar in behavior and the evidence they leave, it is important to be careful in examining sign. The front foot on the left is that of a 35-pound male collie dog. That on the right is of a 30-pound male coyote. Note the difference in the shape of the feet, toes and pads, as well as the nails.

This coyote scat is composed almost entirely of mohair from an Angora goat. The appearance of scat is based on the diet and differs a great deal with dietary content.

Coyote scats composed almost entirely of pig hair.

This ewe exhibits the type of injuries that often result from attack by dogs.

After the ewe was killed, the dog began feeding in the flank area in a manner similar to that of coyotes.

Coyote scat composed almost entirely of wild plums.

This ewe was mutilated and partially disemboweled by dogs which killed her.

The Rambouillet lamb was killed by a large dog which attacked at the throat and fed on the hindquarters. This attack could have been confused with that of a coyote.

A Rambouillet wether show lamb that was attacked by dogs.

These Angora kids also exhibit the indiscriminate mutilation caused by dogs; three were killed and two were badly injured. Multiple kills are quite common where dogs are the predators responsible.

The feeding on the hindquarters is also much more typical of coyotes since pet dogs do not normally feed on animals they kill. However, this lamb was killed by pets in the backyard of a home.

These ewes exhibit the indiscriminate mutilation that commonly results from dog attacks.

Some dogs, through innate instinct or experience, learn to kill as efficiently as wild carnivores. This ewe was killed by a German Shepherd attack at the throat.

These are the feet of a gray fox; the front foot is on the left, the hind foot is on the right.

These are the tracks of a gray fox in soft soil.

This is a 15-pound Angora kid bitten in the throat and below the left ear by a gray fox. The size and spacing of the tooth punctures as well as the history of gray fox attacks in this vicinity helped determine that this was a gray fox attack.

This 25-pound Angora kid was also attacked at the throat by a gray fox.

An Angora kid, weighing approximately 8 pounds, that was attacked and killed by a gray fox through repeated bites to the back. The size and spacing of tooth punctures as well as the lack of any broken bones, in addition to the history of gray fox predation, were the determining factors for confirming this as a gray fox kill.

Examination of the Angora kid during necropsy confirmed that it was well nourished and well fed. Note the milk in the stomach.

This is an Angora kid that was killed by a red fox through bites to the throat and back of the skull. Size and spacing of the tooth punctures, as well as the history of red fox predation in the vicinity were the determining factors.

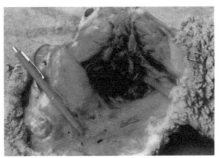

This is a 20-pound lamb killed by a red fox through an attack at the throat. Again, the size and spacing of the tooth punctures, as well as the history of red fox predation in the area were the determining factors.

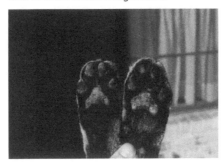

These are the feet of an adult male bobcat. The hind foot is at the left. The shape and spacing of the pads, as well as the lack of claw marks are evident in bobcat tracks.

The characteristics of a bobcat's track are evident in this track made in snow.

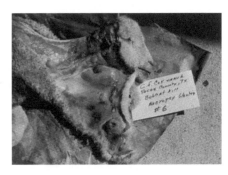

A 20-pound lamb killed by a bobcat bite in the back of the head. Size and spacing of the tooth punctures and claw marks on the skin were the determining factors.

After killing the lamb, the bobcat took a small feed from the flank area.

This mule deer fawn was killed by a bobcat attack at the throat. The bobcat ate a small amount from the hindquarter.

This is a small lamb (approximately 6 pounds) killed by a bobcat bite to the throat and jaws.

This is a male cougar track in the mud. Note the distinct characteristics.

This is the carcass of a male mule deer that was killed, fed upon and partially covered by a cougar. "Caching" by cougars is a relatively common occurrence with larger prey.

Skinning the lamb's neck and shoulders reveals massive injuries to the larynx, as well as claw punctures and scratches on the neck and shoulders.

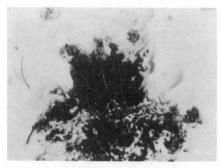

This is a cougar scratch in snow at which the cougar defecated and urinated. This appears to be a territorial activity along cougar travel-ways, particularly by males.

This sheep was killed by a cougar which bit the top of the neck behind the head.

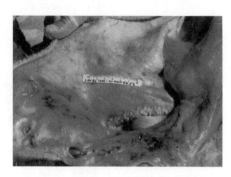

The opposite side of the lamb also shows scratches and punctures in the skin. The hemorrhage which accompanied these indicates that this occurred while the lamb was alive.

The pile of leaves in the center were scratched up by a male cougar near a kill. This may be a territorial marker.

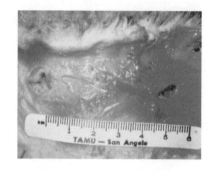

The size and spacing of the tooth punctures in this kill demonstrate that it was made by a large animal. The tooth punctures were nearly $3/8$ inch in diameter and 2 ¼ inches apart.

This is the front foot of a 125-pound male cougar. Note the distinct characteristics of the toes and the rear pad.

The tracks in this photo which straddle the drag marks were made by the front feet of a male cougar as it dragged a deer carcass to cover for feeding. It is relatively common behavior for cougars to drag their kills into cover for seclusion while feeding.

A rancher and technician are examining one of numerous kills made by a cougar one night at this sheep bed-ground.

This lamb carcass shows the abnormal position in which it was dropped while being dragged by a cougar.

This ewe was attacked and her udder eaten by a black bear, although the ewe escaped and survived for a short period of time.

This calf was attacked by a black bear which began feeding at the shoulders while the calf was still alive. The bear was shot at the site and the calf had to be destroyed.

These are the tracks of a black bear made in soft soil. Note the distinct pattern of the toes and rear pads in the tracks.

This ewe was killed and fed upon by a black bear. It is relatively common for black bear to feed on the udders of lactating ewes.

This is an eagle nest near lambing grounds which contains an eaglet and lamb remains.

This rather formless pile of scat was deposited by a black bear which had been feeding on huckleberries.

These are the remains of a lamb that weighed approximately 70 pounds which was killed and almost entirely consumed by a black bear. The skinning of the carcass and almost total consumption indicates an adult bear's huge appetite, as well as its feeding behavior.

This skull of a lamb killed by an eagle exhibits the talon punctures which are relatively common in such predation.

The claw marks on this tree made by a black bear may be a territorial mark.

After killing and eating the lamb shown in the previous illustration, the bear then killed this ewe and fed heavily on the neck and shoulders. Note the distinct difference in the feeding pattern compared to that of other carnivores.

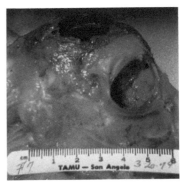

The skull of this lamb indicates the massive injuries and hemorrhage caused by an eagle which opened the skull and fed on the brain.

The head and neck of this lamb show the characteristics of an eagle attack. Pencils are inserted into the talon punctures and the fracture in the right side of the skull was caused by the eagle's grip.

This Angora kid carcass was almost entirely skinned out and the carcass, including the small bones, was consumed by an eagle.

This is the carcass of a moribund lamb which died from shock and blood loss when fed upon by two red-tailed hawks.

The back of this lamb exhibits the talon punctures made by an eagle which killed the lamb.

This is a carcass of a lamb that was killed and had its intestines stripped out by ravens.

These are the remains of a lamb that was killed and fed upon by a wild domestic hog.

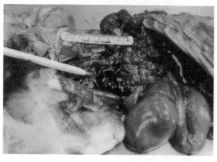

During necropsy it was found that the eagle's talons had penetrated through the ribs into the dorsal aorta and caused the massive hemorrhage shown at the tip of the pencil.

This ewe survived an attack by gulls.

This is the carcass of a lamb that was killed and fed upon by a raccoon.

This carcass exhibits the characteristics of extensive eagle feeding with the carcass skinned out and the ribs clipped off close to the spine.

This first-calf heifer had trouble calving and was fed upon by vultures while unable to rise. The heifer had to be destroyed.

This is the carcass of a lamb which died from a rattlesnake bite. The discolored tissue is evident at the point of the arrow.

Selected References

Livestock Diseases

Agriservices Foundation. 1980. *Sheep and Goat Handbook,* Vol. 1, Agriservices Foundation, P.O. Box 429, 648 West Sierra Ave., Clovis, CA 93612.

Agriservices Foundation. 1981. *Sheep and Goat Handbook,* Vol. 2, Agriservices Foundation, P.O. Box 429,648 West Sierra Ave., Clovis, CA 93612.

Jensen, R. 1974. *Diseases of Sheep,* Leo and Febiger, Philadelphia, PA.

Scott, G. E. (Editor). 1970. *The Sheepman's Production Handbook,* Sheep Ind. Dev. Pro. Inc., 200 Clayton Street, Denver, CO 80206.

Smith, H. A. and T. C. Jones. 1966. *Veterinary Pathology,* Leo and Febiger, Philadephia, PA.

Poisonous Plants

Gay, C. W. and D. D. Dwyer. 1967. *Poisonous Range Plants,* Cooperative Extension Service Circular No. 391, New Mex. State Univ., Las Cruces, 21 pp.

Keeler, R. F., K. R. Van Kampen, and L. F. James (Editors). 1978. *Effects of Poisonous Plants on Livestock,* Academic Press, N.Y. 600 pp.

Kingsbury, J. M. 1964. *Poisonous Plants of the United States and Canada,* Prentice-Hall, Inc., Englewood Cliffs, NJ. 626 pp.

Sperry, O. E., J. W. Dollahite, G. O. Hoffmann and B. J. Camp. 1968. *Texas Plants Poisonous to Livestock,* Bulletin B-1028, Texas A&M Univ., College Station, TX. 57 pp.

U.S. Department of Agriculture. 1968. 22 *Plants Poisonous to Livestock in the Western States.* USDA, U.S. Gov. Print. Off., Wash., DC. 64 pp.

Predators and Predation

Bowns, J. E. 1976. Field criteria for predator damage assessment, *Utah Science* 37 (1): 26-36.

Bowns, J. E., and D. A. Wade, 1980. *Physical Evidence of Carnivore Depredation* (35 mm slide series and 40 pp script), Texas Agri. Ext. Serv., College Station, TX.

Connolly, G. E. 1978: Predators and predator control, in: *Big Game of North America,* (J. B. Schmidt and D. L. Gilbert, Editors) Stackpole Books, Harrisburg, PA. pp. 359-394.

Connolly, G. E. 1980. *Use of Compound 1080 in Livestock Neck Collars to Kill Depredating Coyotes, A Report on Field and Laboratory Research.* November 1978–March 1980, U.S. Dept. of Int., Denver Wildl. Res. Center, Denver, CO, 125 pp and 12 appendices.

Connolly, G. E., R. M. Timm, W. E. Howard, and W. M. Longhurst. 1976. Sheep killing behavior of captive coyotes. *J. Wildl. Manage.* 40 (3): 400- 407.

Denny, R. N. 1974. The impact of uncontrolled dogs on wildlife and livestock. *N. Am. Wildl. Nat. Res. Conf.* 39: 257-291.

Dorrance, M. J., and L. D. Roy, 1976. Predation losses of domestic sheep in Alberta. *J. Rge. Manage.* 29 (6): 457-460.

Eide, S. 1965. The nature of brown bear predation on cattle on Kodiak Island. *Trans. 45th West. Assoc. State Game and Fish Comm. Conf.* pp. 113-118.

Fisher, R. J. (Editor). 1976. *Transactions: Mountain Lion Workshop of the Western United States and Western Canada,* U.S.F.W.S., Div. Fed. Aid, Portland, OR. 213 pp.

Fitzwater, W. D. 1981. Reptilian and Small Mammalian Predators of Livestock in America, in: *Pests, Predators and Parasites,* Volume 21A, World Animal Science, W. E. Howard and R. E. Marsh, (eds.), Elsevier Publ. Co., Amsterdam, Holland, (in press).

Foster, H. A., and R. E. Crisler. 1978. *Evaluation of Golden Eagle Predation on Domestic Sheep, Temperance Creek-Snake Sheep and Goat Allotment,* Hell's Canyon National Recreation Area, Oregon. U.S.F.W.S.-ADC, Portland, Ore. 26 pp.

Gee, C. K. 1979. Cattle and calf losses to predators—feeder cattle enterprises in the United States, *J. Rge. Manage.* 32(2): 152-154.

Gee, C. K., R. S. Magleby, W. R. Bailey, R. L. Gum, and L. M. Arthur. 1977. *Sheep and Lamb Losses to Predators and Other Causes in the Western United States,* USDA-ERS, A.E.R. Rep. No. 369, USDA, Wash., D.C. 41 pp.

Glover, F. A., and L. G. Heugly, 1970. *Final Report: Golden Eagle Ecology in West Texas,* Cooperative Wildlife Research Unit, Colo. State Univ., Fort Collins, Colo. 84 pp.

Hawthorne, D. W. 1980. Wildlife damage control techniques. Chapter 22, *Wildlife Management Techniques Manual,* The Wildl. Soc., Wash. D.C. pp. 411-439.

Henne, D. R. 1975. Domestic sheep mortality on a western Montana ranch, M. S. Thesis, Univ. of Mont., Missoula. 53 pp.

Hornocker, M. G. 1970. *An Analysis of Mountain Lion Predation on Mule Deer and Elk in the Idaho Primitive Area.* Wildl. Monogr. No. 21. The Wildl. Soc., Wash., DC. 39 pp.

Jones & Stokes Associates, Inc. 1977. *Dog Depredation on Wildlife and Livestock in California,* Cal. Dept. Fish and Game, Sacramento, CA. 64 pp.

Kalmbach, E. R., R. H. Imler, and L. W. Arnold. 1964. *The American Eagles and Their Economic Status—1964.* U.S. Dept. Int., Wash., DC. 85 pp.

McBride, R. T. 1976. The Status and Ecology of the Mountain Lion *(Felix concolor stanleyana)* of the Texas-Mexico Border. M.S. Thesis, Sui Ross State Univ., Alpine, TX. 160 pp.

Mech, L. D. 1970. *The Wolf.* Natural History Press, N.Y. 384 pp.

Mitchell, G. J. 1980. *The Pronghorn Antelope in Alberta.* Univ. of Regina, Saskatchewan, Canada, 165 pp.

Murie, O. J. 1954. *A Field Guide to Animal Tracks.* The Riverside Press, Cambridge, Mass. 374 pp.

Neilson, D. B. 1975. Coyotes and deer. *Utah Sci.* 36 (3): 87-90.

O'Gara, B. W. 1978. Sheep depredation by golden eagles in Montana. *Proc.: Eighth Vert. Pest Conf.,* March 7-9, 1978. Sacramento, CA. pp. 206-213.

Plant, J. W., R. Marchant, T. D. Mitchell, and J. R. Giles. 1978. Neonatal lamb losses due to feral pig predation. *Aust. Vet. J.,* Vol. 54: 426-429.

Robinette, W. L., J. S. Gashwiler, and O. W. Morris. 1959. Food habits of the cougar in Utah and Nevada. *J. Wildl. Manage.* 23(3): 261-273.

Robinson, W. B. 1952. Some observations on coyote predation in Yellowstone National Park. *J. Mammal.* 33(4): 470-476.

Rowley, I. 1970. Lamb predation in Australia: Incidence, predisposing conditions, and the identification of wounds. *CSIRO Wildl. Res.* 15: 79-123.

Roy, L. D., and M. J. Dorrance. 1976. *Methods of Investigating Predation of Domestic Livestock.* Alberta Agri. Dept., Edmonton, Alberta, Can. 54 pp.

Shaw, H. G. 1979. *A Mountain Lion Field Guide.* Special Report No. 9, Ariz. Game and Fish Dept., Phoenix. 27 pp.

Simmons, V. L. 1935. *Sheep Killing Dogs.* USDA, Wash., DC. 37 pp.

Storer, T. I., and L. P. Tevis, Jr. 1955. *California Grizzly.* Univ. of Cal. Press, Berkeley. 335 pp.

Truett, J. C. 1979. Observations of coyote predation on mule deer fawns in Arizona. *J. Wildl. Manage.* 43(4): 956-958.

U.S. Fish and Wildlife Service. 1978. *Predator Damage in the West: A Study of Coyote Management Alternatives.* U.S. Dept. Int., Wash., DC. 168 pp.

Wade, D. A. 1978. Coyote damage: A survey of its nature and scope, control measures and their application, in: *Coyotes: Biology, Behavior and Management.* Academic Press, Inc., N.Y. pp. 347-368.

Wade, D. A. 1980. Predator damage control, 1980: Recent history and current status, in *Proc.: Ninth Vert. Pest Conf.* Cal. Dept. Food and Agri. Sacramento. pp. 189-199.

Wade, D. A. 1981. Large Mammal and Bird Predators of Livestock in North America, in: *Pests, Predators and Parasites, Vol. 21A,* World Animal Sci., W. E. Howard and R. E. Marsh, (Eds.). Elsevier Pub. Co., Amsterdam, Holland, (in press).

Wade, D. A., and S. L. Beasom. 1979. The effects of environmental-political factors on predator research. *Vertebrate Pest Control and Management Materials*, ASTM STP 680, J. R. Beck (Ed.) Am. Soc. Test. and Mat. pp. 294-303.

Wade, D. A., and C. W. Livingston, Jr. 1979. Lamb and kid necropsies and mortality factors found in Operation Dead Lamb—1978-79, in: *Research Reports: Sheep and Goat, Wool and Mohair—1979*. Texas Agri. Exp. Sta. Texas A&M Univ., College Station, TX.

Wade, D. A., and G. E. Connolly. 1980. Coyote predation on a Texas goat ranch. *Texas Agri. Prog.* 26 (1): 12-16.

Wade, D. A. 1982. *Impacts, Incidence and Control of Predation on Livestock in the United States with Particular Reference to Predation by Coyotes*. Counc. for Agri. Sci. and Technol. Spec. Publ. 10. 20 pp.

Western Regional Coordinating Committee, WRCC-26. 1980. *Predation on Domestic Animals*, A Response to Secretary of Interior Andrus' Policy Statement Pertaining to the Animal Damage Control Program. Utah Agri. Exp. Sta. Utah State Univ., Logan. 91 pp.

White, M. 1973. Description of remains of deer fawns killed by coyotes. *J. Mammal.* 54(1): 291-293.

Young, S. P. 1958. *The Bobcat of North America*, Univ. of Nebr. Press, Lincoln. 193 pp.

Young, S. P., and E. A. Goldman. 1944. *The Wolves of North America*. Am. Wildl. Inst., Wash., DC. 660 pp.

Young, S. P., and E. A. Goldman. 1946. *The Puma: Mysterious American Cat*. Am. Wildl. Inst., Wash., DC. 350 pp.

Young, S. P., and H. H. T. Jackson, 1951. *The Clever Coyote*. The Stackpole Co., Harrisburg, PA. 411 pp.

Appendix A

Some North American carnivore species are listed that prey on livestock, poultry and game animals and may also scavenge carcasses.

Mammals

Kodiak bear, *Ursus arctos middendorfi*
Grizzly bear, *Ursus arctos horribilis*
Black bear, *Ursus americanus*
Cougar, *Felis concolor*
Jaguar, *Felis onca*
Bobcat, *Lynx rufus*
Lynx, *Lynx canadensis*
Ocelot, *Felis pardalis*
Jaguarundi, *Felis yagouarundi*
Gray wolf, *Canis lupus*
Red wolf, *Canis rufus* (now considered extinct)
Coyote, *Canis latrans*
Dog, *Canis familiaris*
Coydog, primarily coyote-dog crosses (*Canis latrans* × *familiaris*)
Red fox, *Vulpes fulva*
Gray fox, *Urocyon cinereoargenteus*
Arctic fox, *Alopex lagopus*
Wolverine, *Gulo luscus*
Badger, *Taxidea taxus*
Striped skunk, *Mephitis mephitis*
Hooded skunk, *Mephitis macroura*
Hognosed skunk, *Conepatus leuconotus*
Spotted skunk, *Spilogale putorius*
Mink, *Mustela vison*
Weasels, *Mustela frenata, M. erminea, M. rixosa*
Raccoon, *Procyon lotor*
Opossum, *Didelphis marsupialis*
Hogs (domestic, feral and wild), *Sus scrofa*

Birds

Golden eagle, *Aquila chrysaetos*
Bald eagle, *Haliaeetus leucocephalus*
Redtailed hawk, *Buteo jamaicensis*
Great horned owl, *Bubo virginianus*
Caracara, *Carcara cheriway*
Black vulture, *Coragyps atratus*
Turkey vulture, *Cathartes aura*
White-necked raven, *Corvus cryptoleucus*
Common raven, *Corvus corax*
Common crow, *Corvus brachyrhynchos*
Blackbilled magpie, *Pica pica*
Yellowbilled magpie, *Pica nuttalli*
Various gull species, e.g.,
  California gull, *Larus californicus*
  Herring gull, *Larus argentatus*

Acknowledgments

The authors acknowledge the assistance of the following individuals in preparing this publication: Robert J. Burgee, Milton J. Caroline, Guy E. Connolly, Donald W. Hawthorne, Darrell C. Juve, Norman C. Johnson, Robert A. Kriege, James M. Laughlin, Charles W. Livingston, Jr., Roy L. McBride, Gary L. Nunley, Charles W. Ramsey, Milo J. Shult, Ronald A. Thompson and Shirley E. Bovey.

Numerous contributors of the slides and photos for use in the slide series and this bulletin include among others: U.S. Forest Service; U.S. Fish and Wildlife Service; Colorado Division of Wildlife; Texas Rodent & Predatory Animal Control Service; V. W. Howard, Jr., New Mexico State University, Las Cruces; Donald A. Klebenow, University of Nevada, Reno; Darwin B. Nielsen, Utah State University, Logan; Donald G. Delorenzo, Oregon State University, Eugene; Guy E. Connolly, U.S. Fish & Wildlife Service, Twin Falls, Idaho; Alex T. Cringan, Colorado State University, Fort Collins; Bart W. O'Gara, University of Montana, Missoula; Jeff A. Brent, U.S. Fish and Wildlife Service, Grand Junction, Colorado; Jerry P. Clark, Department of Food and Agriculture, Ceres, California; Charles W. Livingston, Jr., Texas A&M University, San Angelo; J. Maurice Shelton, Texas A&M University, San Angelo; Robert M. Timm, University of Nebraska, Lincoln; Jack Clucas, U.S. Fish & Wildlife Service, Shell, Wyoming; Warren Montague, U.S. Forest Service, Waldron, Arkansas; Clell Lee, Blue, Arizona; James M. Laughlin, U.S. Fish & Wildlife Service, Miles City, Montana; Saidor H. Turman, U.S. Fish & Wildlife Service, Uvalde, Texas; F. Robert Henderson, Kansas State University, Manhattan; Robert A. Kriege, U.S. Fish & Wildlife Service, Buffalo, South Dakota; Jerry H. Scrivner, Texas A&M University, College Station; Donald V. Bynum, Texas Agricultural Extension Service, San Angelo; James R. Tigner, U.S. Fish & Wildlife Service, Rawlins, Wyoming.

The publication reprinted here was originally produced in 1984 by the Texas Agricultural Extension Service, The Texas Agricultural Experiment Station of The Texas A&M University System, and the United States Fish and Wildlife Service of the Department of the Interior. It is used by permission.

General Appearance of Animal Tracks

Illustrations show general appearance only and are not necessarily drawn to scale.

Coyote

Dog

Red Fox

Gray Fox

Badger

Bobcat

Raccoon

Cougar

Black Bear

Armadillos Nine-Banded Armadillo (*Dasypus novemcinctus*)

Biology

Size: Not sexually dimorphic but males heavier than females. Range 12 to 17 lbs (5.5 to 7.7 Kg). Total length is 24 to 31 in (615 to 800 mm) including a 9.7 to 14.5 in (245 to 370 mm) tail.

Diet: 90% is various invertebrates (earthworms, beetles, beetle larvae, fly larvae), within the top 3.94 in (10 cm) of soil, the rest consists of grapes, persimmon, other vegetation, salamanders, small frogs, lizards, neonatal mice, and carrion.

Habitat: Habitat generalists. But may prefer dense ground cover and scrub near riparian areas. No differences found between male and female habitat selection preferences.

Activity: Highly correlated to temperature. More diurnal during winter months and more nocturnal in summer months. Most activity occurs between 1700 hours and sunset. Do not hibernate. 77 to 90% of above ground time is spent foraging.

Behavior: Jump when startled. Tend to be loners. Sleep up to 20 hours/day.

Procreation: Mate in July. Delayed egg implantation to November followed by a 120 to 150 day development. Females give birth to quadruplets in early spring and young emerge May to July.

Capabilities: Outstanding diggers. Can cross streams by swimming or walking across the bottom. Poor eyesight and hearing. Excellent sense of smell. Cannot tolerate cold. Can climb fences at least up to 5 ft (1.5 m) tall.

Symptoms

Owners will complain of torn up turf.

Signs

Avg. Hole Size: The average diameter 8.8 in (22.4 cm), with a range of 6 to 20 in (15 to 51 cm) (Fig. 1). Maximum head width ranges from 1.7 to 1.8 in (42.3 to 44.7 mm). Dens may have more than 1 entrance. Opening may be sealed with a leaf ball. Average burrow length is 4 ft (1.2 m) but can reach 15 ft (4.5 m).

Access: They may dig underneath homes lacking full foundations (Fig. 2).

Damage to structures: Burrowing can undermine slabs, decks, driveways, and structures.

Damage to Lawn/Garden: Can cause substantial damage to turf. Their damage may be difficult to distinguish from that done by raccoons (Fig. 3). Holes tend to be 1 to 5 in (2.5 to 12.7 cm) wide and 1 to 5 in (2.5 to 12.7 cm) deep. Others say holes typically are 3 to 5 inches (7.6 to 12.7 cm) wide and 1 to 3 inches (2.5 to 7.6 cm) deep. Remember an animal will only dig as deep as necessary to find food. Watered lawns will keep food near the surface. In Texas, most complaints occurred between July to November.

Tracks:. Front track (Fig. 4) is 1½ to 2 in (3.8 to 5.1 cm) long and 1 3/8 to 1 5/8 in (3.5 to 4.1 cm) in width.

Fig. 1. Den hole by house foundation. Photo by Ron Frye.

Fig. 2. Shallow depression reveals an access point created by an armadillo in this home's crawl space. Photo by Tom Holmes.

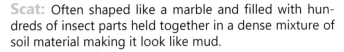

Fig. 3. Armadillo diggings in mulch. Photo by Tom Holmes.

Fig. 4. Front foot of armadillo. Image by Kim Cabrera.

Scat: Often shaped like a marble and filled with hundreds of insect parts held together in a dense mixture of soil material making it look like mud.

Hair: Rarely found even though they have a few hairs in between the horny plates on their back, and a patch on their unshielded belly.

Sounds: Quite noisy during foraging. Utter a buzzing noise (like bees) when frightened.

Bite Marks: Rare since they lack front teeth. Their 28 to 32 teeth consist of only molars and premolars that are peg-like in shape that they use to grind their food.

Associated Animals: Been known to share their den with opossum, cotton rat, and cottontail rabbit.

Health/Safety

Leprosy: Armadillos have been known to carry leprosy (*Mycobacterium leprae* is the causative agent). People who handle or eat armadillos are 2 times as likely to contract the disease.

Chagas Disease: Chagas disease (*T. cruzi* infection; also referred to as American trypanosomiasis) is a parasitic infection that is commonly transmitted by the infected feces entering through the bite of insects known as "kissing bugs" (family *Reduviidae*, subfamily *Triatominae*). This insect has been found in an armadillo burrow and studies of Chagas disease infection in Louisiana armadillos ranged from 1.1% to 28.8%.

Coccidioidomycosis: The fungus (*Coccidioides immitis*) occurs in alkaline soil receiving annual rainfall averaging 5 to 20 in (12.7 to 51 cm), hot summers, and rare freezes. Armadillo hunters and those who disturb contaminated soil may contract the infection.

Resources

Thanks to Tom Olander of Olander's Wildlife Control and Rob Russell of Wildlife Pro Network for providing some information for this module.

Ancona, K. A., and W. L. James. 2009. Time Budgets of Wild Nine-banded Armadillos. *Southeastern Naturalist* 8(4):587-598.

Armstrong, J. 1997. Controlling Armadillo Damage in Alabama. Alabama Cooperative Education System (May):1-2.

Centers for Disease Control. 2010. Chagas Disease. (Nov. 2). http://www.cdc.gov.

Chamberlain, P. A. 1980. Armadillos: Problems and Control. *Proceedings of the 9th Vertebrate Pest Conference*, pp. 163-169.

Clark, W. K. 1951. Ecological Life History of the Armadillo in the Eastern Edwards Plateau Region. *American Midland Naturalist*. 46:2(Sep):337-358.

Controlling Armadillo Damage. N.D. Texas Cooperative Extension, Texas A & M University. 2 pp.

Deps, P. D., B. L. Alves, C. G. Gripp, R. L. Aragão, B.V.S. Guedes, J. B. Filho, M. K. Andreatta, R. S. Marcari, I.C.A. Prates, and L. C. Rodrigues. 2008. Contact with armadillos increases the risk of leprosy in Brazil: A case control study. *Indian Journal of Dermatology, Venereology & Leprology* 74:4 (Jul/Aug):338-342.

Dorn, P. L., L. Perniciaro, M. J. Yabsely, D. M. Roellig, G. Balsam, J. Diaz, and D. Wesson. 2007. Autochthonous Transmission of *Trypanosoma cruzi*, Louisiana. *Emerging Infectious Diseases* http://www.cdc.gov/eid 13:4(April): 605-7.

Elbroch, M. 2003. *Mammal Tracks and Sign: A Guide to North American Species*. Mechanicsburg, PA: Stackpole Books.

Fitch, H. S., P. Goodrum, and C. Newman. 1952. The Armadillo in the Southeastern United States. *Journal of Mammalogy* 33:1(Feb):21-37.

Freeman, P. W. and H. H. Genoways. 1998. Recent Northern Records of the Nine-Banded Armadillo (Dasypodidae) in Nebraska. *The Southwestern Naturalist,* 43:4(Dec):491-495.

Gammons, D. J., M. T. Mengak, L. M. Conner. 2009. Armadillo Habitat Selection in Southwestern Georgia. *Journal of Mammalogy* 90:2(Apr):356-362.

Hawthorne, Donald W. "Armadillos." in *Prevention and Control* of Wildlife Damage. Editors, S. E. Hygnstrom, R. M. Timm, G. E. Larson. 1994. University of Nebraska-Lincoln. 2 vols.

Inbar, M. and R. T. Mayer. 1999. Spatio-Temporal Trends in Armadillo Diurnal Activity and Road-Kills in Central Florida. Wildlife Society Bulletin 27:3 (Autumn):865-872.

Merriam, D. F. 2002. The Armadillo [Dasypus novemcinctus (Linnaeus)] Invasion of Kansas. Transactions of the Kansas Academy of Science. 105:1/2 (Apr):44-50.

Petersen, L. R., S. L. Marshall, C. Barton-Dickson, R. A. Hajjeh, M. D. Lindsley, D. W. Warnock, A. A. Panackal, J. B. Shaffer, M. B. Haddad, F. S. Fisher, D. T. Dennis, and J. Morgan. 2004. Coccidioidomycosis among Workers at an Archeological Site, Northeastern Utah. Emerging Infectious Diseases 10:4(April): 637-642.

Pierce, R. A. II. 2007. Armadillos in Missouri: Techniques to Prevent and Control Damage. University of Missouri Extension (Mar):1-2.

Sikes, R. S., G. A. Heidt, and D. A. Elrod. 1990. Seasonal Diets of the Nine-banded Armadillo (Dasypus novemcinctus) in a Northern Part of Its Range. American Midland Naturalist 123:2(Apr):383-389.

Schaefer, J. M. and M. E. Hostetler. The Nine-banded Armadillo (Dasypus novemcinctus). 2009. Publication #WEC 76. The Institute of Food and Agricultural Sciences, University of Florida (Apr):1-4.

Schwartz, C. and E. Schwartz. 1981. The Wild Mammals of Missouri. University of Missouri Press and Missouri Department of Conservation.

Whitaker, Jr. J. O. and W. J. Hamilton, Jr. 1998. Mammals of the Eastern United States. 3rd ed. Ithaca, NY: Comstock Publishing Associates.

Bats

Order Chioptera. A variety of bats may enter structures, however, most are colony bats consisting of Small Brown (*Myotis lucifugus*) and Big Brown (*Eptesicus fuscus*).

Biology

Size: Small browns weigh 0.25 to 0.35 oz (7 to 10 g). females larger than males. Big browns weigh 0.42 to 0.56 oz (12 to 16 g).

Diet: Little browns. Eat a variety of flying insects but tend to select 0.12 to 0.4 in (3 to 10 mm) in size. Big browns. Beetles comprise almost 58% of their diet.

Habitat: Large Buildings within ½ mile (0.8 km) of standing water that have good sun exposure and 20 ft (6 m) of clear flying to den hole. Big browns tend to move to cooler areas of a roost when temperature rises above 95°F (35°C). If they hibernate in buildings, these tend to be buildings that are heated (attics stay above freezing) and the structure did not have a maternity colony.

Activity: Nocturnal/Spring/Summer/Fall; may migrate. Bats tend not to leave the roost when temperature is below 50°F (28°C) or in heavy precipitation. They hibernate in the winter when insect prey is absent. But they can wake up, move around creating scratching noises during warm spells Temperature >40°F (4° C). If the house has them in the winter time, then the bat(s) are hibernating in the house.

Little browns. Tend not to hibernate in buildings. Enter torpor when temperatures fall below 90°F to 97°F (32° to 36°C) winter; 102°F to 108°F (39° to 42°C).

Big browns tend to leave roosts 30 min or more before dark. Small brown bats that are nursing will reduce their flight area by 35% and generally fly less than 600 yards (0.55 km) from roost.

Procreation: Spring, 1 to 2 young per year. Young are flightless till third week, June to July. No nests are created. They rely on body-warmth and ambient temperature (Fig. 1a). Young are weaned in 40 to 60 days. Bats tend to choose nursery sites with temperatures between 85 to 104°F (30 to 40°C). Big brown maternity colonies tend to select structures with larger openings and taller than surrounding structures, with metal roofs, near more water and agriculture than forest, and are hotter than alternative buildings (122°F/50°C at 1400 to 1600 hours).

Little browns. Young raised in colonies of almost exclusively made up of females, though some males may be present. Non-pregnant females and males typically roost alone or in small groups away from maternity colonies. Nursing bats return to roost 1 to 2 times per night with initial visit around 3 hours after emergence. Nursing colonies begin to disperse in mid-summer.

Capabilities: Outstanding fliers but cannot fly directly from ground-level. Use echolocation to identify objects while flying at night. They are not blind but see better in dim light. They also can climb and crawl. The late Kirk LaPierre has said that little browns can chew through foam. But bats lack the ability to chew through solid/hard items.

Symptoms

Owners will complain of scratching sounds or feces that keeps appearing on patio etc.

Signs

Avg. Hole Size: ½-inch (1.27 cm) wide and 2 to 3 inches (5 to 7.6 cm) long (Fig. 1b). Widest head measurements for the little brown range from 0.3 to 0.4 in (8.1 to 10.5 mm). However bats can enter a hole as small

Fig. 1a. Bats clustered in attic rafter. Photo by Mark Casaleggi of ABC Animal and Insect Innovations, LLC.

Fig. 1b. Gap in the slate roof accessed by bats.

Fig. 2a. Brown rubmarks surround entrance to hole.

as 3/8 in (9.5 mm). The edges of primary entrances will be darkened from the rubbing of their bodies against the edges (Fig. 2a). Look for urine stains on windows (Fig. 2b).

Access: Bats typically enter structures at joints (where 2 items abut) which have expanded to allow bat entry. Bats have entered behind siding.

Damage to Structures: Bats do not gnaw or otherwise create holes to enter structures. Neither do they create nests.

Bats damage homes through their urine (Fig. 3) and feces which can form large piles and feces. Volume depends on the number of bats and the years they were allowed to remain in a structure. Big browns maintain high levels of fidelity to roosts.

Urine can crystallize and form stalactites in heavy infestations. Odor, once it penetrates wood and other porous materials, can be very difficult to remove.

Sometimes you will find bats in toilettes.

Damage to Lawn/Garden: None. Bats are actually beneficial due to the crop damaging insects they eat.

Tracks: Typically not found, although crawl marks may be seen in dusty locations.

Scat: About the size of a grain of rice. $3/16$ to $1/4$ in (4.8 to 6 mm) in length (Fig. 4a). When examined one will find silver speckles. These speckles are the undigested wings of the insects they eat. This will be in direct contrast to mouse droppings, which will lack the specks. Bat droppings tend to be concentrated in 1 area due to roosting behavior. They also defecate/urinate before entering the building (Fig. 4b). Two cubic yards (1.8 m^3) of dry guano weighs around 40 lbs (18 kg). Elbroch says little brown scat is $1/16$ to $1/8$ in (2 to 3 mm) in diameter and $1/8$ to $11/16$ in (3 to 17 mm) in length.

Fig. 2b. Dried bat urine on window.

Fig. 3. Urine stains on this wall stemmed from more than 20 years of bats living in the attic.

Fig. 4a. Bat scat.

Fig. 4b. Note droppings and staining where bats entered this attic vent.

Attic inspections will reveal concentrated droppings in one area. This is proof that bats were here. Bat droppings when crushed, will break apart into dust. This is in contrast to mouse droppings that remain hard when they dry. Wet droppings suggest recent deposit (Fig. 4c).

Hair: Rarely found.

Sounds: High-pitched clicking, wing flapping, and sounds of scratching as they climb walls. Research using specialized sound equipment has shown promise in identifying bat species and even individual bats.

Bite Marks: So small and pin-like that a person who is bitten may not even know he/she was bitten (Fig. 5). The marks can be very difficult to see even when the victim knows the location of the bite.

Associated Animals: Bats have been known to dwell in houses also occupied by flying squirrels. So says Tom Logan of Wild Things LLC Stratford, CT 06614. He had a house in New Canaan CT. He estimates the house as 2,000 to 2500 ft^2 (609 to 762 m^2).

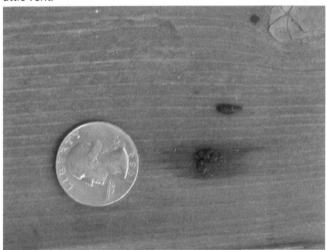

Fig. 4c. Oil stain around scat means dropping was deposited within 48 hours according to Dennis Ferraro.

Health/Safety

Rabies: Bats are endemic carriers of rabies. However, prevalence of rabies among bats is believed to be <1%. Among bats submitted for rabies testing, the rate jumps to 3 to 5%. Be sure to know the rabies protocols of your state. Many states now require people to assume they have been bitten if they awake in a room with a bat. Interestingly, between 1958 and 2000, 36 cases of indigenous rabies cases occurred in the U.S. Of the 28 cases known to be "cryptic exposures (i.e. nature of exposure unknown)" 26 were associated with strains of rabies from insectivorous bats. Of the 26, 19 exposures came from 2 species of bats not normally associated with dwellings, namely the silver-haired bats (*Lasionycteris noctivagans*) and eastern pipistrelles (*Pipistrellus subflavus*).

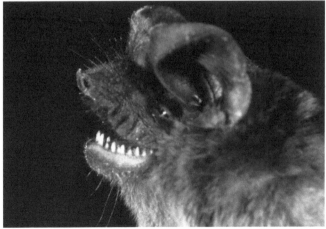

Fig. 5. Note the needle-like structure of bat teeth. Photo by CDC.

Histoplasmosis: Histoplasmosis is caused by exposure (typically through respiration) to fungal spores growing in the droppings of bats. It is essential that proper respiratory and vision protection be worn during attic inspections.

Bat Bugs: Bat bugs include the eastern bat bug (*Cimex adjunctus*), the western bat bug (*Cimex pilosellus*, and the swallow bug (*Oeciacus* spp.). As their name suggests, they focus their feeding efforts on bats. However, when bats are no longer available (e.g. young achieve flight and/or the colony relocates), these bugs sometimes search for blood meals from humans.

White-nosed Syndrome: Caused by a fungus. No known risk to humans but care should be taken to decontaminate one's self and equipment between bat inspections to prevent transferring the infection.

Resources

Acknowledgements: Some of the information on this species was gained from Eric Arnold, Kirk LaPierre (d. 2010), and Tom Logan.

Elbroch, M. 2003. *Mammal Tracks and Sign: A Guide to North American Species*. Mechanicsburg, PA: Stackpole Books.

Fenton, M. B. and R. M. R. Barclay. 1980. *Myotis lucifugus*. Mammalian Species No. 142 (Nov. 20):1-8.

Greenhall, A. M. and S. C. Frantz. "Bats." in *Prevention and Control of Wildlife Damage*. Editors, S. E. Hygnstrom, R. M. Timm, G. E. Larson. 1994. University of Nebraska-Lincoln. 2 vols.

Handbook of Pest Control: The Behavior, Life History, and Control of Household Pests. 2011. S. A. Hodges, Ed. 10th Edition. Mallis Handbook Co.

Harding, J. 1979. *An Animal Damage Identification Guide for Massachusetts*. Amherst, MA: Cooperative Extension Service, University of Massachusetts, SP-113.

Henry, M., D. W. Thomas, R. Vaudry, and M. Carrier. 2002. Foraging Distances and Home Range of Pregnant and Lactating Little Brown Bats (*Myotis lucifugus*). *Journal of Mammalogy* 83:3 (Aug):767-774.

Link, R. 2004. *Living with Wildlife in the Pacific Northwest*. Seattle, WA: Univ. of Washington Press.

Messenger, S. L., J. S. Smith, and C. E. Rupprecht. 2002. Emerging Epidemiology of Bat-Associated Cryptic Cases of Rabies in Humans in the United States. *Clinical Infectious Diseases*, 35:6 (Sep. 15):738-747.

Murray, K. L., E. R. Britzke, and L. W. Robbins. 2001. Variation in Search-Phase Calls of Bats. *Journal of Mammalogy* 82:3 (Aug):728-737.

Nuebaum, D. J., K. R. Wilson, and T. J. O'Shea. 2007. Urban Maternity-Roost Selection by Big Brown Bats in Colorado. *The Journal of Wildlife Management* 71: 3(May):728-736.

Whitaker, J. O. Jr., and S. M. Barnard. 2005. Food of Big Brown Bats (*Eptesicus fuscus*) from a Colony at Morrow, Georgia. *Southeastern Naturalist*. 4(1):111-118.

————, and S. L. Gummer. 2000. Population Structure and Dynamics of Big Brown Bats (*Eptesicus Fuscus*) Hibernating in Buildings in Indiana. *American Midland Naturalist* 143:2(Apr):389-396.

————, and L. R. Douglas. 2006. Bat Rabies in Indiana. *The Journal of Wildlife Management* 70:6 (Dec):1569-1573.

Williams, L. M., and M. C. Brittingham. 1997. Selection of Maternity Roosts by Big Brown Bats: *The Journal of Wildlife Management* 61:2 (Apr):359-368.

Beavers *(Castor canadensis)*

Biology

Size: 35 to 69 lbs (16 to 31 kg). Males and females are not visually dimorphic. Length 40 in (100 cm).

Diet: Tree bark (Fig. 1a). Willow (*Salix spp.*) and Aspen (*Populus spp.*) are particularly preferred, but will thrive in areas lacking these plants. Herbaceous plants, water plants, and row crops will be eaten, usually during summer months. Strict vegetarians.

Habitat: Wherever there is slow moving water and suitable plants. Rocky areas and rapids are avoided. One study on characteristics of beaver selection of streams found that beaver population density and fidelity to stream sites depended on 7 key variables: watershed size, stream width below dam, stream gradient, soil drainage. Beaver stream habitat was then categorized into 3 classes: class 1, hardwoods within 109 yds (100 m); class 2, hard-woods within 218 yds (200 m); and class 3, abandoned fields within 109 yds (100 m).

Class 1 habitat could sustain multiple colonies per km². Beaver density will not exceed 1 colony per ½ mi (0.8 km) of stream in even the best of conditions.

Fig. 1b. Pond lodge. Photo by Hans Stuart of USFWS.

Fig. 1c. Entrances to bank den revealed after water level dropped. Yard stick in image. Photo by Aaron Hildreth.

Class 2 habitat could sustain 1 colony per 0.6 mi² (1 km²).

Class 3 habitat is unable to sustain a colony per 0.6 mi² (1 km²).

Behavior: Central location foragers, meaning beavers gather food in various places but tend to eat the food in 1 place. They also choose smaller trees farther away from water. Create mounds on banks with mud and deposit scent (castor) as a territorial marker.

Activity: Crepuscular, nocturnal/year-round. 12 hours/day during Spring/Summer/Fall. Typically between 1600 to 0600 hours. Spring: dam construction activity is greatest (following flooding period). Fall: food caching in fall by northern populations.

Procreation: Mating: Mid January-mid-March. Gestation is 107 days. One litter of 2 to 4 young per year born in May/June. Young remain with adults for 1¾ years be-

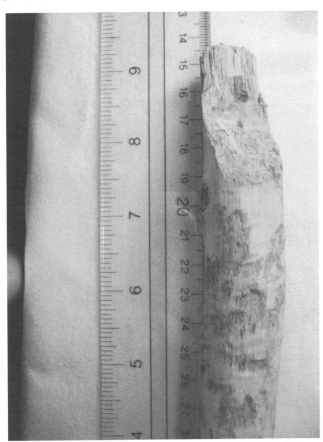
Fig. 1a. Gnawed stick shows the angled cut typical of beaver cutting as well as the stripped bark.

Fig. 2. Beaver dam about 6 ft in height.

Fig. 4. Trench cut by beaver from their lodge (out of view) through this isthmus.

fore being evicted. The distance evicted beavers travel depends on habitat. Sometimes the 2-year-olds remain in the area. A couple of studies found that dispersed beavers traveled an average of 5 mi (8 km).

Beaver homes (called lodges) fall into 2 types. In bear country, but may be found elsewhere, lodges are piles of mud and logs surrounded by water (Fig. 1b). Beavers may den in the bank of streams (Fig. 1c) or rivers. Lodges may or may not have log and mud coverings.

Capabilities: Poor eyesight. Excellent smell and hearing. Able to stay submerged for 15 min. Nature's engineers able to build substantial dams (Fig. 2) that cause significant upstream flooding. Some claim that an adult beaver can fell 300 trees in a year. Cannot climb.

Beavers can cut trees of less than 6 in (15 cm) diameter in just a few minutes (Fig. 3).

Symptoms

Clients may complain of rising water and loss of trees and plants.

Signs

Avg. Hole Size: Varies to size of beaver. Adults will require at least 4 in (10 cm) diameter holes. Skull size 3.425 to 4.25 in (87 to 108 mm). Living chamber in the lodge is at least 3 ft (0.9 m) in diameter.

Access: Beaver will travel over land to find new territories. They also will cut trenches (Fig. 4) to give them access to other areas. These trenches usually have muddy bottoms and are filled with 15 to 25 in (38 to 62 cm) of water and are 1 to 4 ft (0.3 to 1.3 m) wide.

Damage to House: Beaver dams can flood homes, septic systems, and wells. In addition, cut trees can fall on buildings. Otherwise, direct damage to structures typically does not occur with beavers.

Damage to Lawn/Garden: Beaver remove plants, fell (Fig. 5a) and girdle trees, and flood vegetation. Trees tend to fall in the direction of the dam. Branches <1/4-in (6.35 mm) wide have slanting cut and no teeth marks. Branches <¾ inch (2 cm) may be eaten completely. Larger branches show tooth marks. Tree stumps have conical shape (Fig. 5a). Most harvesting occurs within 165 ft (50 m) of water.

Fig. 3. Note the chunks of wood cut by a beaver's teeth.

Fig. 5a. Tree 6 to 8 in (15 to 20 cm) wide cut by a beaver.

Beavers also create slides measuring 15 to 20 in (38 to 50 cm) wide perpendicular to water where they regularly enter (Fig. 5b).

Fig. 5b. Beaver slide.

Damage to Pets & Livestock: Beaver will stand and defend themselves, snapping at enemies with their incisors. Beaver activity will reduce the presence of trout in waterways.

Tracks: Dimorphic. According to Elbroch, front tracks 2½ to 3 7/8 in (6.4 to 9.8 cm) in length and 2¼ to 3 ½ in (5.7 to 8.9 cm) wide. Hind feet are 4 ¾ to 7 in (12.1 to 17.8) in length by 3¼ to 5¼ in (8.3 to 13.3 cm). Tail will also be dragged.

Scat & Scenting: Typically not found as beavers defecate in the water. Scats are cylindrical with length reaching 2½ in (6.4 cm). Diameter of scat signifies animal size, 1 in (2.5 cm) for adult. Fresh scats are dark brown speckled with undigested wood fragments. Over time, the scat turns pale. Alan Huot says that feces are compacted sawdust. However, castor mounds consisting of slicked piles of mud accompanied with a deposit of sweet smelling beaver castor may be found as these are territorial markers for beaver. Mounds can number over a 100 for mature colonies.

Hair: Typically not found.

Sounds: Beavers slap their tails against the water as a warning to others of danger. Seven vocalizations noted, but only 3 used outside the lodge, namely whine, hiss, and growl.

Fig. 6. These tracks made from rubber replicas shows how the front foot (left) differs dramatically from the rear foot (right).

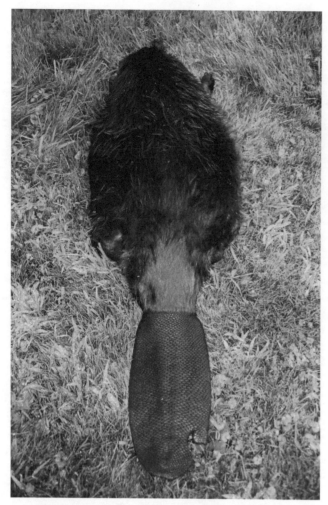

Fig. 7. Beaver tail suffering damage from a fight.

Bite Marks: Beavers do bite each other as the tail of the pictured beaver shows. Beaver incisors ~½ in (1.27 cm) wide. Average width of tooth mark is 0.20 in (5 mm). Twin grooves are left in wood. Each groove tends to measure 1/8 in (3 mm) or more.

Associated Animals: Beaver ponds create habitat for a wide variety of water-loving species, including raccoons, river otter, mink, muskrat, waterfowl, and more.

Health/Safety

Beavers carry a number of diseases that threaten human health.

Rabies: Cases of rabies infection among beaver have been confirmed. Rabies infection amongst beavers is rare and little is known about its origin.

Giardia: Beaver are a key reservoir for the protozoa known as *Giardia lamblia*. "Beaver fever" (which involves

intestinal dysfunction such as diarrhea, vomiting, and abdominal cramps) is caused by ingestion of infective cysts of this organism usually by drinking contaminated water. Beavers disseminate the cysts through their feces. Cysts can remain viable for several months.

Tularemia: (*Francisella tularensis*) Beavers can carry Type B version of Tularemia bacteria which rarely causes serious infection in humans. Type A Tularemia is a serious infection and is associated with rabbits.

Flooding: Beaver flooding also can undermine roads, threaten wells and septic systems. Occasionally beaver dams undergo catastrophic collapse resulting in life-threatening flash flooding. Dams on first order streams (the smallest) are less likely to collapse than second and third order streams.

Resources

Baker, B. W., and E. P. Hill. 2003. Beaver (*Castor canadensis*). Pages 288-310 in G. A. Feldhamer, B. C. Thompson, and J. A. Chapman, editors. *Wild Mammals of North America: Biology, Management, and Conservation*. Second Edition. The Johns Hopkins University Press, Baltimore, MD.

Busher, P. E. 1996. Food Caching Behavior of Beavers (*Castor canadensis*): Selection and Use of Woody Species. *American Midland Naturalist* 135:2 (Apr):343-348.

Connecticut Wildlife. Nov/Dec 2001 p. 18.

Dunlap, B. G. and M. L. Thies. 2002. Giardia in Beaver (*Castor canadensis*) and Nutria (*Myocastor coypus*) from East Texas. *The Journal of Parasitology* 88:6 (Dec.):1254-1258.

Elbroch, M. 2003. *Mammal Tracks and Sign: A Guide to North American Species*. Mechanicsburg, PA: Stackpole Books.

Fryxell, J. M. 2001. Habitat Suitability and Source-Sink Dynamics of Beavers, *Journal of Animal Ecology* 70:2 (Mar):310-316.

Harding, J. 1979. *An Animal Damage Identification Guide for Massachusetts*. Amherst, MA: Cooperative Extension Service, University of Massachusetts, SP-113.

Howard, R. J. and J. S. Larson. 1985. A Stream Habitat Classification System for Beaver Rebecca J. Howard, Joseph S. Larson. *The Journal of Wildlife Management* 49:1 (Jan):19-25.

Jenkins, S. H. 1980. A Size-Distance Relation in Food Selection by Beavers. *Ecology* 61:4 (Aug):740-746.

—— and P. E. Busher. 1979. *Castor Canadensis*. Mammalian Species, No. 120, (Jun. 8):1-8.

Link, R. 2004. *Living with Wildlife in the Pacific Northwest*. Seattle, WA: Univ. of Washington Press.

McCarty, S. L., D. J. Decker, and J. W. Kelley. 1984. Beaver: *Castor canadensis*. New York's Wildlife Resources. Cornell University Extension. No. 18. 1-11.

Miller, J. E., and G. K. Yarrow. "Beavers." in *Prevention and Control of Wildlife Damage*. Editors, Scott E. Hygnstrom, Robert M. Timm, Gary E. Larson. 1994. University of Nebraska-Lincoln. 2 vols.

Samways, K. M., R. G. Poulin, and R. M. Brigham. 2004. Directional Tree Felling by Beavers (*Castor canadensis*). *Northwestern Naturalist* 85:2 (Autumn):48-52.

Canada Geese *(Branta canadensis)*

Biology

Size: Avg. 6.6 to 19.8 lbs (3 to 9 kg, National Geographic). Weight range is due to the number of various subspecies within Canada geese. Adults ~2.45 ft (0.75 m) tall with a wingspan range of 43 to 60 in (1.1 to 1.5 m).

Diet: Vegetarians, primarily grass, particularly new shoots, grains and submerged freshwater plants. Will eat 3 to 4 lbs (1.36 to 1.81 kg) of grass per day. Canada geese will feed on almost any short grass or legume, including the following: Kentucky bluegrass *(Poa pratensis)*, brome grasses *(Bromus spp.)*, new growth on canary grass *(Phalaris arundinacea)*, colonial bentgrass *(Agrostis tenuis)*, perennial ryegrass *(Lolium perenne)*, quackgrass *(Agropyron repens)*, red fescue *(Festuca rubra*, a grass), new growth on mowed or burned switch grass *(Panicum virgatum)*.

They tend to avoid the following plants: mature tall fescue *(Festuca arundinaceae*, a grass), periwinkle *(Vinca spp.*, a groundcover), myrtle *(Myrtus spp.*, a groundcover), pachysandra *(Pachysandra terminalis*, a groundcover), English ivy *(Hedera helix*, a groundcover), hosta or plantain lily *(Hosta spp.*, a groundcover), *Euonymous fortuni* (an evergreen prostrate vine or shrub), ground junipers *(Juniperus spp.*, an evergreen shrub).

A study in South Dakota found that Canada geese foraged up to 39.37 ft (36 m) from the pond. They will pull out young sprouts. Sometimes geese will eat insects.

They require grit to digest their food.

Habitat: Lakes and ponds with low grade banks surrounded by short grass. Will not remain in areas where water freezes.

Activity: Year round. Some migrate others don't. They are also diurnal, but may honk at night.

Procreation: Mating (Feb to Mar). Nesting (April to May). Eggs hatch in 25 to 30 days. Brood size averages 4.5 per brood. Males and females share in raising young and have been known to mate for life. Molting (June to July), geese are flightless, young will often be present. Nests are simple round depressions consisting of sticks, leaves, moss, and feathers (Fig. 1). Nests tend to be placed within 200 yds (183 m) of water.

Female will lay an egg every 8 to 16 hours till completion. They will return to nest sites year after year. Male will guard the nest.

Access: Since geese can fly their access is quite expansive. Dirk Shearer reports of 1 nest on a second floor patio/deck.

Fig. 1. A typical nest of a Canada goose.

Capabilities: Can climb a bank up to 56° slope. Marathon fliers but their size makes take off, landing, and tight maneuvering difficult. Look for their classic "V" formation during migratory flights.

Behavior: Canada geese can be quite aggressive especially when protecting their nest. Hissing (Fig. 2), head down and extended, head pumping (up and down movement of head) charging and extending their wings are ways geese attempt to intimidate perceived threats. Bites from Canada geese, although not lethal, can be quite painful and pose an infection risk. People frightened by geese also may injure themselves trying to flee.

Fig. 2. Geese will hiss when threatened.

Fig. 3. Track of Canada goose.

Fig. 4a. Fresh scat of a Canada goose.

Fig. 4b. Old scat of Canada Geese on pavement.

Symptoms

Clients may complain of loud noises (honking of geese) and of being attacked.

Signs

Avg. Hole Size: Not applicable.

Damage to House: No known reports of Canada geese damaging structures. Nests may be found on second floor balconies.

Damage to Lawn/Garden: On clay soils, their constant walking will compact and erode grass denuding it into a slippery mess.

Tracks: Normally not needed to identify Canada geese problems. Tracks will exhibit a 3-prong look with the middle prong longer than the rest. Webbing between toes may not show depending upon sensitivity of ground. Walking pattern will alternate (Fig. 3) and toes will point inward toward the other foot.

Scat: A single Canada goose can leave 100 lbs (45.36 kg) of excrement per year. (National Geographic). Others say 1 to 3 lbs (0.45 to 1.36 kg) of feces per day per goose. Fresh Canada goose feces will be tubular (5 to 8 times longer than wide), green and wet (Fig. 4a). After drying, it will take on a more white-wash appearance with black areas (Fig. 4b). Canada goose droppings can get quite dense.

Feathers: Recognizable by its long length (Fig. 5).

Sounds: Distinctive honking (ahonk) when greeting, calling mates, and in groups. They hiss when angry (Fig. 2).

Bite Marks: Vegetation will be torn as it is plucked from the ground.

Associated Animals: Canada geese are a flocking species preferring the safety of numbers. But they can be found in isolated pairs. Don't believe the myth that swans will keep Canada geese from a pond.

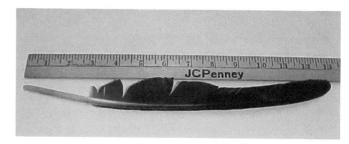

Fig. 5. Feather of Canada goose.

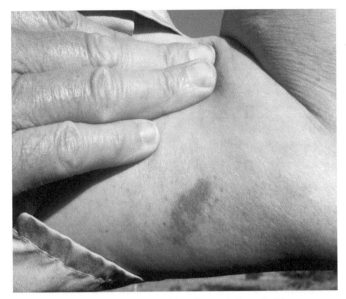
Fig. 6. Goose bite on inside of an adult male bicep.

Health/Safety

Diseases: Canada geese droppings have been known to contain various infectious organisms can wreak havoc on your intestines. Diseases include *Cryptosporidium*, *Giardia*, and *Campylobacter*. Primary route of infection is ingestion of feces. The significance and impact of goose droppings on water and soil quality and the threat to human-health is debated.

Slip & Fall: Note, however, that feces can make for walking hazards by making walkways quite slippery. So all the threats related to goose droppings cannot be directly related to disease.

Attacks: Geese can injure people by biting (Fig. 6). Others can be injured in falls while trying to flee attacking geese.

Resources

Art Smith provided some information contained in this module.

Elbroch, M. 2003. *Mammal Tracks and Sign: A Guide to North American Species.* Mechanicsburg, PA: Stackpole Books.

Hygnstrom, S. E., et al. 2010. Canada Geese http://icwdm.org University of Nebraska-Lincoln.

Jehl, J. R. Jr., 2004. Carnivorous Canada Geese. *The Wilson Bulletin* 116:2(Jun):179-180.

Lenhart. S. W., M. P. Schafer, M. Singal, and R. A. Hajjeh. 2004. *Histoplasmosis: Protecting Workers at Risk.* Dept. of Health and Human Services. Centers for Disease Control and Prevention National Institute for Occupational Safety and Health. National Center for Infectious Diseases (December).

Link, R. 2004. *Living with Wildlife in the Pacific Northwest.* Seattle, WA: Univ. of Washington Press.

N.H. State Report. 2000. The Wildlife Sampler, Summer p. 4.

Purdy, K. and R. Malecki. 1984. Canada Goose: *Branta canadensis.* New York's Wildlife Resources. Cornell University Extension. No. 8. 1-12.

Sibley, D. A. 2000. *The Sibley Guide to Birds.* NY, NY: Alfred A. Knopf.

Smith, A. E., S. R. Craven, and P. D. Curtis. 1999. *Managing Canada Geese in Urban Environments: A Technical Guide.* Jack Berryman Institute Publication 16, and Cornell University Cooperative Extension, Ithaca, N.Y.

Coyotes *(Canis latrans)*

Biology

Size: 33 to 47 lbs (15 to 21 kg). Western coyotes tend to be several pounds less. Western coyotes stand 18 to 25 in (46 to 65 cm) at shoulder. Male coyotes slightly larger than females.

Diet: Omnivores eating berries, small mammals, herptofauna, house cats, birds, deer, garbage, compost, pet food, fruit, insects (e.g. grasshoppers), grill drippings, carrion, and other artificial food sources to supplement their natural diet.

Habitat: Forests broken by fields (home range is 4 to 30 mi² (6 to 48 km²), 2× that of Western Coyotes). In Massachusetts coyote home range averages 15 mi² (24 km²).

Activity: Crepuscular, year round. Heavy hunting during June to feed the growing young. Coyotes can travel 10 to 15 mi (16 to 24 km) per night making them appear more numerous than their actual numbers indicate.

  Scent stations. Coyotes will designate territory with scat and urine at various locations (e.g. rocks, trails). Within 6 ft (1.8 m) they will scratch the soil. Halfpenny and Furman (2010) contend coyotes mark every 1/8 to ¼ mi (200 to 400 m). Wolves ¼ to 3/8 min (400 to 600 m).

Procreation: Mating in Feb. 5 to 7 young born in April to May after a 58 to 63 day gestation period. In contrast, coy-dogs mate in the fall. Young will explore outside of den in 3 weeks and learn hunting at 8 to 12 weeks. Mating pair works together to tend young. Dr. Way says coyotes are bolder during the period of raising young.

Capabilities: You have to look at your fences or for trails to see where they are entering. They can get over fences up to 6 ft (1.8 m). They can perform limited climbing. They also can crawl under fences: look for a 5 to 6 in (13 to 15 cm) gap. If their head can go through their body can fit through.

Symptoms

Clients will note howling and missing pets.

Signs

Avg. Hole Size: Generally an enlarged woodchuck den about 12 to 24 in (31 to 60 cm) wide. Egg shaped, taller than wide. Skull width is 3.36 to 4.5 in (85 to 114 mm). In Wyoming, sage brush will be darker around dens (Dr. Bob Wendt, 2007). It is not uncommon for coyotes to have multiple home sites that can be used throughout the year. Spooked coyotes will move pups to

Table 1. California Landscape plants having fruits or seeds often preferred by coyotes.

Common name	Scientific name
Indian laurel fig	*Ficus microcarpa* var. *nitida*
Ornamental strawberry	*Fragaria chiloensi*
Date palm	*Phoenix dactylifera*
Passion fruit, Passion vine	*Passiflora* spp.
Lychee	*Litchi chinensis*
Sugar bush	*Rhus ovata*
Strawberry bush	*Euonymus americanus*
Strawberry tree	*Arbutus unedo*
Jujube, or Chinese date	*Ziziphus jujuba*
Brush cherries	*Eugenia* spp.
Elderberry	*Sambucus* spp.
Avocado	*Persea americana*
Fig	*Ficus carica*
Guava	*Psidium guajava*
Loquat	*Eriobotrya japonica*

a new den 54.7 yds (50 m) to 0.6 mi (1 km) away. Look for prey remains around den entrance. Stale dens have no bones. Dens often located in areas with brush cover and can be 5 to 30 ft (1.5 to 9 m) long.

Damage to House: Typically don't damage buildings but have been known to den under sheds and hollow trees.

Damage to Lawn/Garden: Usually not much to speak of but coyotes will eat watermelon and other fruit and gnaw on irrigation lines. Lines will look compressed, with bite marks like a dog. We also know through anecdotal information that coyotes can scale 5 ft (1.5 m) high cinder block fences in Arizona.

Damage to Pets & Livestock: Coyotes typically attack the throat and kill by crushing the trachea (Fig. 1). Domestic dogs often attack at an animal's flank and are more random in biting (Fig. 2). Tend to kill sheep between October to March. Intestines and hindquarters eaten first. Coyotes feed for 25 min and consume ~4 lbs (1.8 kg) in the first meal. Pets < 30 lbs (13.6 kg) in weight are particularly vulnerable to predation according to Paul D. Curtis of Cornell University.

  Coyotes also can transmit diseases such as distemper and parvo virus to pets.

Tracks: Tracks of large coyotes are 3.5 in (8.9 cm) tall by 1.75 in (4.5 cm) wide (Fig. 3). They have small feet that leave 4-toed, claw tipped tracks that are generally more elongated than those of domestic dogs and nails tend to point towards each other (Fig. 4). Coyote tracks are more rounded than domestic dog tracks. Their nails are less pronounced as well due to greater use. Coyote

Fig. 1. Coyote with chicken. Photo by Applied Mammal Research Institute.

Fig. 2. Goat killed by domestic dogs. Photo by John Consolini.

nails will be worn even more in urban areas. You also can see coyote tracks at the end of the "Procedures for Evaluating Predation on Livestock and Wildlife" booklet included in this book (p. 97).

Trails. Coyotes tend to walk in straight lines versus meandering of dogs. Straight-line trails average 2¼ to 5¼ in (5.7 to 13.3 cm) in width. Seldom move in packs.

Scat: Single droppings average 3 to 4 in (7.5 to 10 cm) in length and 1 in (2.5 cm) in width (Fig. 5). Halfpenny and Furman (2010) say scats tend to be 0.91 in (23 mm) or less in width. Black and more liquid scat signifies diet of meat. Scat full of hair tends to be larger. Scat consisting of fruit tends to crumble.

Hair: Typically black-tipped but will also have bands of color on individual strands. Look for hair snagged on fences and logs along trails.

Sounds: Coyotes have a number of calls, barks, grunts, whines, howls, and yip howls to signify threats, greetings, and other communications.

Bite Marks: Measurements taken from coyote specimens yielded distances from 1.012 to 1.38 in (28 to 35 mm) between canine teeth. Dr. Bob Wedt (2007) puts fang distance at 1¼ to 1½ in (3.2 to 3.8 cm). Timm's article suggests 1 to 1.375 in (2.5 to 3.5 cm).

Associated Animals: Coyotes are territorial. They will kill other canines in their area, including foxes and dogs.

Health/Safety

Attacks: Dr. Robert M. Timm's research has revealed that coyote aggression goes through several stages which can help people determine potential threats.

Sequence of increasingly aggressive coyote behaviors.
1. Increase in coyotes on streets and in yards at night
2. Increase in coyotes approaching adults and/or taking pets at night
3. Coyotes on streets, and in parks and yards, in early morning/late afternoon

Fig. 3. Coyote track in sand. Scale in inches.

Fig. 4. Coyote track in mud. Photo by Rich Westin.

4. Coyotes chasing or taking pets in daytime
5. Coyotes attacking and taking pets on leash or near owners; chasing joggers, bicyclists, other adults
6. Coyotes seen in and around children's play areas, school grounds, and parks in midday
7. Coyotes acting aggressively toward adults in midday

Rabies: Coyotes can suffer from a number of diseases including, mange, rabies, and distemper.

Toxoplasmosis: Coyotes can carry *toxoplasma gondii*.

Mange: Coyotes can suffer from mange. But many recover from the infection.

Plague: Coyotes are sentinels for the presence of the disease. If 1 tests positive then assume exposure over a 100 mi (161 km) radius. Increased positive tests in winter can foretell epizootic outbreaks in summer.

Tularemia: Coyotes are sentinels for tularemia infection.

Resources

Thanks to Paul D. Curtis, Dallas Virchow, University of California-Davis, and Bob Wendt for the information they provided.

Dubey, J. P., N. Sundar, C. A. Nolden, M. D. Samuel, G. V. Velmurugan, L. A. Bandini, O.C.H. Kwok, B. Bodenstein and C. Su. 2007. Characterization of *Toxoplasma gondii* from Raccoons (*Procyon lotor*), Coyotes (*Canis latrans*), and Striped Skunks *(Mephitis mephitis)* in Wisconsin Identified Several Atypical Genotypes. *The Journal of Parasitology*. 93:6(Dec):1524-1527.

Elbroch, M. 2003. *Mammal Tracks and Sign: A Guide to North American Species*. Mechanicsburg, PA: Stackpole Books.

Freeman, M. W., R. E. Marsh, and T. P. Salmon. 2008. UC IPM Pest Management Guidelines: Citrus. UC ANR Publication 3441. Vertebrates (Sept).

Green, J. S., F. R. Henderson, and M. D. Collinge. "Coyotes." in *Prevention and Control of Wildlife Damage*. Editors, Scott E. Hygnstrom, Robert M. Timm, Gary E. Larson. 1994. University of Nebraska-Lincoln. 2 vols.

Halfpenny, J. C. and T. D. Furman. 2010. *Tracking Wolves: The Basics*. A Naturalist's World.

Howard. W. E., R. Teranishi, R. E. Marsh, and J. H. Scrivner. 1985. Understanding Coyote Behavior. *California Agriculture*. March-April: 4-7.

Klippel, W. E. and J. A. Synstelien. 2007. Rodents as Taphonomic Agents: Bone-Gnawing by Brown Rats and Gray Squirrels. *J Forensic Sci, 52*:4(July):1556-4029.

Link, R. 2004. *Living with Wildlife in the Pacific Northwest*. Seattle, WA: Univ. of Washington Press.

Massachusetts Wildlife Press Release on 6-4-01.

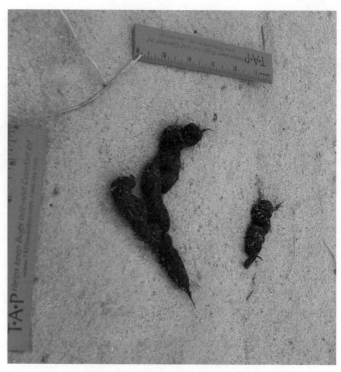

Fig. 5. Coyote scat. Scale in inches.

Mirick. P. 1998. Coyotes and Other Questions," Massachusetts Wildlife No. 4:10ff.

Murie, O. J. and M. Elbroch. 2005. *A Field Guide to Animal Tracks*. 3rd. ed. NY: Houghton Mifflin Harcourt.

Robinson, S. A., J. A. Parkhurst, and J. E. Cardoza. 2003. *Co-existing with Black Bears in Massachusetts: Guidelines for the Prevention and Management of Bear Damage*. University of Massachusetts Cooperative Extension System, Amherst, MA. 15 pp.

Schmidt, R. H. and R. M. Timm. 2007. Bad Dogs: Why Do Coyotes and Other Canids Become Unruly? *Proceedings of the 12th Wildlife Damage Management Conference* (D. L. Nolte, W. M. Arjo, D. H. Stalman, Eds).

Schwartz, C. and E. Schwartz. 1981. *The Wild Mammals of Missouri*. University of Missouri Press and Missouri Department of Conservation.

Smith, C. R. 1994. Wild Carnivores as Plague Indicators in California—A Cooperative Interagency Disease Surveillance Program. *Proc. 16th Vertebr. Pest Conf*. W. S. Halverson & A. C. Crabb Eds. U.C. Davis.

Timm, R. M. Timm, C. C. Coolahan, R. O. Baker, and S. F. Beckerman. 2007. *How to Manage Pests: Coyotes*. Produced by IPM Education and Publications, University of California Statewide IPM Program.

Way, J. G. 2007. *Suburban Howls: Tracking the Eastern Coyote in Urban Massachusetts*. Indianapolis, IN: Dog Ear Publishing.

Eastern Chipmunks *(Tamias striatus)*

Biology

Size: 2.5 to 4 oz. (70.87 to 113.4 g). Size of head and body ranges in length from 4.5 to 6.3 in (115 to 160 mm). The tail length ranges from 2.8 to 6.3 in (70 to 115 mm).

Diet: Fungi, nuts, berries, vegetables and some animal matter such as insects, salamanders and young birds. One of their 2 cheek pouches can hold 60 black sunflower seeds. Requires free water, up to 25% of its body weight per day.

Habitat: Prefers environmental edges like rock walls, woods abutting fields that are well drained.

Activity: Diurnal usually beginning their day 2 to 4 hours after sunrise and then active again in the afternoon. They do not hibernate but in extremely cold weather they enter torpor for 1 to 8 days. Young tend to stay active longer in the fall than adults. Chipmunks do defend territories of 50 ft (50.24 m) of burrow.

Procreation: One to 2 litters per year (late April to early May and late July to mid-Aug) of 1 to 8 young per litter. Young born 31 days after conception. Males do not help raise young. Young can stand at 2 weeks and wean at 35 to 43 days.

Capabilities: Can climb trees up to 40 ft (12 m).

Symptoms

Client will hear noises along eaves or baseboards. Client will know that chipmunks live in the area.

Signs

Avg. Hole Size: 1.5 to 2.0 inches (3.81 to 5 cm) or silver dollar in size, clean around the edges (no dirt pile) and it will go straight down into the ground (Fig. 1). Width of skull ranges from 0.78 to 0.9 in (19.93 to 22.87 mm). Burrows tend to be about 12 ft (3.66 m) long with a nesting chamber about 3 ft (0.91 m) below the surface.

Access: Chipmunks rarely enter buildings. But when they do the entryways tend to center around the front stoop (Fig. 2a) and along the sill plate. Chipmunks may climb downspouts (Fig. 2b). They also will climb up the corner openings of sided (particularly vinyl) buildings and take advantage of branches or vines.

Fig. 2a. Chipmunks will enter homes around the foundation.

Fig. 1. Chipmunk den. Penny used for scale.

Fig. 2b. This chipmunk was trying to climb up the downspout but couldn't make it.

Fig. 3. Chipmunks can enter under garage doors.

Damage to Structures: Like any rodent chipmunks can chew wires etc. Often they will bring in large amounts of sand into the home near where they have entered the building (unless they have entered at the eave level). They also have been known to chew on the corners of wooden buildings, typically garage door moldings because they abut the ground (Fig. 3). I have seen instances where chipmunks burrowed under pool liners. The weight of the water ultimately collapsed the den causing a bulge in the liner (Fig. 4).

Damage to Lawn/Garden: They will eat bulbs, vegetables (Fig. 5), and uproot plants. They will feed on bird seed if they can reach the feeder.

Tracks: Rarely found (Fig. 6) except in snow. Front track is ~1 in wide (~2.5 cm) and each set of 4 tracks may be 2.5 in (6.25 cm) wide. Rear track is ½ to ⅞ in (1.3 to 2.2 cm) in length and ⅝ to ¹⁵/₁₆ in (1.6 to 2.4 cm in width. Nails will be noticeable.

Fig. 4. Chipmunk burrowed under this pool. When filled, the weight of the water collapsed the den, stretching the liner.

Fig. 5. Chipmunk damage to a tomato. Photo by Marne Titchenell.

Scat: Pellets are ³/₃₂ to ⁵/₃₂ in (0.24 to 0.4 cm) in diameter and ⅛ to ⁹/₃₂ in (0.3 to 0.7 cm) in length. Others say 0.3 in (0.75 cm) long, but can vary significantly.

Hair: Rarely found.

Sounds: Chipmunks exhibit 4 noises. The high-pitched "chip" is a warning shriek and is often heard when a chipmunk sees you approach. Sometimes the chipmunk utters a series of "chips" that can occur at a rate of up to 130 per minute. Other sounds are "chip-rrrr" and "cuk".

Bite Marks: Some research suggests chipmunks are not known to gnaw bones.

Associated Animals: Weasels are key predator.

Health/Safety

Chipmunks are not a significant threat to humans either through disease or damage with our present knowledge. However, like other rodents, they can pose a threat through their damage to electrical lines (potential of fires). Additionally, their denning activity can undermine retaining walls and walkways leading to the potential of collapse.

Fig. 6. Tracks of eastern chipmunk. Image by Kim Cabera.

Resources

Elbroch, M. 2003. *Mammal Tracks and Sign: A Guide to North American Species.* Mechanicsburg, PA: Stackpole Books.

Elbroch, M. 2006. *Animal Skulls: A Guide to North American Species.* Mechanicsburg, PA: Stackpole Books.

Falker, S. T. and M. C. Brittingham. 1998. Chipmunks. Wildlife Damage Control 13. Penn State University. Pp. 1-4.

Gao, G., D. Dyke, and G. Comer Jr. ND. The Eastern Chipmunk (*Tamias striatus*) in the Home, Yard, and Garden. Ohio State University Extension Factsheet. HYG-1034-99.

Harding, J. 1979. *An Animal Damage Identification Guide for Massachusetts.* Amherst, MA: Cooperative Extension Service, University of Massachusetts, SP-113.

Heinrich, B. 2003. *Winter World: The Ingenuity of Animal Survival.* New York: HarperCollins.

Klippel, W. E. and J. A. Synstelien. 2007. Rodents as Taphonomic Agents: Bone Gnawing by Brown Rats and Gray Squirrels. *J Forensic Sci,* 52:4(July 2007):1556-4029.

McCarty, S. L., D. J. Decker, and J. W. Kelley. 1987. Eastern Chipmunk: *Tamias striatus.* New York's Wildlife Resources. Cornell University Extension. No. 15. 1-12.

Myers, P., R. Espinosa, C. S. Parr, T. Jones, G. S. Hammond, and T. A. Dewey. 2008. The Animal Diversity Web (online). Accessed at http://animaldiversity.org. on 12/4/2011.

Reid, F. A. 2006. *Mammals of North America.* 4th ed. Peterson Field Guides. NY, NY: Houghton Mifflin Co.

Rezendes, P. 1992. *Tracking and the Art of Seeing: How to Read Animal Tracks and Sign.* Charlotte, VT: Camden House Publishing, Inc.

Snyder, D. P. 1982. *Tamias striatus.* Mammalian Species No. 168, (May 25):1-8.

Williams, D. E. and R. M. Corrigan. "Chipmunks." in *Prevention and Control of Wildlife Damage.* Editors, S. E. Hygnstrom, R. M. Timm, G. E. Larson. 1994. University of Nebraska-Lincoln. 2 vols.

Eastern Cottontail Rabbits *(Sylvilagus floridanus)*

Biology

Weight: 1.8 to 3 lbs (0.8 to 1.4 kg) in weight and 15 to 19 in (37 to 48 cm) in length.

Diet: Rabbits eat a wide variety of plants, consult bibliography for the extensive list. However, they tend not to eat corn, squash, cucumber, tomatoes, potatoes, and some peppers. In winter, rabbits eat stems, bark, and inner bark.

Habitat: Varies by region. Home range can be a small as 0.95 to 2.8 ha. Prefers woody habitat with sufficient undergrowth for cover. Males will maintain territories. Other males may stay provided they remain subordinate.

Activity: Crepuscular and nocturnal. Rabbit activity is highest in summer when nights are the shortest. Moonlighted nights also are times of peak activity. Rabbits are less active on rainy nights.

Procreation: Breeding season tied to temperature and rainfall (water needed for vegetation). Southern states have longer season and northern states have shorter. Female rabbits can have 3 to 4 litters of 5 to 7 young per year. Gestation is 25 to 35 days (mean 28 to 29). Eyes open in 5 to 7 days and young leave nest in 12 to 16. Males do not help rear young.

Nests: Nests, also called "forms", are slanting holes (not tunnels) in the soil. Avg. size length × width × depth 7 × 4.9 × 4.7 in (180 mm × 126 mm × 119 mm). Others have found nest sizes to be 4¾ × 4 × 5¾ in (121 × 102 × 146 mm). Nests are directional in that 1 side has a more gradual slope than the other. Size of nest does not correlate with litter size. Nests may be lined with the mother's fur, herbaceous plants, and leaves. Rabbits will use sheltered areas such as brush piles, stumps, and other structures to hide their nests. But you also can find them in the middle of a lawn (Fig. 1).

Rabbits will utilize underground dens dug and abandoned by other animals (e.g. woodchuck) and tend not to dig their dens but use what is already there.

Capabilities: Rabbits seem to avoid digging through snow with a crust. Maximum running speed is 20.5 to 25 mph (33 to 40 km/hr). Excellent vision.

Symptoms

Owners will complain of damaged landscape plants and missing vegetables.

Fig. 1. Grass depression made by a cottontail rabbit. Photo by Marie Boulier.

Fig. 2. Rabbit trail outlined in black.

Fig. 3. The 2 front feet are in a vertical line and overstepped by the 2 larger rear feet which are side by side.

Fig. 4. Rabbit scat 3/8 inch (1 cm) in diameter.

Signs

Avg. Hole Size: Highly variable. But skull size of an adult averages 1.07 in wide (27.2 mm; range 26.4 to 29.9 mm). In tall grass, rabbit trails can be identified (Fig. 2). They average 4 to 5 in (10 to 12 cm) in diameter.

Damage to Structures: Minimal to none.

Damage to Lawn/Garden: Rabbits can cause significant damage to a wide variety of woody, herbaceous, flowering, and garden plants. Damage will extend up to 24 in (60 cm). Damage higher on plants suspect deer. Prefer young vegetables. Plants may be completely eaten when tender. They tend to avoid cucumbers, squash, potatoes, tomatoes, corn, and some types of peppers. Suspect other animals, such as woodchucks, if the aforementioned plants are eaten. Grass and succulent plants may be clipped to within 1 in of ground (2.5 cm).

Rabbits also create dust baths in sandy or dry soil. These tend to be about 1 ft (30 cm) across.

Tracks: Hind foot (the larger foot) measures 3.0 to 4.1 in (7.7 to 10.6 cm). Easily distinguished from squirrel by the T pattern (1 by 1 by 2; Fig. 3). Squirrel tracks are 2 by 2.

Cottontails also flee predators by running in zig-zag and circular running patterns.

Scat: Rabbits have 2 types. The soft-form is re-ingested. The hard type is discarded (Fig. 4).

Hair: Rarely found but do look for hair snags at fence crawl-unders. They molt twice per year.

Sounds: Three types of vocalizations.
1. Distress cries are high-pitched screams emitted by frightened or injured rabbits. Sound alerts other rabbits of danger.
2. Squeal sounds occur during copulation by either gender.
3. Grunts are emitted by nesting females to repel intruders from their nest.

Bite Marks: On thin branches, rabbits clip. Note the distinct 45° angle of the cutting. In winter, particularly with heavy snow cover, rabbits will gnaw the bark of woody plants. Clippings typically on twigs ¼ in (6.35 mm) or less in thickness (Fig. 5). Will browse up to 2½ ft (76.2 cm) above surface level (don't forget snow depth will add height).

Gnawing. Softwood with thin bark will leave a ragged appearance. Hardwood with thicker bark will leave a cleaner appearance. Avg. width of incisor 0.10 in (2.54 mm). Avg width of tooth mark 0.08 in (2 mm; Figs. 6a,b).

Associated Animals: Rabbits are an important prey species for a wide variety of carnivores and raptors.

Health/Safety

Tularemia: Tularemia is caused by the bacterium (*Francisella tularensis*). The infection can be contracted from parasites and contact with contaminated fluids (eating or aerosolized). Rabbits infected with tularemia appear to be tame and will die in 7 days.

Ectoparasites: Rabbits can host a variety of ticks, including deer ticks (*Ixodes damini*), fleas, and other parasites on their bodies.

Shope's Fibroma Virus "Jackalope": Rabbits infected with this virus have fleshy finger-like growths protruding from various parts of their body. These growths occasionally make rabbits look like they have antlers and led early Europeans to believe that infected rabbits were a different species. This may have given rise to the mythical "jackalope." Whereas rabbits afflicted with the Shope's fibroma virus can raise concern among onlookers, it mostly affects cottontail rabbits and is not contagious to humans.

Fig. 5. Stem clipped by a rabbit.

Fig. 6a. Woody plant gnawed by rabbits during the winter. Scale in mm.

Resources

Biggins, E. and D. M. Biggins. 2006. Bobcat Attack on Cottontail Rabbit. *The Southwestern Naturalist,* 51:1 (Mar):119-122.

Casteel, D. A. 1966. Nest Building, Parturition, and Copulation in the Cottontail Rabbit. *American Midland Naturalist,* 75:1 (Jan.):160-167.

Chapman, J. A., J. G. Hockman, and M.O.C. Magaly. 1980. *Sylvilagus floridanus.* Mammalian Species 136 (Apr):1-8.

Craven, S. R."Cottontail Rabbits." in *Prevention and Control of Wildlife Damage.* Editors, Scott E. Hygnstrom, Robert M. Timm, Gary E. Larson. 1994. University of Nebraska-Lincoln. 2 vols.

Goff, G. R., D. J. Decker, P. Curtis, and J. W. Kelley. 1992. Cottontail Rabbit: *Sylvilagus floridanus.* New York's Wildlife Resources. Cornell University Extension. No. 5. 1-10.

Harding, J. 1979. *An Animal Damage Identification Guide for Massachusetts.* Amherst, MA: Cooperative Extension Service, University of Massachusetts, SP-113.

Link, R. 2004. *Living with Wildlife in the Pacific Northwest.* Seattle, WA: Univ. of Washington Press.

Llewellyn, L. M. and C. O. Handley. 1945. The Cottontail Rabbits of Virginia. *Journal of Mammalogy,* 26:4 (Nov):379-390.

Sweetman, H. L. 1944. Selection of Woody Plants as Winter Food by the Cottontail Rabbit. *Ecology* 25:4 (Oct):467-472.

———. 1949. Further Studies of the Winter Feeding Habits of Cottontail Rabbits. *Ecology* 30:3 (Jul):371-376.

Fig. 6b. White areas due to stripped bark exposing the white wood beneath.

Thurston, S. N. and M. C. Brittingham. 1997. Cottontail Rabbits. Wildlife Damage Control 7. Penn State Univ. 1-4.

Todd, J. B. 1927. Winter Food of Cottontail Rabbits. *Journal of Mammalogy* 8:3 (Aug):222-228.

Vantassel, S. M. et al. 2010. *Managing Rabbit Damage.* NebGuide G2019. University of Nebraska-Lincoln pp. 1-4.

Websites: http://wildlife1.wildlifeinformation.org/s/0mlagomorph/leporidae/Sylvilagus/sylvilagus_floridanus.html consulted 5/16/2011.

Flying Squirrels

(*Glaucomys volans*) Southern flying squirrel (SF)
(*Glaucomys sabrinus*) Northern flying squirrel (NF)

Biology

Size: **SF** weight ranges is 1.8 to 2.8 oz (51 to 79 g). Length range 7.8 to 10 in (198 to 255 mm) including a tail that measures 3.2 to 4.7 in (81 to 120 mm) in length.

NF weighs 4.0 to 6.5 oz (113 to 184 g). Total length (body + tail) is 10.2 in (260 mm). Tail is 4.25 to 6.3 in (108 to 160 mm) in length.

Diet: Various nuts, fruits, bugs, small mammals (the most carnivorous of all tree squirrels), mushrooms, and lichens.

Habitat: **SF** prefer hardwood forests but can be found in mixed woods. **NF** prefers dense forests of hemlocks and birch or hemlock and maple forests.

Activity: Nocturnal/Year round. **SF** active throughout the night in summer but reduces to excursions during colder weather. **NF** tend to be active during 2 periods, 1 after sundown for ~2 hours and another a few hours before sunrise for ~1 hour.

Procreation: **SF** mates in Feb/Mar and in June/July. Two to 6 young born 40 days later. Young furred in 2 weeks and independent in 10. Males do not assist with rearing young. **NF** mate Mar to May. Gestation is 37 to 42 days. Births of 2 to 4 young normally occur in May and June but have been found in Dec. Females may have 3 litters.

According to Ravenelle, numbers of flying squirrels residing in a structure tends to diminish as you move south, e.g. MD avg 7; NC avg 4 to 5; FL avg 1 to 2.

Capabilities: Outstanding gliders able to glide up to 270 ft (82 m). They also can climb and crawl. Poor walkers.

Symptoms

Clients will complain of noises in the wall, generally at night, especially windy nights when the flyers are less likely to be out foraging for food.

Signs

Due to its small size, identifying this squirrel as the culprit is very difficult. A careful search of the building is necessary.

Avg. Hole Size: ½ to 1 in (1.27 to 2.5 cm). Head width of **SF** is (18.5 to 22.2 mm). Head width of **NF** is (260 mm).

Damage to Structures: Generally, the entry point will permit clear jumping and landing for these gliding squirrels. They seem to like to have 10 to 20+ ft (3 to 6 m) of unobstructed flight paths. You will want to keep your eyes high, with close attention being paid to screens and vents, especially the ends of ridge vents.

Since these squirrels don't have the strong jaws of gray squirrels, damage should be minimal at best. Of course wires may be chewed, but one shouldn't find the chew damage as would be found with a gray or fox squirrel. It is said that when a flyer eats an acorn he will do so by cracking the top and hollowing it out like a mouse. This is in contrast to a gray squirrel which will open an acorn by cutting it in half.

According to LaPierre, flyers will bore holes through insulation and also create a tornado stack.

Droppings may stain building soffit (Fig. 1).

Damage to Lawn/Garden: I have not heard of any significant damage.

Damage to Pets & Livestock: Flying squirrels can predate on bird nests and eggs.

Fig. 1. Brown stains in soffit caused by feces and urine of flying squirrels.

Tracks: Typically not found even though they may spend a fair amount of time foraging on the ground.

SF front foot is 5/16 to ¾ in (0.8 to 1.9 cm) in length and 5/16 to ¾ in (0.8 to 1.9 cm) in width. Rear foot is ½ to 1.36 in (1.3 to 3.5 cm) in length and 3/8 to 7/8 in (1 to 2.2 cm) in width.

NF front foot is 11/16 to 1.25 in (1.7 to 3.2 cm) in length and ½ to ¾ in (1.3 to 1.9 cm) in width. Rear foot is 1.25 to 1.88 in (3.2 to 4.8 cm) in length and 5/8 to 11/16 (1.6 to 2.4 cm) in width.

Scat: SF scat has a pellet character and is 1/16 to 5/32 in (0.2 to 0.4 cm) in diameter and 3/16 to 5/16 in (0.5 to 0.8 cm) in length. **NF** deposit pellets 3/32 to 3/16 in (0.2 to 0.5 cm) in diameter and 1/8 to 3/8 in (0.3 to 1 cm) in length. These squirrels don't like to defecate in their nest and so use toilettes.

However, you can find feces around the hole they use to access the house. I have found feces on the inside of an attic just below their exit through the vent (Fig. 2). The feces and staining can be quite severe. Their urine will also cause brown staining (think spilled molasses). Flyers often come in bunches so don't be surprised if you see a great deal of urine and fecal staining. It will differentiate itself from bat dropping because of the staining. Bat droppings will tend to be less sticky. Urine and feces has a distinctive odor.

Hair: Varies in color from white to cinnamon to black.

Sounds: Clucking noise may occur when fighting over food.

Bite Marks: Unknown.

Associated Animals: Flyers are quite gregarious. They will share homes with each other.

Health/Safety

Typhus: Typhus is caused by *Rickettsia prowazekii*. Typically, typhus is spread by lice but in the U.S. infections have been associated with flying squirrels. This rodent inhabits the eastern United States, frequently nests in the attics of houses during the winter, and is a known host of *R. prowazekii*. It is presumed that infection is acquired from this animal, although the mechanism of transmission is unknown.

The disease is rare (e.g. 30 cases in ~6 years) with 21 of 30 cases occurring between Dec to Jan.

Fig. 2. Droppings and urine left by flying squirrels exiting the vent above (not in photo).

Symptoms of infection in order of decreasing occurrence include fever, headache, skin rash, confusion, and myalgia. The skin rash has been characterized as maculopapular, usually involving the trunk and spreading to the extremities.

Rabies: Rabies amongst squirrels is rare. However, 1 SF was found with rabies which it possibly contracted from a bat.

Resources

I would like to thank Kirk LaPierre (d. 2010) and Mark Ravenelle for the information they provided.

Center for Disease Control. 1982. Epidemic Typhus Associated with Flying Squirrels-United States. *MMWR* 31:41 (Oct. 22):555-6,561.

Dolan, P. G. and D. C. Carter. 1977. *Glaucomys volans*. Mammalian Species, No. 78, (Jun. 15):1-6.

Ford, W. M. and J. L. Rodrigue. Northern flying squirrel, *Glaucomys sabrinus*. in *The land manager's guide to mammals of the South*. Ed. M. K. Trani, W. M. Ford, B. R. Chapman. Durham, NC: The Nature Conservancy; Atlanta, GA: U.S. Forest Service: 389-394.

Jackson, Jeffery J. "Tree Squirrels." in *Prevention and Control of Wildlife Damage*. Editors, S. E. Hygnstrom, R. M. Timm, G. E. Larson. 1994. University of Nebraska-Lincoln. 2 vols.

Harding, J. 1979. *An Animal Damage Identification Guide for Massachusetts*. Amherst, MA: Cooperative Extension Service, University of Massachusetts, SP-113.

Link, R. 2004. *Living with Wildlife in the Pacific Northwest*. Seattle, WA: Univ. of Washington Press.

Wells-Gosling, N. and L. R. Heaney. 1984. *Glaucomys sabrinus*. Mammalian Species, No. 229, (Nov. 14):1-8.

Gray & Fox Squirrels

Gray Squirrel (*Sciurus carolinensis*) GS
Fox Squirrel (*Sciuris niger*) FS

Biology

Size: GS 12 to 24 oz (340 to 680 g) and 14 to 21 in (35.5 to 53.3 cm) in length including a 7 to 10 in tail (17.7 to 25.4 cm). **FS** 16 to 48 oz (453 to 1,360 g) in weight. 19 to 29 in (48.2 to 73.6 cm) in total length including a 7 to 14 in (17.7 to 35.5 cm) tail.

Diet: Nuts (Fig. 1a), tree leaf buds, and corn; they also eat flowers, bark, fungi, birds' eggs, insects and occasionally animal matter. Greatest amount of food consumed in spring and fall. Seeks salt during the breeding season.

Habitat: Urban woods and deciduous forests. **GS** prefer areas closer to water and **FS** prefer more upland areas.

Activity: Year-round/crepuscular and diurnal. Avoids extreme cold, heat, and high winds. Feeds 6 to 9 A.M. and 3 to 6 P.M. It adjusts these times during winter so that activity occurs during the warmer parts of the day.

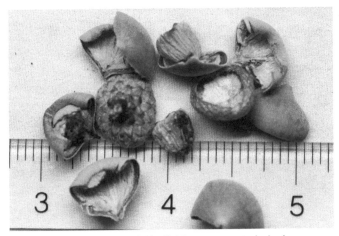
Fig. 1a. Acorns cut in half. Measurements in inches.

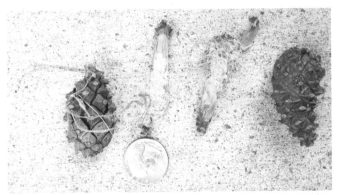
Fig. 1b. Green pine cones may be eaten like corn on the cob.

Fig. 2. Squirrels walk wires.

Procreation: Mating occurs twice a year. **FS** behaviors occurs 2 weeks earlier than **GS**. **GS**—Dec to Feb with young born in April to May and weaned in June to July. Second mating occurs in May to July with young born in July to Sept and weaned in Oct to Nov. Gestation averages 44 to 45 days and weaning occurs 42 to 49 days later. Female raises 3 to 5 young alone. Carl Carnahan of Oklahoma noted that a first season litter occurred around Feb 28. Kirk LaPierre of New Jersey found a first litter on Mar 1. LaPierre says (2007) that females with pink nipples means they are still nursing. If the nipples are black then the young are old enough to capture.

Nests may be in tree holes (or human structures) or leaf nests. Leaf nests tend to be 12 to 19 in (30.5 to 48.3 cm) in diameter.

Capabilities: Squirrels can climb bricks, stucco, wooden shingles, aluminum downspouts, power lines (Fig. 2). They can swim but don't prefer it. Don't under estimate their gnawing power (Figs. 3a,b,c). GS-Good vision with 40° binocular vision. GS-Can jump laterally up to 6 ft (1.8 m) and can achieve speeds of 15 mph (24 km/h) for short distances. **FS** can achieve speeds up to 12 mph (19 km/h).

Symptoms.

A. Noises in walls and attic: Typically, the customer will complain of scratching in the walls and ceiling. Often this will occur in the late evening or early (predawn) morning during the colder months of Sept to April. The noises may not be heard every day.

B. Noises in cellar/chewed window panes (see special situations).

C. Noises in fireplace (see special situations).

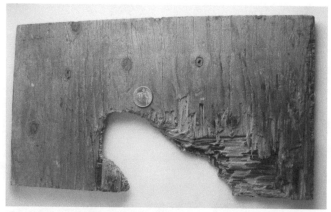

Fig. 3a. ½-in (1.25-cm) plywood placed over a hole. The female gray squirrel wanted to return to young.

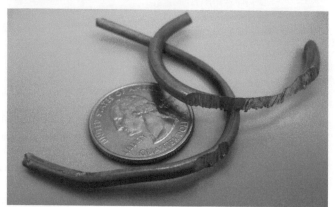

Fig. 3b. Fox squirrel gnawing on aluminum fasteners for a chain-link fence.

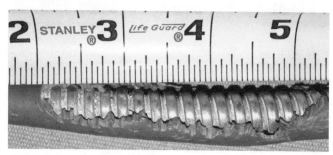

Fig. 3c. Gnawing to gas line by squirrel. Photo by Noreen Esposito.

Signs

Avg. Hole Size: Hole range 1.5 to 3 in (3.8 to 7.6 cm) in diameter (Fig. 4). **GS** mean head width is 1.4 in (34.5 mm). **FS** mean head width is 1.5 in (37.8 mm) The longer the squirrels have been resident, the closer the hole size will be to 3 in (7.6 cm) or larger. Holes typically found where 2 boards/surfaces meet, such as corners, eaves, dormers or in vents such as mushroom vents and flat vents. I have only witnessed squirrels entering a building at ground level on 2 occasions, so inspection emphasis should be on heights.

Check structure closely looking for brown oil-like smudges on vents which are left as it squeezes through tight areas.

Fig. 4. Screened gray squirrel hole.

Fig. 5. Squirrels caught in basements will gnaw in an attempt to escape.

Access: Gray squirrels, like most creatures, will always use the easiest way to enter a building. Typically, they access buildings from overhanging branches. If no branches are available they will use power lines (usually if they are taut) and aluminum gutters. In these situations, look closely at the gutters for small ¼- to ½-in (6.4 to 12.7 mm) long scratches in the paint. The scratches will look like they have been made by a pin. So be sure to look very closely at each of the gutters, especially the ones that reach all the way to the top of the roof.

Damage to Structures: If you enter the attic area, look for the pink fiberglass insulation that will be stripped to the paper. They also will pile up the insulation into a corner during nest construction or bore holes through it. Cardboard boxes will be gnawed. Distinguish from mouse or rat by the absence of droppings. On rare occasions, you will notice chewed beams, rafters and wiring. Usually these signs are found when the house has had long term problems, i.e. years of untreated squirrel problems or multiple infestations.

In these kinds of heavy damage, you often will be able to smell the squirrels. Get to know that smell as you will probably smell it again. Another sign is when the homeowner complains that a small hole is appearing in the ceiling and growing larger each day. Grays also will chew lead flashing used around chimneys and walls.

Special Situations

A. Noises in the basement: Sometimes the owner will tell you that they have heard noises in the basement and items on shelves have been knocked over.

Typically this occurs in the months of December through February when female squirrels are scouting nesting sites and males seek females. Often it will happen just before an impending snowstorm. (90% of the time the furnace will be fired with gas not oil. New Hampshire has the opposite stats). Ask the owner, if branches overhang the house/chimney. Again the majority of the time the answer will be "yes." Don't trust him when he says his chimney is capped. Often people don't know what capping means or they screened the chimney 10 years ago with hardware cloth that has long since rusted through or blown off.

A careful look at the draft diverter (in Gas furnaces) will often reveal small smudge marks where the squirrel climbed out. Once in the chimney, the squirrel cannot climb back out because the flue tile is too smooth.

If there is damage to the window pane wood or to bottom of a basement door then you know that a squirrel has been trapped inside (Fig. 5). Generally speaking, squirrels cannot live much longer than 3 days without water. There have been exceptions, but they are < 10%.

B. Noises in fireplace: Could be caused by raccoon, bird or a squirrel. Fluttering suggests birds, chirping suggests raccoons. Before looking down the chimney, investigate the sides of the house for access. Try to rule out other animals. Remember, just because you cannot see an animal from the top of the chimney, doesn't mean 1 isn't there. Many times animals are off to the side out of view. Always keep in mind that the smoke chamber is usually larger than the flue. In the final analysis, you will need to open the damper narrowly first (Fig. 6) and use your mirror to see if it is squirrel. Be careful, the squirrels sometimes run out once they see the light. Make sure breakables are out of the way and that you have sectioned off the area by closing doors. Other times, you may have difficulty seeing the squirrel because he has climbed part way up the flue (Fig. 7).

Damage to Lawn/Garden: Generally damage will be minimal.

Lawn. Occasionally, you will hear complaints about squirrels digging up the grass when they bury or uncover hidden acorns (Fig. 8a). Holes can reach a depth of 1.5 in (cm) and can be quite extensive (Fig. 8b).

Trees: Fox squirrels will clip the tip of branches up to $3/8$ inch in diameter (Fig. 9). Buds and fruits will be consumed. Both species will strip/gnaw bark of smooth-barked trees (Fig. 10). Look for strips of bark found on

Fig. 6. Gray squirrel peering over the slightly ajar fireplace damper.

Fig. 7. Squirrel climbed up the brick smoke chamber. Photo taken from the damper.

ground (Fig. 11). Squirrels may mark their territory by gnawing a small portion of the tree (Fig. 12).

Gardens. When food is scarce squirrels will eat flowers, pumpkins (Fig. 13) and their seeds, and even tomatoes. Squirrels eat the hearts of corn (Fig. 14).

Damage to Pets & Livestock: Squirrels can predate on bird eggs.

Tracks: Squirrel hop pattern is hind feet land ahead of front feet. Tracks will be in groups of 4. Rear foot has 5 toes and front shows 4 (Fig. 15).

GS front foot is 1.25 to 1.75 (3.2 to 4.4 cm) in length and $5/8$ to 1.12 in (1.6 to 2.9 cm) in width. Rear foot is 1.25 to 3.25 in (3.2 to 8.3 cm) in length and 1 to 1.5 (2.5 to 3.8 cm) in width.

Fig. 8a. Lawn damage by fox squirrel. Note how the soil is pulled to 1 end.

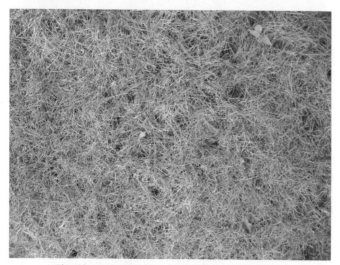

Fig. 8b. Holes caused by fox squirrel digging.

Fig. 9. These evergreen branches were clipped by fox squirrels and found scattered around the base of the tree.

Fig. 10. Branches stripped by fox squirrels.

Fig. 11. Strips of bark on the ground are evidence of bark stripping above.

Fig. 12. Territorial marking of a fox squirrel.

FS front foot 1.25 to 2 (3.2 to 5.1 cm) in length and 1⅜ in (2.5 to 3.5) in width. Rear foot is 1.25 to 3.5 in (3.2 to 8.9 cm) in length and ⅞ to 1.75 in (2.2 to 4.4 cm) in width.

Scat: You will not find abundant fecal material in an attic. Squirrels, unlike raccoons, don't have toilets per se. Any feces that is found will probably be few and far between. Generally, the feces look like a black piece of rice.

Fig. 13. Pumpkin gnawed by a fox squirrel.

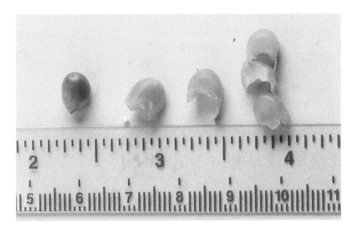

Fig. 14. Hearts removed by squirrel feeding.

Fig. 15. Gray squirrel front track in sand. Front track shows 4 toes

Fig. 16. Droppings of gray squirrel. Photo by Kirk LaPierre (d. 2010), A1Saver.com.

Fig. 17. Squirrel gnawing on a 1-inch (2.5 cm) thick electrical cable.

Sometimes it will be more round like an enlarged brown BB pellet. **GS** scat is $^1/_8$ to $^7/_{32}$ (0.3 to 0.6 cm) in diameter and $^5/_{32}$ to $^3/_8$ in (0.4 to 1 cm) in length. It has a rough texture (Fig. 16). **FS** scat is ¼ in (6.4 mm) in length.

Hair: GS's guard hairs are tipped with white. **FS** guard hairs are tawny or orange but eastern **FS** may have white-tipped guard hairs.

Sounds: Churrs (anger), cherks (warning), quacks (contentment), and squeals (injury, fear).

Bite Marks: **GS** tend to gnaw bones for minerals so bones with flesh or fat on them tend to avoided in favor of bleached and weathered "dry" bones (usually after 16 months of exposure). Gnaw marks tend to be 0.1 inch (2.54 mm). Thickest part will be gnawed on first (see Bone ID chapter). As noted elsewhere, they also gnaw on other items (Fig. 17).

Associated Animals: Don't be misled if you see birds using a hole in the house. I have had at least 1 job where birds and squirrels used the same hole to enter their nests.

Leaf girdler. Damage to trees should not be confused with the damage by the twig girdler, an insect that strips the bark around the leaf stem causing the leaf cluster to die, while remaining attached to the tree. When squirrels clip branches, the branch will be green and fall off the tree (Fig. 18).

Fig. 18. Branch killed by leaf girdler (left) and a branch clipped by a squirrel (right). A close look at the branch will show that the leaf girdler cut is around the outside bark and is smooth and even. The squirrel cut is rough (Fig. 19).

Fig. 19. Branch on left cut by a leaf girdler and the branch on right cut by a squirrel.

Health/Safety

Squirrels are subject to fibromas (tumors), cutaneous warbles (larvae of flies that infest the skin), and ectoparasites. The majority of these diseases do not threaten human health.

Resources

Davidson, W. R. editor. 2006. *Field Manual of Wildlife Diseases in the Southeastern United States.* Third edition. Athens, GA: Southeastern Cooperative Wildlife Disease Cooperative.

Elbroch, M. 2003. *Mammal Tracks and Sign: A Guide to North American Species.* Mechanicsburg, PA: Stackpole Books.

Harding, J. 1979. *An Animal Damage Identification Guide for Massachusetts.* Amherst, MA: Cooperative Extension Service, University of Massachusetts, SP-113.

Klippel, W. E. and J. A. Synstelien. 2007. Rodents as Taphonomic Agents: Bone Gnawing by Brown Rats and Gray Squirrels. *J Forensic Sci,* 52:4(July):1556-4029.

Jackson, J. J. "Tree Squirrels." in *Prevention and Control of Wildlife Damage.* Editors, S. E. Hygnstrom, R. M. Timm, G. E. Larson. 1994. University of Nebraska-Lincoln. 2 vols.

Koprowski, J. L. 1994. *Sciurus carolinensis.* Mammalian Species, No. 480, (Dec. 2):1-9.

Koprowski, J. L. 1994. *Sciurus niger.* Mammalian Species, No. 479, (Dec. 2):1-9.

Link, R. 2004. *Living with Wildlife in the Pacific Northwest.* Seattle, WA: Univ. of Washington Press.

Rezendes, P. 1992. *Tracking and the Art of Seeing: How to Read Animal Tracks and Sign.* Charlotte, VT: Camden House Publishing, Inc.

Schwartz, C. and E. Schwartz. 1981. *The Wild Mammals of Missouri.* University of Missouri Press and Missouri Department of Conservation.

House Cats *(Felis catus)*

Biology

Size: Avg. 3 to 15 lbs (1.36 to 6.8 kg) and 29.5 in (75 cm) in total length of which approximately half is the tail.

Diet: Opportunistic predators, eating small rodents, birds, shrews, reptiles, amphibians, handouts, and cat food (dry and moist). Australian research shows that on the mainland, cats can kill mammals up to 4.2 lbs (2000 g) and birds up to 2.1 lbs (1000 g) but most kills are on mammals <7.8 oz (220 g) and birds <7.1 oz (200 g). On islands, kills on land mammals can reach 6.6 lbs (3000 g). Adult females require ~200 to 300 calories/day. Adult males need 250 to 300 calories/day.

Habitat: Urban and suburban areas where food can be gleaned from human enablers and/or trash cans. But can be found in areas 1 mi (1.6 km) from the nearest home.

Activity: Nocturnal/Year round. An Illinois study found that owned cats loafed 80% of the time while un-owned cats loafed only 67%. In the study, the most mobile stray cat traveled 1,351-acre area. Less active during colder temperatures.

Procreation: Cats can breed any time of the year, and a single pair of cats can produce 2 or more litters a year. Litters range from 2 to 10 kittens. The mother cat will keep the kittens hidden until they are about 5 or 6 weeks old. Males do not help in rearing young. Nursing continues up to 8 weeks. Young become independent in 6 to 8 months.

Capabilities: Under, over, or through fences. Being good jumpers (able to jump 5× their height), they can even live in basements and jump out through basement windows (provided they have a raised launching point). I have personally witnessed a cat climb a ladder 10 ft (3 m) high to a roof and then climb back down. Note (Figs. 2a,b) the cat climbed the tree in the rear of house (2-floor house) and then walked to the opposite corner and then needed rescue. White marks are due to the fact that it was snowing.

Behavior: Cats are territorial and have a variety of methods for marking their territory. They will spray urine on objects, scratch trees and posts, rub their faces on things, and leave scat, or droppings, as a marker to let other cats know whose territory they occupy. Male cats do more spraying than females do, although females do sometimes spray. If a cat feels threatened by the presence of a new cat, it may go out and remark its territory. Scratching trees and upright objects is a way for a cat to display its size to other cats. Higher scratches suggest a taller cat. When a cat rubs on something, scent glands on the side of the face leave behind odors for other cats to find. House cats do this a lot, even rubbing their faces on their owners to mark them. Cats also will butt heads in displays of affection for one another.

Fig. 2a,b. This house cat climbed to the roof by the tree in the opposite end of the house.

Fig. 1. Cat with a small rodent in its mouth (arrow). Note the time and temperature printed on the photo. Photo by University of Nebraska-Lincoln.

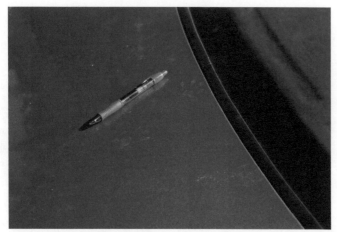

Fig. 3. Tracks on car from cat.

Fig. 4. Cat scrape over its urine spot

Fig. 5. Feather field from a cat kill.

Damage to Lawn/Garden: I have not heard of any significant damage but they will scrape and defecate in gardens (Fig. 4).

Damage to Pets & Livestock: Cats are instinctive hunters. If they can kill it, they will (Fig. 5). They often pounce on their prey and kill by biting the back of the neck. Larger animals may be bitten and struck repeated by front paws.

Tracks: Front track is 1 to 1.6 in (2.5 to 4.1 cm) long and $7/8$ to 1.75 in (2.2 to 4.4 cm) wide. Rear track is 1.12 to 1.5 in (2.9 to 3.8 cm) long and $7/8$ to 1.6 in (2.2 to 4.4 cm) long. Note there are no claws as cats have retractable claws (Fig. 6a). Note the linear way the cat walks as if walking on an invisible tight rope. This is classic cat gait. (Fig. 6b).

Scat: Normally 2 to 4 in (5 to 10 cm) long (Fig. 7). Scat will be segmented and somewhat blunt on one end. Look for hair inside from their grooming. Domestic cats bury their scat, but wild cats will sometimes leave it exposed as a way of claiming territory.

Hair: Hair can exhibit diverse coloration.

Sounds: Meow, purrs, and hisses.

Bite Marks: Distance between lower incisors of medium-sized cat 0.6 in (16 mm).

Associated Animals: Cats are sometimes taken by fox and coyotes.

Most cats remain within 984 ft (300 m) of human structures according to an Illinois study.

Sometimes they climb a tree but then can't get back down. At University of Nebraska-Lincoln, a cat was so high in a tree that a bucket loader was needed to reach it.

Symptoms

Clients may complain of the loss of birds and small wildlife around their property. Odors may be perceived from males spraying.

Signs

Avg. Hole Size: 3 to 5 inches (7.6 to 12.7 cm) whatever they can fit their head through). Skull width range is 2.16 to 2.7 in (54.82 to 68.4 mm).

Damage to Structures: Shredded furniture, cat hair and feces. The smell is unmistakable. Once you learn it, you will never forget it. They will climb onto cars for warmth (Fig. 3).

Health/Safety

Rabies: In 2009, cases of rabies in cats increased 2.0% over 2008. The number of rabies cases reported in cats is routinely 3 to 4 times that of rabies reported in cattle or dogs. In 2009 approximately 1% of cats and 0.3% of dogs tested for rabies were found positive.

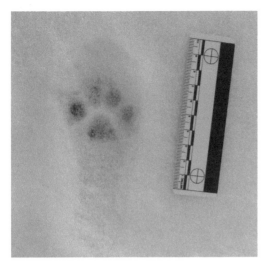

Fig. 6a. Cat track in snow. Note no claws are showing.

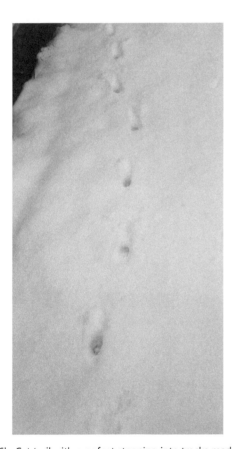

Fig. 6b. Cat trail with rear feet stepping into tracks made by front.

Toxoplasmosis: A parasitic disease and felines are the definitive host. Eggs viable in stool for 48 hours after defecation.

Cat Scratch Fever: Cat scratch fever is caused by the bacteria *Bartonella henselae*. Approximately 40% of all cats carry the bacteria. It is spread through scratches and bites.

Fig. 7. Scat of house cat.

Bite Infections: Pasturella is common in the saliva of cats.

Resources

Thanks to Kim A. Cabrera of Beartracker's Animal Tracks Den, www.geocities.com/wind_tracker/ for the information she provided.

Anna Toenjes, N. 2011. *"Felis catus"* (On-line), Animal Diversity Web. http://animaldiversity.ummz.umich.edu/site/accounts/information/Felis_catus.html visited December 31, 2011.

Blanton, J.D., D. Plamer, and C. E. Rupprecht. 2010. Rabies surveillance in the U.S. during 2009. *JAVMA* 237:6 (Sept 15):646-657.

CDC.gov. 2011. Cat Scratch Disease (*Bartonella henselae* Infection) updated April 23. http://www.cdc.gov/healthypets/diseases/catscratch.htm visited January 1, 2012.

Dickman, C. R. 1996. Overview of the Impacts of Feral Cats on Australian Native Fauna: Invasive Species Program. Sydney, NSW: Australian Nature Conservation Agency and University of Sydney. 1-97. http://www.feral.org.au/wp-content/uploads/2010/03/impacts-feral-cats.pdf.

Elbroch, M. 2003. *Mammal Tracks and Sign: A Guide to North American Species.* Mechanicsburg, PA: Stackpole Books.

Elbroch, M. 2006. *Animal Skulls: A Guide to North American Species.* Mechanicsburg, PA: Stackpole Books.

Fitzwater, William D. "House Cats (Feral)." in *Prevention and Control of Wildlife Damage.* Editors, Scott E. Hygnstrom, Robert M. Timm, Gary E. Larson. 1994. University of Nebraska-Lincoln. 2 vols.

Horn, J. A., N. Mateus-Pinilla, R. E. Warner, and E. J. Heske, Home range, habitat use, and activity patterns of free-roaming domestic cats, *Journal of Wildlife Management* 75:5 (2011).

"Researchers track the secret lives of feral and free-roaming cats," http://news.illinois.edu/news/11/0526_cat_study_Horn-Mateus-Warner.html visited June 11, 2011.

http://whyfiles.org/2011/the-secret-life-of-cats/ visited June 11, 2011.

Whitaker, Jr. J. O. and W. J. Hamilton, Jr. 1998. *Mammals of the Eastern United States.* 3rd ed. Ithaca, NY: Comstock Publishing Associates.

House Mice

House Mouse (*Mus musculus*) HM
Deer Mouse (*Peromyscus maniculatus*) DM
White-footed Mouse (*Peromyscus leucopus*) WFM

Note: Research is stronger for house mice. Information is separated by abbreviations **HM**, **DM**, and **WFM** when able. **Mice** or **ALL** will refer to all 3 species.

Biology

Size: **HM** Weight 0.5 to 1 oz (1.2 to 2.5 g). Length 2.5 to 3.75 in (65 to 95 mm) **DM** Weight $\frac{1}{3}$ to 1 oz (9 to 28 g) length 4 $\frac{3}{8}$ to 8 in (11.1 to 20.3 cm). **WFM** weight $\frac{2}{5}$ to 1 oz (11 to 28 g) length 5 $\frac{1}{2}$ to 8 $\frac{3}{8}$ in (13.9 to 21.2 cm)

Diet: **HM**. Omnivores, partial to grains. They will eat cockroaches and can be significant predators of eggs and bird young. They prefer grains and sweets. Eat $\frac{1}{10}$ oz (3 g) per day or ~2.2 lbs (1 kg) per year. **DM/WFM** Eat seeds, green vegetation, insects, berries, and mushroom. **ALL** They also are "opportunistic foragers", meaning they will indulge when food is available. Look for acorns and other mast crops such as, partially chewed walnuts (Fig. 2a) and acorns (Fig. 2b) also can be found. Mice tend to open a nut only as much as needed to eat. By contrast, gray squirrels will often split the walnut and acorn in half.

Need minimal water, as they can generate their own from metabolism but will drink 0.14 to 0.27 fl oz (4 to 8 ml) per day if available. This small amount could be gained from condensation on pipes.

Habitat: **HM** Houses, wood piles, debris, trees. Wherever humans live, house mice can live. In structures, mice select for areas that are warm, quiet, and near food resources. Mice prefer areas of the home with heat (water heaters, refrigerators/freezers and other appliances that remain on constantly) and walls with vertical chases. **DM/WFM** can live in the ground, bird nests, trees, etc. Though **WFM** are more likely to live in elevated nests and **DM** in ground nests.

Fig. 2a. Gnaw marks on black walnut typical of mice. Squirrels would slice the nut in sections. Closest measurement is inches

Fig. 2b. Gnaw marks on acorns typical of mouse feeding. Measurement cm.

Activity: **ALL** nocturnal/year round. Pressure to enter structures increases as temperature declines. **HM** will adjust activity to take advantage of quiet times in human activity.

Behavior: **HM** Will make multiple trips from nest to feeding sites each night. Usually don't travel more than 30 ft (9 m) from a nest. Will create territories as population density increases. **DM** may travel 500 ft (150 m) from nest. **All.** Nests made from fine material to enhance insulation capabilities (Figs. 3a, 3b).

Procreation: **HM** 5 to 8 litters annually. A litter consists of 5 to 7 young. Females can have multiple litters per year. Gestation is 19 to 21 days. Young sexually mature in 6 weeks. Gender ratio of male to female is 1:1. **DM** Most mating in spring and fall, females give birth

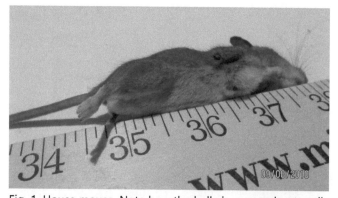

Fig. 1. House mouse. Note how the belly is gray and not easily distinguishable from the tan back fur. This coloration helps distinguish HM from DM whose bellies are bright white.

Fig. 3a. The pole on the left used to have a vine that gave the mice easier access to the eave.

Fig. 3b. Volume of nesting material removed from the eave.

Fig. 4a. Damage to insulation by mice. Photo by Robert M. Timm.

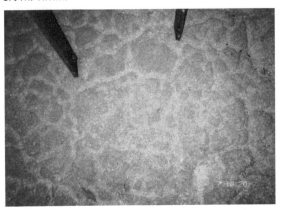

Fig. 4b. Trails in blown insulation made by mice.

to 1 to 9 young (3 to 4 most common) after 21 to 23 days and up to 37 days when females are nursing. Young wean in 2 to 3 weeks. **WFM** mate in early spring and late summer. Some females have up to 8 litters per year.

Capabilities: HM Research has shown they can jump 9.8 inches (25 cm) vertically from ground to flat surface. They are excellent climbers. I once found a portion of a corn cob stuck in a second floor hole because it was too wide to fit through the mouse hole. Superb sense of taste, hearing, smell, and touch. Visual acuity limited to 1 to 2 ft (31 to 60 cm), can see movement up to 45 ft (13.7 m). Color blind to the color red. Have been known to travel 1.5 mi (2.4 km). **DM/WFM** enter garages and can climb into attic areas. **ALL** Don't underestimate what they can carry.

Symptoms

ALL Clients will complain of noises in the attic or walls. Ask the owner if birdfeeders are present on the property. You also will find it difficult to find entries into structure (sometimes mice enter as stowaways in boxes). Sometimes the noise of their activity will seem quite loud to residents. Pets, particularly cats, may stare at vents and walls as they hear the mice activity.

Signs

Avg. Hole Size: HM 0.52 inches (1.3 cm) is the diameter that research has shown to be the minimum size hole for mice of all sizes to enter/exit. However, given that holes in structure are rarely perfectly round and that substrates may "stretch", it is best to consider the minimum hole size as $3/16$ in (4.8 mm). Mice can enter almost anywhere, along the roof line, along pipes, through vents, anywhere they can find an opening or wood soft enough to chew through. Dr. Corrigan says, "House mice don't like vertical gaps (space between the floor and bottom of the furniture) 8 in or taller." So when looking for scat, place your effort in areas where items provide mice with low cover.

Damage to House: Mice chew wires, eat food, deposit feces, and urine. Don't be surprised to see shredded toilet paper or shredded cloth. Look for holes and trails through insulation in the attic (Figs. 4a,b). Though not a building, mice will take advantage of cars (Fig. 4c) and the cars don't have to be idle long.

DM shred styrofoam.

Fig. 4c. Mice can create nests in cars too.

Damage to Lawn/Garden: ALL typically eat only the kernel of the grain. **HM** is normally not found in locations 50 ft (15 m) or more from a structure.

Damage to Pets & Livestock: Mice can damage bee hives during the winter and will eat eggs and chicks.

Tracks: HM typically not found, although crawl marks may be seen in dusty locations.
   DM hind foot ⅝ to 1 in in length (15 to 25 mm)
   WFM front foot is ⅜ in (9.5 mm) wide and hind foot is ¾ to 1 in (19-25 mm).

Scat: HM Scat ⅛ to ¼-in (4 to 6 mm) in length with 2 or both ends pointed (Fig. 6a) but can be rounded like a pellet. Color will vary. Mice don't have toilets so you will find the feces randomly deposited during their activities (40 to 100 droppings/day). Fresh droppings will smear when pressed with a spatula. Old droppings will be hard. Distinguish scat from insect by the presence of hair.
   Urine. House mice communicate primarily through urine. An adult dominant house mouse can release up to 3,000 micro-droplets of urine in 24 hours.
   A black light will also reveal the stains caused by their urine. Mice can leave 1000 to 3000 micro-droplets of urine per day.

Fig. 5. House mouse tracks by Kim Cabrera.

DM/WFM scat (Figs. 6b, 6c). Deer mouse and white-footed mouse droppings tend to be rougher and longer than those of house mice.

Fig. 6a. HM droppings on top of paper in a file folder.

Fig. 6b. Scat of *P. maniculatus*, measurement mm.

Fig. 6c. Scat of *P. leucopus*, measurement cm.

Hair: Rarely found but frequently shed in their travels.

Sounds: Squeaks, scratching, and gnawing. Noise is louder than people think. **DM** high-pitched squeaks, trills, and even a buzz that can extend for 5 to 10 seconds and can be heard up to 50 ft (15.24 m)

Bite Marks: **HM.** Gnaw marks are 0.125 ($^1/_8$ in; 3.1 mm) others say 0.08 inches wide (2 mm). Incisors rate 5.5 on Moh's hardness scale. Will gnaw holes in cardboard boxes up to 1.5 in (3.8 cm) wide.

Miscellaneous: If your bait keeps getting stolen and the trap doesn't fire, the culprit is most likely mice.

Associated Animals: Mice are curious and easily trapped. If you are finding it difficult to attract mice to a trap consider the possibility of shrews.

Health/Safety

Hantavirus: Although **HM** mice don't carry Hantavirus, the difficulty in distinguishing **HM** droppings from **DM** suggest using caution with all rodent droppings. Always treat mouse infested areas as potential biological hazard zones. Consult with the Centers for Disease Control website in order to learn more about preventing Hantavirus infection.

Asthma: **HM** mouse urinary protein has been implicated as an asthma trigger.

Food Poisoning: Campylobacteria recently has surpassed salmonella as the most significant cause of food poisoning. Salmonella can remain viable in **HM** droppings for 86 days.

Insulation: Mice can significantly reduce the R-value of insulation through their burrowing through and defecating on insulation (Fig. 4b).

Resources

Some material provided here has been provided by Robert Corrigan.

Brooks, J. E. and L. A. Fielder. N.D. Vertebrate Pests: Damage on Stored Foods. United States Department of Agriculture (USDA) Edited by AGSI/FAO: Danilo Mejia (Technical), Beverly Lewis (Language & Style), http://www.fao.org/fileadmin/user_upload/inpho/docs/Post_Harvest_Compendium_-_Pests-Vertebrates.pdf ; visited October 21, 2011. 26 pp.

CDC. N.D. Facts about Hantaviruses: What You Need to Know to Prevent The Disease Hantavirus Pulmonary Syndrome (HPS). Department of Health and Human Services, Centers for Disease Control and Prevention. 11 pp.

Corrigan, R. M. 2000. Using Liquid Rodenticide Baits. *Pest Control Technology.* (Aug):42-47.

Corrigan, R. M. 2001. *Rodent Control: A Practical Guide for Pest Management Professionals.* Cleveland, OH: GIE Media. 353 pp.

Corrigan, R. M. 2011. Rats and Mice, in *Handbook of Pest Control: The Behavior, Life History, and Control of Household Pests* edited by A. Mallis et al. Mallis Handbook, LLC. 11-149 pp.

Frishman, A. 2002. Rodent Control Safety Tips. *Pest Control Magazine* 70:8 (Aug):14-15.

Harding, J. 1979. *An Animal Damage Identification Guide for Massachusetts.* Amherst, MA: Cooperative Extension Service, University of Massachusetts, SP-113.

Heinrich, Bernd. 2003. *Winter World: The Ingenuity of Animal Survival.* New York: HarperCollins.

Link, R. 2004. *Living with Wildlife in the Pacific Northwest.* Seattle, WA: Univ. of Washington Press.

Minnesota Public Health Dept. N.D. Domestic Rats and Mice. http://www.health.state.nm.us/erd/HealthData/documents/DomesticRatsandMice_001.pdf visited October 21, 2011.

Pitt, W. C., R. T. Sugihara, L. C. Driscoll, and D. S. Vice. 2011. Physical and Behavioral Abilities of Commensal Rodents Related to the Design of Selective Rodenticide Bait Stations. *International Journal of Pest Management* 57:3 (July-Sept):1-5.

Rezendes, P. 1992, 1995. *Tracking and the Art of Seeing: How to Read Animal Tracks & Sign.* Charlotte, VT: Camden House Pub., Inc.

Schwartz, C. W. and E. R. Schwartz. 2001. *The Wild Mammals of Missouri.* Second Revised Edition. Columbia, MO: University of Missouri Press.

Timm, R. M. "House Mouse." in *Prevention and Control of Wildlife Damage.* Editors, Scott E. Hygnstrom, Robert M. Timm, Gary E. Larson. 1994. University of Nebraska-Lincoln. 2 vols.

Timm, R. M., R. E. Marsh, R. M. Corrigan, and K. Holscher. N.D. Controlling Rats and Mice in Swine Facilities. Purdue University. Cooperative Extension. PIH-107. Lafayette, IN. http://www.animalgenome.org/edu/PIH/107.html visited Oct 21, 2011.

House Sparrows *(Passer domesticus)*

Biology

Size: Both genders weigh about 1 oz. (27 to 29 g) and are 6 to 7 in (15 to 17 cm) long with a 9 to 9.5 -in (23 to 24 cm) wingspan.

Diet: ~96% of diet consists of grains (including livestock feed), seeds, flowers, buds, and human garbage. When rearing young, they consume insects.

Habitat: Comfortable in urban settings and other human-impacted environments. Not found in wilderness areas.

Activity: Diurnal/year round.

Procreation: Mating can occur anytime of year, typically when it is above freezing. Females can have 1 to 4 clutches of 2 to 6 eggs per clutch per year. Nesting begins around April 10 in Nebraska. Incubation is 10 to 17 days. Nests fill the cavity (Fig. 1) and are made of grasses, leaves, and feathers. Male chooses site. Young leave 14 to 23 days later. Males assist in rearing young. Parents stay within 1.25 mi (2 km) of nest during nesting period.

Capabilities: Can travel 5 to 6 mi (6 to 8 km) from nesting area to feeding sites. Can rapidly rebuild nests.

Symptoms

Owners may complain of nesting material in vents, droppings, and noise.

Signs

Avg. Hole Size: Can enter holes ¾ in (2 cm) wide. Nests are messy, piles of dried grass that fill the void or crevice.

Damage to Structures: Nests can clog drains and vents risking flooding and fires (Figs. 2a,b,c). Nests also can uplift ceramic tiles on roofs. They have been known to peck at the solid insulation of buildings (Fig. 5).

Droppings are acidic aiding decay and are unsightly as well.

Damage to Lawn/Garden: Little to none, but droppings below roost and nesting sites may a nuisance.

Damage to Pets & Livestock: Consume livestock feed and consume bird seed. They compete with native bird species by predation and taking over nesting areas. Males defend their territory (Fig. 3).

Tracks: 1.12 to 1.31 in (2.8 to 3.3 cm) in length and 3/8 to 9/16 in (1 to 1.4 cm) in width (Fig. 4).

Scat: Non-descript but contains the white nitrogenous material typical of bird droppings (Fig. 5).

Fig. 2a. Nests in power lines have caused fires.

Fig. 1. House sparrow nest in a sign.

Fig. 2b. Note male nearby nest.

Fig. 2c. Nest on downspout.

Feathers: Primary feathers are short only 2.5 in (6.4 cm) length and dark in coloration.

Sounds: Sharp "yew, yew".

Bite Marks: N/A

Associated Animals: House sparrows compete with native bird species.

Health/Safety

House sparrows have been implicated in transmitting a number of diseases including salmonellosis, encephalitis, psittacosis, and diseases affecting poultry and hog farms.

Histoplasmosis: Histoplasmosis is caused by exposure (typically through respiration) to fungal spores that are growing in the soil enriched with bird dropping.

Ectoparasites: House sparrows suffer from a number of fleas, ticks, and mites (e.g. fowl mite).

Fig. 3. Male house sparrow outside a Purple martin house.

Fig. 4. Image by Dee Ebbeka.

Resources

I would like to thank Bird Barrier for some of the information used on this page.

Brown, N. S. and G. I. Wilson. 1975. A Comparison of the Ectoparasites of the House Sparrow (*Passer domesticus*) from North America and Europe. *American Midland Naturalist* 94:1(Jul):154-165.

Cornell Lab of Ornithology. http://www.allaboutbirds.org/guide/House_Sparrow/lifehistory Accessed December 20, 2011.

Elbroch, M. 2001. *Bird Tracks & Sign: A Guide to North American Species.* Mechanicsburg, PA: Stackpole Books.

Elphick, C., J. B. Dunning Jr., and D. A. Sibley (eds). 2001. *The Sibley Guide to Bird Life & Behavior.* National Audubon Society. NY: Knopf Press.

Fitzgerald, W. D. "House Sparrows." in *Prevention and Control of Wildlife Damage.* Editors, S. E. Hygnstrom, R. M. Timm, G. E. Larson. 1994. University of Nebraska-Lincoln. 2 vols.

Gulmahamad, H. 2008. An Unwelcome Guest. *Wildlife Professional* (August):64-66; 68,70.

Johnson, S. A. and H. Violett. 2009. Florida's Introduced Birds: European House Sparrow (*Passer domesticus*). University of Florida IFAS Extension. WEC260. June. 1-7 pp.

Link, R. 2004. *Living with Wildlife: In the Pacific Northwest.* Seattle, WA: University of Washington Press.

McNeely, S. 2011. *Vertebrate Pests in Handbook of Pest Control: The Behavior , Life History, and Control of Household Pests* edited by A. Mallis et al. Mallis Handbook, LLC. 1119-1189 pp.

Sappington, J. N. 1977. Breeding Biology of House Sparrows in North Mississippi. *The Wilson Bulletin* 89:2(Jun):300-309.

Sibley, D. A. 2000. *The Sibley Guide to Birds.* NY, NY: Alfred A. Knopf.

Fig. 5. House sparrow droppings. Photo also shows damage to Styrofoam by house sparrows. Photo by University of Nebraska-Lincoln.

Moles

Eastern Mole (*Scalopus aquaticus*) **EM**
Hairy-tailed Mole (*Parascalops breweri*) **HM**
Star-nosed Mole (*Condylura cristata*) **SNM**

All data refers to eastern mole unless other wise signified by the use of abbreviations.

Weight: **EM** weight 1.5 to 5 oz (28 to 141 g) and are 5.7 to 7.2 in (144 to 184 mm) in total length with a 0.6 to 1.2 in (15 to 30 mm) tail. Females lighter and smaller than males. **HM** weigh 1.4 to 2.3 oz (40 to 64 g) with females smaller than males. Total length ranges from 5.9 to 6.9 in (150 to 170 mm) with a 1 to 1.1 in (24 to 30 mm) tail. **SNM** average 1.8 oz (52 g) and total length averages 7.4 in (188 mm) including a 2.6 in (66.5 mm) tail.

Diet: Carnivorous, earthworms, grubs, scarab beetle larvae, centipedes, and other insects. Ants are primarily eaten in sandy soils. Reported to eat 70 to 100% of their weight in food per day. **SNM** aquatic insects, earth worms, snails etc. Consumes 45 to 50 lbs of food per year.

Habitat: Woods with well drained but moist soil or sand. **SNM** prefer wetter soil.

Activity: Moles will dig at all times of the day because their activity is not governed by the sun. Moles are active primarily active between 0800 to 1600 hr and 2300 to 0400 hr.

SNM are 2× as active between 0900 to 1800 hr than the rest of the day. Moles do not hibernate and can be active even at 10°F (-12 C). Moles have been recorded to travel in a deep tunnel at 78.75 ft/min (24 m/min).

Males are significantly more likely than females to be trapped between Jan to Mar. This is due to their larger home ranges.

Procreation: Breeding occurs in March-April. One litter of 2 to 5 young are born which leave the next 4 weeks later. **SNM** mating occurs in March to April and 3 to 7 young are born 45 days later.

Mole nests are located 6 to 9 in (15 to 25 cm) below the surface and connected to deep tunnels. Nests filled with coarse grass and/or leaves. Nests were 7 to 8.7 in (18 to 22 cm) long and 4 to 4.7 in (10 to 12 cm) wide. Moles may have more than 1 nest but they tend to remain with a single nest for many days before moving to another particularly in cold weather. During warm weather they are less attached to a particular den.

Capabilities: Outstanding diggers, able to create surface runs at ~1 ft/min (30.5 cm/min). Deep tunnels can be dug at a rate of 12 to 15 ft/hour (3.7 to 4.6 m/hour). Can swim. One researcher found evidence against the notion of moles being loners, observing 2 moles extending the same run.

Symptoms

Owner will complain of soft mushy grass or will identify trails. Owner will find erratic runs on the ground which lie below dead or dying grass.

Signs

Avg. Hole Size: Moles rarely come to the surface. The tunnels they dig tend to be about 1.25 to 1.5 in (3.2 to 3.8 cm) in diameter. **SNM** more likely to come to the surface than **EM**. Their tunnel holes are ~1 to 1⅜ in (2.5 to 3.5 cm) wide.

Access: Usually will enter the lawn from the side that abuts woods. However, moles will dig under streets and other flat stone structures. You can even find them well inside a housing development hundreds of yards from the nearest wood lot. **SNM** is the same. I have heard that moles occasionally enter buildings. But I will assure readers that this is an extremely rare occurrence. Pay close attention to homes that have dirt floor basements or field stone foundations.

Damage to Structures: None for all species. Sometimes brick/stone patios and walkways will be disturbed by burrowing activity.

Damage to Lawn/Garden: **Surface Runs.** Moles damage the grass by separating the roots of the grass from the soil beneath it. Surface runs tend to be 0.75 to 1 in (2 to 3 cm) below the surface (Fig. 1). They have no interest in the eating grass or plants. All they want is the food in the ground. If the owner complains of food missing from the garden, it is not because of the mole.

Deep runs tend to be more permanent are 4 to 16 in (10 to 40 cm) below the surface. Older runs will have dead and dying grass above them (Fig. 5).

Fig. 1. Travel run of eastern mole. Photo by Tom Olander.

Fig. 2. Boil of soil created by a mole.

Mounds. The owner may also complain of dirt boils that have emerged on the grass. These are caused by moles bringing soil to the surface because the tunnel is too deep to push the excess dirt above them. Mounds are spherical in shape (Fig. 2), but not always (Fig. 3). Avg. boil size is ~8 in (20 cm) across. These boils also will be found when the mole digs under driveways or heavy objects. Star-nose moles burrow more erratically than eastern moles. You may find push-ups spotted with dirt boils.

Tracks: Typically not found, although crawl marks may be seen in dusty locations.

Scat: If you find some you have found a rare item indeed. Elbroch claims that some species create latrines, typically under an overhead structure such as a log. Depending on diet, scat may be a squirt (when eating worms) or tubes with pointed ends (insects).

Hair: Rarely found. All hairs are identical in length. Under magnification will display a whip-like tip that is unique among the mammals. They also are non-directional, meaning you can stroke the hair in any direction without resistance.

Sounds: High-pitched and guttural squeaks, snorts, and teeth grinding.

Bite Marks: Unknown.

Associated Animals: Some pets may dig at the lawn in an attempt to capture moles.

Health/Safety

Moles are not significant health threats to humans because of their subterranean activity. Humans, however, may twist ankles and suffer falls tripping on runs, mole hills, or collapsed tunnels.

Fig. 3. Mole runs can blur with boils.

Fig. 5. Note how the runs have turned the grass brown.

Resources

Elbroch, M. 2003. *Mammal Tracks and Sign: A Guide to North American Species.* Mechanicsburg, PA: Stackpole Books. 784 pp.

Hartman, G. D. 1995. Seasonal Effects on Sex Ratios in Moles Collected by Trapping. *American Midland Naturalist,* 133:2(Apr):298-303.

Hartman, G. D., J. O. Whitaker Jr., and J. R. Munsee. 2000. Diet of the Mole *Scalopus aquaticus* from the Coastal Plain Region of South Carolina. *American Midland Naturalist* 144:2(Oct):342-351.

Harvey, M. J. 1976. Home Range, Movements, and Diet Activity of the Eastern Mole, *Scalopus aquaticus. American Midland Naturalist* 95:2(Apr):436-445.

Henderson, F. R. "Moles." in *Prevention and Control of Wildlife Damage.* Editors, S. E. Hygnstrom, R. M. Timm, G. E. Larson. 1994. University of Nebraska-Lincoln. 2 vols.

Schwartz, C. and E. Schwartz. 1981. *The Wild Mammals of Missouri.* University of Missouri Press and Missouri Department of Conservation.

Whitaker, Jr. J. O. and W. J. Hamilton, Jr. 1998. *Mammals of the Eastern United States.* 3rd ed. Ithaca, NY: Comstock Publishing Associates.

Yates, T. L. and D. J. Schmidly. 1978. *Scalopus aquaticus.* Mammalian Species. No. 105, (Sep. 21):1-4.

Distinguishing a Mole Mound from a Pocket Gopher Mound.

From the side, mole mounds are shaped like volcanos in a single mound (Fig. 4a). Pocket gopher mounds, in contrast are more oblong (Fig. 4b).

Looking down, mole mounds tend to be round (Fig. 4c) and pocket gopher mounds tend to be kidney or fan-shaped (Fig. 4d).

Fig. 4a. Mole mound from the side. Image by Michael Heller.

Fig. 4b. Pocket gopher mound from the side. Image by Michael Heller.

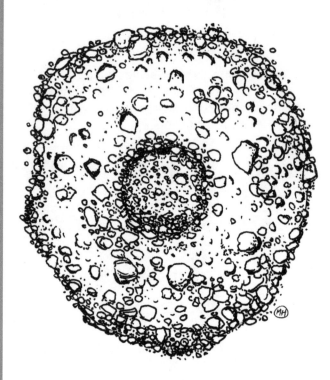

Fig. 4c. Mole mound. Round circle in the middle shows where the mole was tunneling. Image by Michael Heller.

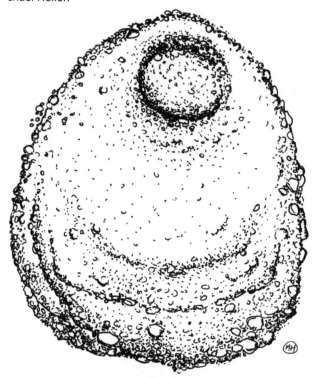

Fig. 4d. Pocket gopher mound with plug. Image by Michael Heller.

Mountain Beavers *(Aplodontia rufa)*

Biology

Size Weight 1.8 to 3.5 lbs (0.8 to 1.6 kg); total length is 13.5 in (34.3 cm) including 1 in (2.5 cm) tail.

Diet: Herbivores, eating a wide variety of plants including all above and below parts of ferns (particularly sword fern, *Polystichum munitum*), nettles, fireweed, salal, huckleberry, brambles, dogwoods, vine maples, willows, alders, and conifers. They also eat rhododendrons (Fig. 1) and other ornamental perennials, shrubs, and trees that they cut off and temporarily store outside their burrow entrances. Mountain beaver require large amounts of water on a daily basis, either from succulent food plants or other sources. They urinate between ¼ to ⅓ of their body weight per day. Can eat plants poisonous to other animals.

Habitat: Moist forests, ferny slopes, occasionally found in damp ravines in urban areas. Live in the coastal lowlands and coastal mountains of southern British Columbia from the Fraser Valley to the Cascade Mountains, western Washington, western Oregon, and south into northern California. Prefer areas dominated by Douglas fir (*Pseudotsuga menziesii*) and western hemlock (*Tsuga heterophylla*). There must be lush plants in the understory for mountain beaver to be present (Fig. 2).

Activity: Nocturnal, primarily fossorial, and territorial. Generally their numbers average 7 per hectare (2.2 acres). Average home range is 0.3 acres with no difference between male and female ranges.

Procreation: Mountain beavers are solitary except during the breeding season. In the Oregon Coast Range, breeding takes place from late February to mid-April. Two to 4 young are born (2 to 3 most common) after a 28 to 30 day gestation period. Development is slow; mountain beavers do not fully mature until their second year. Sex ratio in young is 1:1 but in adults 1:1.6 in favor of males. Subterranean nests, 11.8 to 59 in (0.3 to 1.5 m) below the surface, average 12 in (30 cm) in diameter (Fig. 3).

Fig. 1. Rhododendron fed on by mountain beaver. Photo by John Consolini.

Fig. 2. Mountain beaver habitat with den holes. Photo by Tim Hiller.

Fig. 3. Mountain beaver burrow. Photo by Tim Hiller.

Capabilities: Resemble large, over-grown hamsters or tailless muskrats. They have small ears and eyes, no visible tails, and large curved front claws used for digging, grasping, and climbing. Mountain beavers will climb trees up to 18 ft (5.5 m) high to lop off living branches that are up to an inch (2.5 cm) in diameter. They cut branches off as they climb and use the stubs as footholds when making their descent. Most feeding occurs within 50 ft (15.24 m) of burrow. Can swim well and readily enter water.

Fig. 4a. Evergreen tree damaged by mountain beaver. Photo by John Consolini.

Fig. 4b. Close up evergreen tree damaged by mountain beaver. Photo by John Consolini.

Symptoms

Owners will complain of holes and/or damaged plants.

Signs

Avg. Hole Size: Mountain beaver tunnels range from 5 to 7 in (13 to 18 cm) tall by 6 to 9.8 in (15 to 25 cm) wide, are 6 ft (1.8 m) length, and are 5.9 to 18 in (15 to 46 cm) below the surface. Holes frequently will have plant material sticking out the hole and may be plugged with debris in winter and early spring. Burrow system can have 10 to 30 exit holes that remain open.

Damage to Structures: Minimal to none as they don't attack structures. Their tunneling can encourage erosion.

Damage to Lawn/Garden: Girdling of trunks 3 to 6 in (7.6 to 15 cm) of diameter with no debris left (unlike girdling done by bears or porcupines).

Seedlings <1.5 in (38 mm) in diameter most likely to be eaten. Branches of tall plants will be clipped leaving stubs (1 to 3 in (2.5 to 7.5 cm)) so that mountain beaver can gain footholds (Figs. 4a,b). Cuttings and branches dragged to holes.

Fig. 5. Angle cut of branch by mountain beaver. Photo by John Consolini.

Tracks: Tracks of front foot range $^{15}/_{16}$ to 1.56 in (2.4 to 4 cm) in length and 1 to 1.56 in (2.5 to 4 cm) in width. Rear foot is $^7/_8$ to 1 $^5/_8$ in (2.2 to 4.1 cm) in length and $^{15}/_{16}$ to 1.5 in (2.4 to 3.8 cm) in length.

Scat: $^3/_{16}$ to $^5/_{16}$ in (5 to 8 mm) in diameter and ½ to $^{11}/_{16}$ in (1.3 to 1.7 cm) in length. They eat their feces, preferring the soft over the hard pellets. Hard pellets deposited in underground rooms.

Hair: Rarely found.

Sounds: Only 3 sounds have been identified. Pain is expressed by a soft whining and sobbing. A high-pitched squeal is emitted during fights or when frustrated. The significance of grating teeth is not known.

Bite Marks: Identify damage to conifer seedlings by looking for angular rough cuts on stems ¼ to ¾ inches (0.6 to 1.9 cm) in diameter (Fig. 5).

Associated Animals: Above ground, mountain beavers are prey for coyotes, bobcats, and owls. Below ground, weasels prey on young.

Health/Safety

Mountain beavers are not known to be a significant disease threat to humans. The flea associated with mountain beaver (*Hystrichopsylla schefferi*) does not feed on humans.

Resources

Campbell, D. L. "Mountain Beavers." in *Prevention and Control of Wildlife Damage*. Editors, S. E. Hygnstrom, R. M. Timm, G. E. Larson. 1994. University of Nebraska-Lincoln. 2 vols.

Carraway, L. N. and B. J. Verts. 1993. *Aplodontia rufa. Mammalian Species* No. 431 (Apr. 23):1-10.

Elbroch, M. 2003. *Mammal Tracks and Sign: A Guide to North American Species*. Mechanicsburg, PA: Stackpole Books.

Link, R. 2004. *Living with Wildlife in the Pacific Northwest*. Seattle, WA: Univ. of Washington Press.

Martin, P. 1971. Movements and Activities of the Mountain Beaver (*Aplodontia rufa*). *Journal of Mammalogy* 52:4 (Nov):717-723.

Norway Rats   *(Rattus norvegicus)*

Biology

Size: Weight 10 to 17 oz (284 to 567 g). Total length 12.6 to 18.9 in (320 to 480 mm) including a 6 to 8.6 in (153 to 218 mm) tail.

Diet: Two main feedings a day, one just after sunset and the other prior to dawn. Omnivores, but primarily eat grain, fruit, eggs, small animals. Will kill birds etc. Sub-adults minimum food needs 1.4 oz/day (55 cal/day) of high caloric food, adults need 2.8 oz/day (110 cal/day). Their need for nutritional balance mirrors those of humans (Fig. 1). They will eat pet feces and cockroaches. Require 0.7 to 1.4 fl oz (20 to 40 ml) of water per day.

Habitat: Rats can exist wherever water and humans are present. Prefer to nest near heat source, darkened, and cluttered areas.

Activity: Nocturnal/year round. They will move into homes when disturbed by road construction and flooding. Will adapt to avoid human activity. Home range 90 to 450 ft (27 to 137 m).

Behavior: Territorial. Dominant rats will push out subordinate rats (Fig. 2). Rats that are established in an area will be neophobic. It can take 2 weeks before they interact with an item introduced into their environment.

Procreation: Three to 12 litters per year. A litter consists of 4 to 7 young. Gestation ~22 days. Young wean in 10 to 15 days. Breeding less active during weather extremes (hot and cold).

Capabilities: Good climbers (not quite as good as Roof Rats). Dig subterranean dens. Can jump 15.75 in (40 cm) from floor to horizontal feeding surface. Since this finding was the maximum height that each of the rats tested could reach, clearly some individuals would likely be able to jump higher. Some rats travel 5 mi (8 km) round trip at night. Good swimmers.

Fig. 1. Tears (lower arrow) and food (upper arrow) outside garbage bags can signify rat feeding.

Symptoms

Rats rarely are seen unless numbers are great. Clients will complain about how food has been eaten but not completely.

Signs

Avg. Hole Size: It is customary to say a minimum 1 in (2.5 cm) or about the size of a quarter, however, recent research using 12 rats (different ages represented) found that rats needed 1.58 inch (40 mm) diameter hole for all 12 rats to be able to exit. Hole diameter averages 2 to 3 in (5 to 7.6 cm, Fig. 3). Bolt holes may be plugged to keep out cold air. Active holes are characterized by being smooth, grease marks, lack of cob webs, scratches in dirt, and hair. In soil, they will be located on the upper sides of slopes to reduce flooding risk.

Fig. 2. Posterior of this rat shows the scarring of numerous bite marks.

Fig. 3. Rat hole at the base of a shed.

Fig. 4. Rub marks by rats turning the corner.

Fig. 5. Rat trail network extending from bait station.

Access: Rats can climb, burrow and swim. I have removed a rat that came up a toilet. While rare, it can happen. Typically people will see holes along a foundation. They will be different than chipmunk in that they won't go straight down.

Damage to Structures: They tend to be found around areas with heat, like freezer compressors, electrical conduits, etc. Like any rodent they can chew wires and eat food. Beyond that the damage is usually minimal because people don't stand to have them around. I have seen them eat Camay® beauty soap.

Den hole. Rats dig holes into the ground around foundations and in flower beds. Den entrance often accompanied by 2 or more bolt holes that are hidden. Dens may extend to 12 to 18 in (30.5 to 45 cm) below the surface.

Runways. Look for grease marks that are 2.0 to 2.5 in (5 to 6.4 cm) wide. Grease marks are fresh when they still have a waxy layer (Fig. 4).

Damage to Lawn/Garden: Rats will feed on produce. Trails can scar grass (Fig. 5) and tunneling can undermine soil making it more vulnerable to erosion.

Damage to Pets & Livestock: Rats can kill birds, eggs, chicks, and rabbits. I once identified the culprit as a rat because a rat would have been the only animal able to fit through the chicken wire (weasels aren't common in my area so I didn't consider them). Rats will attack poultry. Prey will often be taken away and consumed under cover or in the den. Adult birds will have throat cut. Will kill more animals than it needs (similar to weasel).

Tree Bark Stripping: Mark A. McKee says bark stripping happens in Texas quite a bit to bios de ark trees (horse apple trees) and its cause is Neotoma (pack rats).

Tracks: One of the ways to distinguish mouse tracks from rat tracks (besides print size) is rats typically don't drag tails when foraging. Older rats are more likely to drag than younger rats.

Scat: Dark, cylindrical like a grain of rice but thicker and up to a ¾ in (19 mm) long and ¼-in (6.35 mm) in diameter (Fig. 6). Ends tend to be blunt. In heavy rat infested areas look for stains on floor which result from accumulated feces (Fig. 7) and urine. They deposit 20 to 50 scat/day.

Hair: Shed millions of them per year.

Sounds: Sometimes they can be heard in walls as they move, squeak, or fight.

Bite Marks: Rats will gnaw bones in search of fat and organic nutrients and thus will prefer fresh "meaty" bones not dry weathered bones preferred by gray squirrels. Gnaw marks will be 0.1 in (2.5 mm) wide. Incisors rate 5.5 on Moh's hardness scale. Can gnaw through wood, uncured cement, plastic, and more.

Associated Animals: Remove rats, and house mice will grow in numbers.

Fig. 6. Tubular rat scat next to the penny.

Fig. 7. Scat can occur in piles as this pile near a trash bin.

Health/Safety

Attacks: Rats have been known to bite children (Fig. 8). Typically around the face where smeared food is present. Leptospirosis, a bacterial infection, is commonly transmitted by rat bites, as is rat bite fever (Streptobacillary fever).

Fleas: Northern rat flea and Oriental rat flea. If you feel something crawling on you, it might not be your imagination. The Oriental rat flea was the vector for the Black Plague (*Yersinia pestis*) that killed millions in the Middle Ages and still kills today. Murine typhus also is transmitted by fleas.

Numerous diseases are associated with rats. Consult Corrigan (2011) for more information.

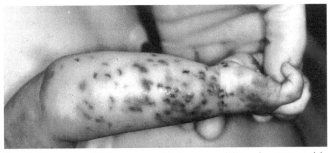

Fig. 8. The arm of this deceased infant was bitten by rats multiple times. Photo by William Jackson.

Resources

Thanks to the following for their information, Mark A. McKee, Mirko Barago, and Robert Corrigan.

Barnett, S. A. 2001. *The Story of Rats: Their Impact on Us, and Our Impact on Them.* Crows Nest, NSW: Allen & Unwin.

Corrigan, R. M. 2000. Using Liquid Rodenticide Baits. *Pest Control Technology.* (Aug):42-47.

Corrigan, R. M. 2001. *Rodent Control: A Practical Guide for Pest Management Professionals.* Cleveland, OH: GIE Media. 353 pp.

Corrigan, R. M. 2011. Rats and Mice in *Handbook of Pest Control: The Behavior, Life History, and Control of Household Pests* edited by A. Mallis et al. Mallis Handbook, LLC. 11-149 pp.

Harding, J. 1979. *An Animal Damage Identification Guide for Massachusetts.* Amherst, MA: Cooperative Extension Service, University of Massachusetts, SP-113.

Klippel, W. E. and J. A. Synstelien. 2007. Rodents as Taphonomic Agents: Bone-Gnawing by Brown Rats and Gray Squirrels. *J Forensic Sci,* 52:4(July 2007):1556-4029.

Pitt, W. C., R. T. Sugihara, L. C. Driscoll, and D. S. Vice. 2011. Physical and Behavioral Abilities of Commensal Rodents Related to the Design of Selective Rodenticide Bait Stations. *International Journal of Pest Management* 57:3(July-Sept):1-5.

Timm, R. M. "Noway Rats." in *Prevention and Control of Wildlife Damage.* Editors, S. E. Hygnstrom, R. M. Timm, G. E. Larson. 1994. University of Nebraska-Lincoln. 2 vols.

Whitaker, Jr. J. O. and W. J. Hamilton, Jr. 1998. *Mammals of the Eastern United States.* 3rd ed. Ithaca, NY: Comstock Publishing Associates.

Opossums *(Didelphia virginianus)*

Biology

Size: Weights range from 2 to 15 lbs (1 to 7 kg), and lengths from 14 to 20 in (37 to 45 cm), plus a 9 to 15 in (28 to 37 cm) tail.

Diet: Omnivores. They will eat bird seed, suet, carrion, grapes, etc.

Habitat: See skunk.

Activity: Nocturnal/year around but will den up for a few weeks in extremely cold weather (<20°F [-7°C]). Will use multiple dens. They are solitary animals.

Procreation: Mating occurs January to mid-July. It seems the farther the northern range of its habitat the earlier in the year the mating occurs. Mating may occur up to 3 times per year in southern regions. About 13 days after mating, females produce 5 to 13 young which they raise alone and carry with them (Marsupial trait). Young stay in pouch for 2 months. Young then remain with mother (usually riding on the mother's back) for an additional 6 to 7 weeks until weaned.

Capabilities: Capable climbers (Fig. 1). Tail is somewhat prehensile. They can run 7 mph (11.3 km/hr). As a defense mechanism, they can leak a skunk-like smelling fluid that is greenish-yellow in appearance.

Symptoms

Occasionally, owners will complain of a skunk odor. Often the odor, if present, won't be as strong as a skunk's would. Usually, this odor will be noticed during the winter months. One client, whose house by the lake was built on posts, complained of noises in the walls. It appeared the opossum crawled underneath the building and up the walls.

Signs

Avg. Hole Size: 3 to 5 in (7.6 to 12.7 cm). Skull width is 2.25 to 2.75 in (57 to 69 mm).

Access: Although opossums climb, I have yet to see them nesting in a building above ground level, i.e. attic, although other WCOs have seen this. They are poor diggers so they will usually take over a den abandoned by another animal, like a skunk or woodchuck. You will often find them under trailer houses, sheds and enclosed porches. Anywhere they can find a secluded spot to nest they will go. They also like to live in the insulation underneath the floor of trailer homes.

Damage to House: Opossums are not known for causing damage, just a lot of panic in people who think

Fig. 1. Opossums use fences for transport. Photo by Steve Stronk of Steve's Wildlife Control.

they are a white rat. Other than living under sheds, porches or trailer homes, most of your calls will arise because the owner left a door open to the shed or basement or some other typically enclosed structure. They have been known to die in the insulation underneath mobile homes. Odor can be a problem also. Sometimes people think they have skunks when in fact they have opossums.

I have received a report (including a photograph) of an opossum building a pile of grass in an attic in Virginia. The pile was similar to those created by starlings. The WCO claimed to have seen an opossum carrying grass. I have not received similar reports from others.

They feed on garbage and sometimes become trapped in garbage cans and fall into window wells (Fig. 2).

Fig. 2. Opossum trapped in a window well.

Damage to Lawn/Garden: They will eat birdseed and will spook homeowners who see them feeding off the seed that falls to the ground. They also have been known to eat grapes. They like ripe fruit and will forage beneath fruit drops. Corn will be eaten during the milk stage.

Damage to Pets & Livestock: Has been known to raid poultry barns. Birds will look mauled. Intestines removed from anus. Smashes eggs. They carry a parasite harmful to horses.

Tracks: Their tracks show 5 toes on the front foot and 5 toes on the rear, including the opposable thumb. The thumb lacks a claw.

The tracks nearly overlap each other in the alternating pattern that is typical of a walking opossum (Fig. 3a,b). The opposable thumb is very prominent in some of these tracks.

Scat: Usually not found. But if it is it will be catlike in that it will be pointed on the ends and about 1 to 3 in (2.5 to 7.5 cm) long. (Fig. 4.).

Hair: Mix of gray, white, and black hair. Hairs on belly area can be white to yellow.

Sounds: Typically silent. Will hiss, click teeth, and/or growl when threatened.

Bite Marks: Has been known to raid poultry barns. Look for numerous punctures in prey.

Associated Animals: Opossums are prey for raptors and carnivores.

Direction of travel

Stride: 6 to 10 inches
Front: 1½" L × 2" W
Hind: 2½" L × 2½ W

Fig. 3b. Opossum walking trail. Images by Kim A. Cabrera of Beartracker's Animal Tracks Den.

Health/Safety

Frightened Opossum: Clients may complain of an opossum (sometimes calling them a big white rat) that "won't leave." Opossums will run when they feel safe enough. Otherwise they hunker down and bare their teeth (most of any animal in North America; Fig. 5) or go into a catatonic state. Clients should leave them alone (keep pets and children away) for 24 hours (assuming no one was bitten). Healthy opossums will leave when they feel safe.

Fig. 3a. Opossum tracks (front and rear) in sand. Front foot at top and right hind foot on the bottom. The hind print partially covers the front one. Photo by Kim A. Cabrera of Bear Tracker's Animal Tracks Den.

Fig. 4.Opossum scat. Photo by Tom Olander.

Rabies: Opossums do contract rabies. However, it takes an estimated 10,000 times more virus to infect them.

Equine Protozoal Myeloencephalitis: EPM is a serious disease that is carried by opossums and shed through their feces. It in infects horses and can lead to their death.

Resources

Thanks to information from Dallas Virchow.

Blanton. J.D., D. Palmer, K. A. Christian, and C. E. Rupprecht. 2008. Public Veterinary Medicine: Rabies surveillance in the United States during 2007. *JAVMA*, 233:6 (Sept. 15):884-897.

Harding, J. 1979. *An Animal Damage Identification Guide for Massachusetts*. Amherst, MA: Cooperative Extension Service, University of Massachusetts, SP-113.

Link, R. 2004. *Living with Wildlife in the Pacific Northwest*. Seattle, WA: Univ. of Washington Press.

Merck Veterinary Manual. 2011. Equine Protozoal Myeloencephalitis. Whitehouse Station, NJ: Merck Sharp & Dohme Corp., Inc. http://www.merckvetmanual.com/mvm/index.jsp?cfile=htm/bc/101000.htm visited December 31, 2011.

Jackson, J. J. "Opossums." in *Prevention and Control of Wildlife Damage*. Editors, S. E. Hygnstrom, R. M. Timm, G. E. Larson. 1994. University of Nebraska-Lincoln. 2 vols.

Reid, F. A. 2006. *Mammals of North America*. Peterson Field Guides. 4th ed. NY, NY: Houghton Mifflin.

Schwartz, C. and E. Schwartz. 1981. *The Wild Mammals of Missouri*. University of Missouri Press and Missouri Department of Conservation.

Fig. 5. Opossum baring its teeth. (Do not pick up opossums with your hands.)

Pigeons *(Columba livia)*

Biology

Size: 10 to 16 oz. (284 to 454 g) and average 11 in (28 cm) in length and a wingspan of 28 in (71 cm).

Diet: Grains, seeds, human food scraps and bread. Eat 1 to 2 oz (28 to 57 g) per day and drink 1 oz/day of water. They love distiller's grain and Spanish peanuts. One publication says that "100 feeding pigeons will eat about 7 to 8 pounds (15 to 18 kg) of whole corn per day."

Habitat: Protected ledges and roof tops, particularly sides with good sun exposure. Tend to select sites between the second and fifth floors. Resides in human-impacted areas.

Activity: Diurnal/year round.

Procreation: Pigeons are monogamous. They can mate year around providing it's above freezing. Mating activity peaks in spring and fall. One to 2 eggs are laid 8 to 12 days after mating. Females incubate them for 17 to

Fig. 1. Pigeon nest with 2 eggs.

Fig. 2. Pigeons like to nest under dormer overhangs. Arrows to scat.

19 days. Young fledge in 4 to 6 weeks. Males help construct and guard nests. Nests are primitive piles of sticks (Fig. 1, sometimes consisting entirely of dried droppings) on ledges protected from rain. Another clutch of eggs may be laid before the previous young leave the nest.

Capabilities: Outstanding fliers. Strong homing ability and fidelity to nesting sites. Can reach flight speeds of 100 mph (161 km/h).

Symptoms

People may complain of mites or flu like symptoms. (There is a debate regarding the danger pigeon droppings have for people. Some contend that pigeon droppings around air-conditioning vents can cause people to be sick).

Signs

Avg. Hole Size: Uncertain. Most of the instances when pigeons were entering buildings the access was through an open/broken window. I would suggest a minimum of 2 × 2 in (5 × 5 cm).

Access: Typically open/broken window, vent, chimney flue.

Damage to Structures: Can deface structures with feces and feathers (Fig. 2).

Fecal contamination can be enormous. These birds also carry a variety of parasites that may enter buildings where they have resided for a long time. Tend to nest in the vowels of lettered signs. Will roost/loaf on structures with sun exposure (Fig. 3).

Damage to Lawn/Garden: Typically none but excrement may bother some landowners.

Tracks: Look trident like. ~2.25 inches in length. Typically not found in urban areas due to the volume of asphalt and concrete (Fig. 4).

Scat: White/gray (Fig. 5). It can be piled very high and it hardens. Rex Helton of A-1 Wildlife Services in Indiana who raises white homers estimates "that if a pigeon ate from 2 to 4 oz. (57 to 113 g) of grain per day average (¼ to ½ cup; 0.06 to 0.12 ltr), plus drank water twice daily, the droppings could be up to 2 oz. (57 g) (or what you might visualize as a tablespoonful). One thing to remember when calculating weight of bird droppings, most of the weight is water or moisture. When allowed to dry, grain fed pigeon waste is quite light." Another publication says a single pigeon excretes 25 lbs (11.3 kg) of feces per year.

Fig. 3. Pigeons loafing on 5th floor ledge.

Feathers: Gray with black tip (Fig. 6).

Sounds: Clicking sound in flight from the tips of their wings touching. Will coo.

Bite Marks: N/A.

Associated Animals: Birds of prey, particularly falcons feed on pigeons.

Fig. 4. Pigeon track.

Health/Safety

Droppings: Pigeon droppings can be a danger simply by their weight. While we are not aware of any definitive study on the average weight of pigeon droppings, we provide this information for comparison purposes only. Doug Hulik says, "I have not performed an exhaustive study of lbs/ft³ and many variables could change the findings (moisture, nesting material, dead birds, grub count, etc). On the last pigeon job a bell tower contained approx 80 ft³ (24.4 m³) with a weight of 1440 lbs (653 kg), so the math indicates a weight of 18 lbs/ft³. I have seen much worse "loading" of similar areas."

Weight of Droppings. Dave LaBellas e-mailed me with the following, "Regarding information recently posted on your website, Doug Hulik is certainly correct in that many variables can worsen the numbers, or loadings of pigeon weight droppings. I have additional but very useful information that should be mentioned on your website. I have spoken to some environmental specialists in this line of work and have found that the density of wet pigeon droppings can be similar to that of water (which is 62.4 lb/ft³ [8.51 kg/m³]), and that a number of 60 to 65 lbs/ft³ (8.18 to 8.86 kg/m³) for wet pigeon droppings is a "convenient and useful estimate" to use. I am involved in a job to clear wet pigeon droppings from an enclosed area that contains feathers, debris, carcasses, etc., and have found on that the debris is very heavy, similar in density to that of mud."

Fig. 5. Pigeon droppings under a bridge.

Fig. 6. Feather from a pigeon.

Fig. 7. Photo courtesy of Alan Huot of www.wildlifecontrolsupplies.com

Diseases: Pigeons are implicated in a number of diseases, including pigeon ornithosis, encephalitis, Newcastle disease, cryptococcosis, toxoplasmosis, and salmonella food poisoning.

Histoplasmosis: Histoplasmosis is caused by exposure (typically through respiration) to fungal spores that are growing in the nitrogen rich droppings deposited by pigeons. It is essential that proper respiratory and vision protection be worn during inspections attic inspections. Check air exchange areas too for bird droppings (Fig. 7).

Mites: Northern fowl mite has been associated with infestations of this bird.

Resources

Would like to thank Alan Huot, Bird Barrier, Rex Helton, and Doug Hulik for some of the information used in this document.

Blechman, A.D. 2006. *Pigeons: The Fascinating Saga of the World's Most Revered and Reviled Bird.* NY: Grove Press.

McNeely, S. 2011. Vertebrate Pests in *Handbook of Pest Control: The Behavior , Life History, and Control of Household Pests* edited by A. Mallis et al. Mallis Handbook, LLC. 1119-1189 pp.

Sibley, D. A. 2000. *The Sibley Guide to Birds.* NY, NY: Alfred A. Knopf.

Williams, D. E. and R. M. Corrigan. "Pigeons." in *Prevention and Control of Wildlife Damage.* Editors, S. E. Hygnstrom, R. M. Timm, G. E. Larson. 1994. University of Nebraska-Lincoln. 2 vols.

Pocket Gophers

Plains Pocket Gopher (*Geomys bursarius*) **PP**
Northern Pocket Gopher (*Thomomys talpoides*) **NP**
Unless otherwise noted, all information applies to both species.

The plains pocket gopher has been divided into 3 species. From a damage identification perspective, differences between the species are not significant enough to merit individual attention.

Biology

Size: **PP** is the largest pocket gopher in North America weighing 4.5 to 13.5 oz (128 to 380 g). Head and body is 6.3 to 8.6 in (160 to 225 mm) in length. The tail is 2 to 4.8 in (50 to 121 mm) tail.

NP weighs 2 to 5.5 oz (60 to 160 g). Head and body can is 4.9 to 7.9 in (125 to 200 mm) in length. Tail is 1.6 to 3 in (40 to 75 mm) in length. Males are much larger than females.

Diet: Herbivores, feeding on roots of grasses, forbs, and alfalfa. They cache food in late fall which can contain large amounts of root fragments such as dandelion, alfalfa, and others. They will feed on vegetables and tree roots. They do not prefer seeds and grains. **NP.** Stem and leaf material is more important in summer. **NP** eat ~3.5 oz (100 g) of fresh plants daily.

Habitat: Grasslands and disturbed woods with drained soils, moist enough to hold tunnel shape. They avoid soils containing 10% or more of rocks in the top 8 in (20 cm) of soil.

Activity: Being fossorial, active any-time of day and year round. Solitary, except during mating or when females raise young. A single pocket gopher tunnel system can extend up to 30 yds (27 m) across and goes below

Fig. 1. Plains pocket gopher mound. Pen pointing to plugged hole.

the frost line. They can feed on plants below ground, pull plants into their tunnels from below, or come to the surface and pull plants into their burrows. Damage on surface plants may be as high as 10 feet (3 m) above ground.

Procreation: Spring. Males do not help rear young. **PP.** Females give birth to 3 to 4 young. **NP.** Females give birth to 3 to 9 young once or twice a year. Nesting chamber may be 12 in (30 cm) below the surface. Young disperse in mid-June which ends in late summer. Mound building increases during this time. During dispersal, young gophers travel above ground, sometimes covering distances exceeding 67 yds (60 m).

Capabilities: Able to move a great quantity of soil yearly. **PP** can move up to 2000 lbs (907 kg) of soil a year. Can create up to 200 mounds a year. **NP** can dig at a rate of 1.6 in (4 cm) per minute.

Symptoms

1. Reduction in crop production, particularly in non-irrigated land.
2. If underground cables or pipes are present, the loss of their use.

Signs

Avg. Hole Size: Holes typically are plugged (Fig. 1). Tunnels below ground are 2.5 to 3.5 in (6.4 to 8.9 cm) in diameter. **PP** range of skull width is 0.95 to 1.4 in (24.2 to 36.3 mm). **NP** range of skull width is 0.71 to 0.97 in (18.04 to 24.7 mm). Soil plugs can secure 1.2 to 3.1 in (3 to 8 cm) diameter holes.

Access: Typically don't enter homes. Young that disperse in late summer, will seek out a territory of their own by surface excursions.

Damage to Structures: None to the structure specifically, however, pocket gophers damage to underground pipes, underground wires, and percolation of the soil could impact a structure with less than rigorous foundation.

Damage to Lawn/Garden: Can be extensive. Pocket gophers kill plants by eating roots (Figs. 2a,b,c) and by burying plants with the excavated dirt (Fig. 3). They also will dig through snow (Fig. 4).

PP activity reduced yield on rangelands by 21% to 49%. Dryland alfalfa yields were reduced up to 46%. Irrigated alfalfa yields were reduced up to 35%. Reduction of up to 30% have been reported for hay meadows.

NP activity may reduce the annual productivity of hay fields by as much as 25%.

Fig. 2a. Alfalfa plant damaged by a Plains pocket gopher. Note tap root at right is cut at an angle.

Fig. 2b. The roots of these chicory plants damaged by Plains pocket gopher. Photo by Dallas Virchow.

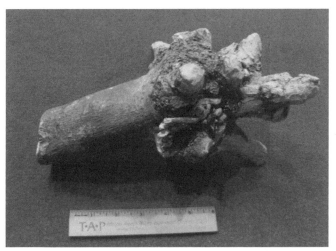

Fig. 2c. Tree roots damaged by a Plains pocket gopher.

Consult the mole chapter for information on how to distinguish mole activity from that of pocket gopher.

Damage to Pets & Livestock: They do not damage livestock and pets. However, mounds may interfere with animal movement.

Fig. 3. Mounds of the Northern pocket gopher. Photo by Gilbert Proulx of Alpha Wildlife Research and Management.

Fig. 4. Pocket gophers sometimes dig tunnels through snow and pack them with soil. These tunnels appear as soil casts when the snow melts. Photo by Gilbert Proulx.

Tracks: Rarely ever seen due to their subterranean activity. **PP** front track is 1.5 to 1.6 in (3.8 to 4.1 cm) in length and 1 in (2.5 cm) in width. Rear track is 1.12 to 1.25 in (2.9 to 3.2 cm) in length and 1.12 and 1.25 in (2.9 to 3.2 cm) in width. **NP** front track is $7/8$ to 1. (2.2 to 3.3

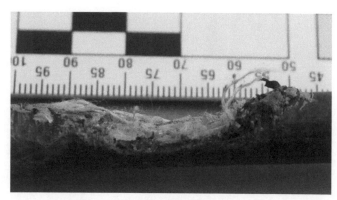

Fig. 5. Underground fiber optic cable gnawed on by a Plains pocket gopher.

Fig. 6. Plains pocket gopher mound in the middle of a gravel road.

cm) in length and $^7/_{16}$ to ½ in (1.1 to 1.3 cm) in width. Rear track is $^5/_8$ to $^7/_8$ in (1.6 to 2.2 cm) in length and $^7/_{16}$ to $^{11}/_{16}$ in (1.1 to 1.7 cm) in width.

Feces: Rarely found.

Hair: Rarely found. Interestingly, despite their subterranean life, their fur is remarkably clean. Fur tends to match the color of the soil.

Sounds: They can click their teeth when angry and cry when injured.

Bite Marks: Can appear similar to other rodents.

Associated Animals: Badgers will hunt pocket gophers and can create large excavations as they dig in their attempt to capture them.

Health/Safety

Pocket gophers can cause serious damage to underground pipes and cables (Fig. 5). Since they can create a gap between upper and lower incisors up to 1 in (2.5 cm)

it is believed that they cannot gnaw on a pipe wider than 2.9 in (7.4 cm) as they would be unable to gain purchase.

The burrowing of pocket gophers also can undermine roads (Fig. 6) and levees.

Due to their fossorial activity, pocket gophers are not known to be a significant disease threat to humans.

Resources

I would like to thank Scott E. Hygnstrom and Gilbert Proulx for the information they provided.

Case, R. M. and B. A. Jasch. "Pocket Gophers." in *Prevention and Control of Wildlife Damage*. Editors, Scott E. Hygnstrom, Robert M. Timm, Gary E. Larson. 1994. University of Nebraska-Lincoln. 2 vols.

Elbroch, M. 2003. *Mammal Tracks and Sign: A Guide to North American Species*. Mechanicsburg, PA: Stackpole Books.

Elbroch, M. 2006. *Animal Skulls: A Guide to North American Species*. Mechanicsburg, PA: Stackpole Books.

Reid, F. A. 2006. *Mammals of North America*. 4th ed. Peterson Field Guides. NY, NY: Houghton Mifflin Co.

Proulx, G. 2002. The Pocket Gopher I: Knowing the Species. *Wildlife Control Technology*, (Jan/Feb):np

Raccoons *(Procyon lotor)*

Biology:

Size: Male raccoons weigh 14.9 lbs (6.76 kg) and females 13.1 lbs (5.94 kg, weights of Missouri raccoons). Northern raccoons are larger than southern. Total length (body + tail) of males is 25 to 37 in (634 to 950 mm) and females is 24 to 36 in (603 to 909 mm). Tail length of males is 7.9 to 16 in (200 to 405) and females is 7.6 to 13.4 in (192 to 340 mm). Weight may drop 50% over winter.

Diet: True omnivores. They will eat whatever is available, provided they can kill it, including but not limited to insects, amphibians, reptiles, crayfish, fish, small birds, and mammals.

Habitat: All over. Raccoons can be found in wooded and urban environments. They are highly adaptable. Prefer to live near water. They live in trees, chimneys, sewers, attics, under sheds and porches etc.

Activity: Nocturnal/year round. Will den up during extreme cold. Research has revealed their movements tend to occur at various times, however, movement to feeding sites often happens between 1600 to 2000 hrs, activity at feeding sites between 2000 to 2400 hrs, and has activity at minor feeding sites 2400 to 0300 hrs. Several raccoons (up to 23) may den together during the winter.

Procreation: Mating occurs once a year in January and February in northern regions and February to early August in northern Florida. Females that lose a litter will re-mate. Note that WCOs have reported finding young in every month of the year. Three to 5 young are born 65 days later. Young remain with mother for 7 weeks and go solo in 12. The father does not assist in raising the young. In fact, if a male finds young raccoons, he will eat them.

Capabilities: Raccoons have an incredible ability to climb (Fig. 1). They have been known to climb, downspouts, steel I-beams (according to Wayne A. Langman), cables, ropes, and corners of buildings.

Symptoms

A. Attic: Owners will complain of something heavy in the attic that moves during early evening and early morning.

B. Chimney: When present, owners complain of bird-like chirping noises emanating from fireplace. This will occur during the spring months when the young are born.

Signs

Avg. Hole Size: Skull width is 2.4 to 3.5 in (60.2 to 89.1) for males, and 2.3 to 3.2 in (58.3 to 81.2 mm) for females. Generally, raccoons need a 4 in (102 mm) diameter hole to enter a structure.

Damage to Structures: Raccoons will typically enter a building somewhere high at least 1 floor off the ground. Attic vents are most common entry ways. Look for bends in attic vent louvers (Fig. 2). You also will find dark smudge marks made by the animal's body oils rubbing off on the wood/metal. Smudge marks on down spouts (Fig. 3). Sometimes climbing is so frequent scratches on wood will give positive sign of raccoon (Fig. 4). If an overhanging tree branch is at least 1 in (2.5 cm) in diameter, then that will be the way the raccoon accesses the building. Look for scratch marks on the tree. During warmer months they have been known to live under porches.

Fig. 1. Female raccoon hanging on the side of a brick chimney.

Fig. 2. Bent louvers reveal raccoon entry.

Fig. 3. Note black smudge marks on the downspout indicating raccoon climbing.

Fig. 4. Climbing by raccoons was so great that the paint wore off.

Don't forget chimney flues. Females especially like to raise young in the chimney smoke chambers. Look for black smudges on the flue tile. Also pay attention to cob webs. If they are present, then you can be reasonably assured that no raccoon has entered that flue. Sometimes even looking down the flue with a light will reveal eyes staring back.

Raccoons damage houses by creating an entrance. They have been known to damage roofing tiles (Fig. 5).

Fig. 5. Raccoon damage to roof. Photo by John Consolini.

They will mash down insulation as they walk around the attic. Occasionally they will enter a building though the shingled roof. Usually there is no damage to the flue tile when entering through the chimney.

Damage to Lawn/Garden: Raccoon like grubs (and worms) as much as skunks do. However, raccoons tend to peel the sod off the soil to get at the grubs. When sod is rolled out, raccoons will unroll it to find invertebrates. Skunks, by contrast, just dig a hole where the grub is.

Raccoons sometimes create trails in grass (Fig. 7).

Fish Ponds: Raccoons can and do raid fish ponds. This damage will generally occur during the night and you may notice damage to the plants caused by the raccoon's struggle to get the fish. If the fish disappear during the daylight hours, think of herons, especially if there is no damage to plant life.

Corn. Eaten just prior to harvest. Ears will be peeled and gnawed (Figs. 8a,b). Sweet corn is a special favorite. Stalks will be bent every which way (Fig. 8c).

Damage to Pets & Livestock: Raccoons will predate on geese and other birds. Typically, they will tear the animals right near where the prey was captured (Source Bob Noonan). Heads will be eaten and crop and

Fig. 6. Raccoon damage to turf. Photo by Dave Varner.

breast torn. Eggs will be smashed. Raccoons will reach through wire cages and pull animals through the cage.

Tracks: All feet have 5 toes but they don't always show. The front print (Fig. 9) is 1.75 to 3.12 in (4.4 to 7.9 cm) in length and 1.5 to 3.25 in (3.8 to 8.3 cm) in width. Rear foot is 2.12 to 3.88 in (5.4 to 10.2 cm) in length and 1.5 to 2.6 in (3.8 to 6.7 cm) in width.

Fig. 7. Sometimes raccoon traffic is so great a trail is left in the grass. Upper arrow points to where raccoon entered structure.

Scat: Typically dark, tubular 2.75 to 5.9 in (7 to 15 cm) long and ¾ in (2 cm) in width with blunt ends and in small sections. Look for evidence of raccoon food particles in feces such as hairs, corn, mulberry seeds etc. (Fig. 11). One researcher found hair in raccoon scat throughout the year. The undigested material in droppings will

Fig. 8a. Raccoon damage. Photo by Brian MacGowan of Purdue University.

Fig. 8b. Raccoon damage to corn. Photo by Brian MacGowan of Purdue University.

Fig. 8c. Stalks will be bent in different directions.

Fig. 9. Tracks of front paw.

Fig. 10. Raccoon toilette in an attic. Photo by Reginald Murray, Oklahoma Wildlife Control, LLC.

often mirror seasonal foods (Be careful when handling feces). They commonly create toilet areas, which may be found inside (Fig. 11) or outside the house. Often raccoons living in attics will defecate on the roof before entering the home. You will find the feces on the flat portions or in the valley between 2 roofs. Otherwise, the feces may be found inside the attic usually well away from the nesting area. The toilet areas also may be identified by the brown staining on the ceiling. Be sure to take appropriate precautions when in close proximity to these toilets.

Hair: Color ranges from brown to black to gray.

Sounds: Young can chatter in a manner that owners think that they are birds. Mating adults can screech in a spine-tingling manner. Growls occur when caught in catch-pole. Mothers call to young with low grumbling purr.

Bite Marks: Raccoons have sharp pointed teeth (Figs. 13a,b). So when they bite you will see definite indentures in the item. In contrast, rodents have 4 incisors. You will see items scraped more than bitten with a ridge line (which is the gap between the front teeth) noticeable.

Associated Animals: Will use abandoned dens of skunks and woodchucks. Will eat pet food.

Health/Safety

Rabies: Raccoons are a primary vector of rabies.

Baylisascaris procyonis: Raccoon feces can harbor eggs of *Baylisascaris procyonis* a rather dangerous roundworm. To learn more visit http://cdc.gov .

Toxoplasmosis: Can carry Toxoplasmosis.

Fig. 11. Raccoon scat with seeds. Photo by Bob Thwaites.

Fig. 12. Sometimes raccoon hair can be found at squeeze points.

Fig. 13a. Bite marks on a corn stalk. Photo by Brian MacGowan of Purdue University.

Fig. 13b. Wood bitten by a raccoon. Note the straightness of punctures. Raccoon teeth are straight not curved like other carnivores.

Resources

Some material was provided by Wayne A. Langman and Bob Noonan.

Boggess, E. K. "Raccoons." in *Prevention and Control of Wildlife Damage.* Editors, S. E. Hygnstrom, R. M. Timm, G. E. Larson. 1994. University of Nebraska-Lincoln. 2 vols.

Dubey, J. P., N. Sundar, C. A. Nolden, M. D. Samuel, G. V. Velmurugan, L. A. Bandini, O.C.H. Kwok, B. Bodenstein, and C. Su. 2007. Characterization of *Toxoplasma gondii* from Raccoons (*Procyon lotor*), Coyotes (*Canis latrans*), and Striped Skunks *(Mephitis mephitis)* in Wisconsin Identified Several Atypical Genotypes. *The Journal of Parasitology.* 93:6(Dec):1524-1527.

Elbroch, M. 2003. *Mammal Tracks and Sign: A Guide to North American Species.* Mechanicsburg, PA: Stackpole Books.

Gavin, P. J. et al. 2005. *Baylisascaris. Clinical Micro Reviews* 18 (Oct):703-718.

Harding, J. 1979. *An Animal Damage Identification Guide for Massachusetts.* Amherst, MA: Cooperative Extension Service, University of Massachusetts, SP-113.

Henner-Lotze, J. and S. Anderson. 1979. *Procyon lotor. Mammalian Species* 119(Jun):1-8.

Huxoll, C. M., T. A. Messmer, and M. Conover. 2010. *Raccoons.* Wildlife Damage Management Series. Utah State University Cooperative Extension. (Dec):1-5.

Link, R. 2004. *Living with Wildlife in the Pacific Northwest.* Seattle, WA: Univ. of Washington Press.

Lotze, J-H. and S. Anderson. 1979. *Procyon lotor. Mammalian Species,* No. 119, (Jun. 8):1-8.

Schwartz, C. and E. Schwartz. 1981. *The Wild Mammals of Missouri.* University of Missouri Press and Missouri Department of Conservation.

Red Squirrels (*Tamiasciurus hudsonicus*)

Biology

Size: Reds weight 5 to 11 oz (135 to 314 g) and total length (body + tail) is 11 to 14 in (280 to 340 mm) with a tail length of 4 to 6 in (100 to 152 mm). Males are a little heavier than females. They are approximately half the size of a gray squirrel.

Diet: They eat all sorts of grasses, flower buds, nuts, berries, fungi (including fly agaric mushroom (*Amanita muscaria*), insects, snails, young rabbits, birds, bird eggs, and deer mice. Reds will snip the buds of young balsam fir trees, particularly the terminal shoot. Need to consume about 117 Kcal/day. Look for piles of debris below favorite feeding areas.

Habitat: Reds tend to live in areas forested with evergreen trees. Seed producing trees must be present. I have found them to be more common in the suburbs rather than in urban areas.

Activity: Diurnal/Year around. Active during the first 2 hours after sunrise and just before sunset. Often rest in the afternoon. Den up during harsh weather and when temperature dips below -13°F (-25°C). Can construct 3 kinds of nests: cavity nests, leaf nests (usually 15 ft (4.6 m) off the ground and 12 in (31 cm) in diameter), and ground nests. Most nests are within 98 ft (30 m) of food caches.

Procreation: Females become sexually mature at 1 year old and can have 2 litters a year. Mating occurs in late February to early April/March and sometimes in June/July. Four to 5 young born in ~31 to 35 days. Young wean in 5 to 7 weeks.

Behavior: Generally solitary, but will share nests. Can be strongly territorial, particularly when defending areas containing food caches. Will drop several cones to the ground before caching.

Capabilities: Can jump 10 ft (3 m) horizontally and 30 ft (9 m) to the ground without injury. Appears to be able to survive without access to free water.

Symptoms

Similar to that of grays. The owner should be able to tell you whether red squirrels live in the area. But don't bet on this. I have done a job where the client didn't know she had red squirrels. Noises in basement also can be a symptom because reds will enter buildings at ground level.

Signs

Avg. Hole Size: ¾ to 1½ in (1.9 to 3.2 cm). Skull width averages 1.1 in (28.19 mm). Reds will typically enter a building at eaves and soffits. Pay special attention to vents because unlike grays, reds will be small enough to pass through the slates without damaging them (Fig. 1). Look closely for the oily smudge mark that will develop as they squeeze through. Pay special attention to houses with stone foundations. Reds will enter the building at ground level through the gaps.

Damage to House: Reds have a tendency to explore more areas of a house than a gray will. So don't be surprised if you are investigating areas some distance from the entry hole. Try to find their food cache. It may be in the attic (Fig. 2). You may find the cache in the gutter. I have removed 10 lbs (4.5 kg) worth of cones from 1 gutter.

Damage to Lawn/Garden: Trees: They will puncture maple trees or exploit the punctures created by other animals to consume the crystallized sugar. Research has shown they will bite into tree trunks 1.6 to 6 in (4 to 15 cm) in diameter at breast height (Fig. 3) or an upright branch to expose the sap carrying vessels.

Reds don't have the jaw power of their larger cousins the grays. Nor would they need as large of an open-

Fig. 1. Holes in the mosquito netting made by red squirrels.

Fig. 2. Arrow points to a cache of pine cones.

ing to get to the seeds. Horse chestnut seeds have been gnawed down in smaller sections (Fig. 4). They will clip pine cones to the string core making them look like a pinecone parachute or thin spindle.

Buds & Twigs: Prefer to clip conifers with large buds. Following species are preferred—Scotch Pine, Norway Spruce, White Pine, and European Larch. Bark stripping occurs when alternative foods are unavailable.

Gardens: Can remove flower buds.

Damage to Pets & Livestock: Reds prey rather carnivorous. They do prey on small animals, including birds, chicks, eggs, and mice.

Tracks: Four toes on front foot and 5 on rear. Front foot is 1 to 1.25 in (2.5 to 3.2 cm) in length and $^9/_{16}$ to 1 in (1.4 to 2.5 cm) in width. Rear foot is $^7/_8$ to 2.25 (2.2 to 5.7 cm) in length and $^5/_8$ to 1.12 in (1.6 to 2.9 cm) in width.

Scat: Will be hard to identify because they will be similar to that of a mouse. One trapper has noted that their feces are round on one end and pointed on the other. Their feces are also about the size of a grain of rice.

Hair: Tips of tail hair is rusty or silvery in coloration.

Sounds: The chirp signals predators in the area, the rattle to defend territory, a screech call (used alone or in sequence with rattles); a growl by females when a male approaches or during aggressive territorial defense, a buzz call used by males encountering females, a threat call is used show host will defend territory, and that the rattle call is used in mating by males, and the squeak and buzz calls, used by young to mother.

Bite Marks: 0.01 inch tooth mark. Others say the grooves are larger at 2 mm (0.08 inches).

Associated Animals: They are prey to many predators.

Fig. 4. Horse chestnut seeds cut by a red squirrel.

Health/Safety

Not known as specific health threats to human interests. However, like many wildlife species, they can carry ectoparasites that can pose risks to humans.

Resources

Elbroch, M. 2003. *Mammal Tracks and Sign: A Guide to North American Species.* Mechanicsburg, PA: Stackpole Books.

Harding, J. 1979. *An Animal Damage Identification Guide for Massachusetts.* Amherst, MA: Cooperative Extension Service, University of Massachusetts, SP-113.

Heinrich, Bernd. 1992. Maple Sugaring by Red Squirrels. *Journal of Mammalogy,* 73.1(Feb):51-54.

Leconti, K. M. and D. J. Decker. 1987. Red Squirrel. Ithaca, NY: Cornell University, No. 31. 1-11 pp.

Lindsay, S. L. 1987. Geographic Size and Non-Size Variation in Rocky Mountain *Tamiasciurus hudsonicus*: Significance in Relation to Allen's Rule and Vicariant Biogeography. *Journal of Mammalogy,* 68:1(Feb), pp. 39-48.

Jackson, J. J. "Tree Squirrels." in *Prevention and Control of Wildlife Damage.* Editors, S. E. Hygnstrom, R. M. Timm, G. E. Larson. 1994. University of Nebraska-Lincoln. 2 vols.

Koprowski, J. L. 1994. Sciurus carolinensis. *Mammalian Species,* No. 480, (Dec. 2):1-9.

Koprowski, J. L. 1994. Sciurus niger. *Mammalian Species,* No. 479, (Dec. 2):1-9.

Rezendes, P. 1992. *Tracking and the Art of Seeing: How to Read Animal Tracks and Sign.* Charlotte, VT: Camden House Publishing, Inc.

Steele, M. A. 1998. Tamiasciurus hudsonicus. *Mammalian Species,* No. 586, (Jun. 1):1-9.

Fig. 3. Cut by red squirrel. Photo by Rod Gehan.

Shrews *(Sorex* spp.)

The number of species in this order is enormous. I have endeavored to generalize the information as much as possible.

Biology

Size: Shrews (Fig. 1) range from ~0.1 to $^3/_5$ oz (2 to 16 g) in weight and 2¾ to 6 in (7 to 15 cm) in length.

Diet: Various insects, slugs, worms, snails, and other invertebrates. Some may predate on bird eggs, mice, amphibians, and other shrews. They have a voracious appetite, eating every 3 to 4 hours.

Habitat: Prefer moist environments (e.g. mulch, leaf litter, etc.) with abundant insects, slugs, worms, and other invertebrates.

Activity: Usually nocturnal. Active year round.

Procreation: Several litters of 1 to 6 young per year from March to April. Gestation may last 23 days. Young weaned at 20 days. Dens dug up to 9 in (23 cm) in the ground. Holes are ¾ in (19 mm) wide.

Capabilities: In loose ground litter may burrow 3 feet in 15 sec. Eyesight is thought to be poor. Rarely jump. Superb abilities in hearing, touch, and smell. Some species can climb. Some can swim.

Symptoms

Owners will complain of odor like a "wet cat" and finding droppings and hard-to-catch mice.

Signs

Avg. Hole Size: Likely similar to house mouse 3/8 in (9 mm) in diameter or greater. They will utilize mole and vole tunnels also.

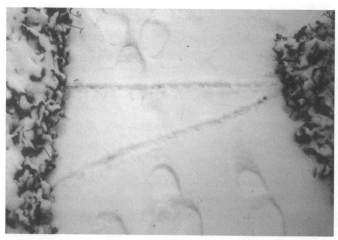

Fig. 2. Two shrew trails in the snow. Scale adult human footprint. Photo by William Jackson.

Access: They may gain entry into buildings at ground level, such as underneath garage doors or foundation cracks.

Damage to Structures: Damage is limited to odor and latrines.

Damage to Lawn/Garden: Trails through bark mulch which is typically avoided by voles. Mulch may have a ruffled look from the burrowing of shrews. Some will consume tree seeds.

Damage to Pets & Livestock: A few species may predate on fish eggs. Others have been known to enter bee hives and feed on larvae.

Tracks: All feet about the same size. Each foot has 5 claws. Trails may be seen in snow when they travel over non-vegetated areas (Fig. 2).

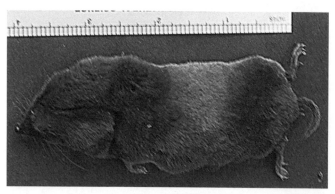

Fig. 1. Short-tailed shrew.

Fig. 3. Shrew scat. Photo by Richard Fuller of Old Saybrook, CT.

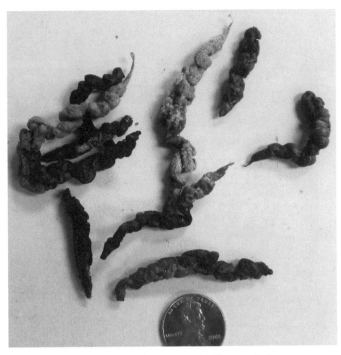

Fig. 4. Shrew scat. Photo by George Williams of ehspest.com

Scat: Tends to be piled (Fig. 3). Often has a corkscrew shape. (Fig. 4). Will smell.

Hair: Does have guard hairs.

Sounds: Great diversity of sounds from the audible to the ultrasonic.

Bite Marks: Some shrews have venomous bites.

Associated Animals: Will eat the heads of trapped mice. Prey for raptors. Most mammals don't eat them, possibly due to the musky odor they release. House cats are a major predator of shrews, but are reported to avoid eating them.

Health/Safety

Pneumocystis carinii: Cyst formations of the fungal parasite (*Pneumocystic carinii*) were found in various shrews in southern California.

Resources

Acknowledgements: Some of the information on this species was gained from Rick Shadel.

French, T. W. 1980. Natural History of the Southeastern Shrew, *Sorex longirostris* Bachman. *American Midland Naturalist*, 104:1 (July):13-31.

Laakkonen, J., R. N. Fisher, and T. J. Case. 2001. Pneumocystosis in Wild Small Mammals from California. *Journal of Wildlife Diseases*, 37(2):408–412.

Link, R. 2004. *Living with Wildlife in the Pacific Northwest*. Seattle, WA: Univ. of Washington Press.

Lund, E. M., M.P. Hayes, T. R. Curry, J. S Marsten, and K. R. Young. 2008. Predation on the Coastal-tailed Frog (*Ascaphus truei*) by a Shrew (*Sorex* spp.) in Washington State. *Northwestern Naturalist*, 89:200–202.

Schmidt, R. H. "Shrews." in *Prevention and Control of Wildlife Damage*. Editors, S. E. Hygnstrom, R. M. Timm, G. E. Larson. 1994. University of Nebraska-Lincoln. 2 vols.

Schwartz, C. and E. Schwartz. 1981. *The Wild Mammals of Missouri*. University of Missouri Press and Missouri Department of Conservation.

Starlings *(Sturnus vulgaris)*

Biology

Size: Average weight is 3.2 oz (90 g). Length averages 6 in (15.24 cm) and has a 16 in (41 cm) wingspan.

Diet: Insects, fruit seeds, and grains. A 3 oz. (85 g) bird can eat 2.2 lbs (1 kg) of feed in 30 days. Transition from grain to protein diet when young emerge.

Habitat: Trees, particularly those with good shade in summer, and lots of branches (winter). Avoid locust trees. Roost on structures.

Activity: Diurnal/year round. Will migrate to flee snow-covered feeding grounds in northern climates, travelling up to 1,700 km. In the Great Plains, generally stay put. Large flocks begin in mid-October (Nebraska). They are an aggressive and determined bird of the invasive species.

Procreation: Two broods per year (4 to 7 eggs/clutch). Eggs hatch in 2 weeks. In Nebraska, 1st fledge mid-July, second mid-August. Incubation is 11 to 14 days and young leave in 21 to 28 days. Both parents assist in rearing young. Bills are yellow January to June (during reproduction).

Nests tend to fill the cavity (Fig. 1). When nesting in attics, they seem to continue to drop grasses in an attempt to fill the "hole." I removed 1 nest that filled a 28 gallon (106 ltrs) trash bag (Fig. 2).

Capabilities: Outstanding fliers. Fly fast and in straight line not up and down like other birds. Can fly 15 to 30 miles/day (24 to 48 km) from roosting to feeding. Able to use beak to pry open holes in soil. Will fly regular routes to and from feeding sites. Starlings may gather in pre-roosting sites before finally reaching the final roost site before nightfall.

Fig. 2. They have a tendency to create large piles of grass for nesting in attics.

Symptoms

Few will be mentioned. You may hear of the client complaining of mites. One lady kept complaining about a thumping sound under her floor. She was elderly and I thought a little crazy. Upon investigating the crawl space under the house, I saw a starling bang the floor trying to get out. Just goes to show you to beware of prejudging your client.

Signs

Avg. Hole Size: Crevice dwellers (like to live in holes and cavities; 6 to 60 ft (1.8 to 18 m) above ground) similar to house sparrow but require a 1.5 in (3.8 cm) opening.

Damage to Structures: Starlings nest in vents and other cavities and deface buildings with excrement (Fig. 3). I have encountered them in basements where they fell down the furnace flue (Fig. 4).

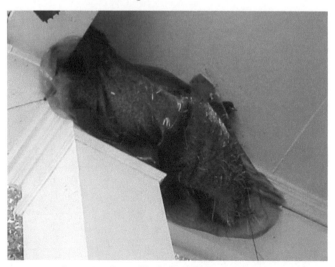

Fig. 1. Starlings filled this netting with grass.

Fig. 3. Starlings like to live in vents.

Fig. 4. Starlings hovering around a chimney to obtain warmth.

Fig. 5b. Excrement covered walk due to starlings roosting in trees overnight.

Fig. 5a. Roosts can range in size.

Damage to Lawn/Garden: Will eat fruit and corn (See Chapter 7). Can damage turf looking for insects, look for tufts of grass that have been pulled up during feeding and the resulting small holes. Their droppings below roosting areas can be extreme as roosts can reach tens of thousands of birds (Figs. 5a, 5b).

Starlings also feed on trash (Fig. 5c).

Damage to Pets & Livestock: Starlings consume and contaminate feed. They also compete with native bird species.

Tracks: 1 $^{13}/_{16}$ to 2.12 in (4.6 to 5.4 cm) in length and $^7/_8$ to 1.12 in (2.2 to 2.8 cm) in width (Fig. 6).

Scat: Can vary in color depending on diet (Fig. 7).

Feathers: Primaries gray to black. During winter, secondaries will have brown tips.

Sounds: Eeu, vibrato. Can mimic the calls of other birds.

Bite Marks: N/A.

Associated Animals: Compete with native bird species.

Fig. 5c. Excrement of starlings that fed in this open dumpster.

Health/Safety

Starlings have been implicated in several diseases including encephalitis, ornithosis, and hog cholera.

Histoplasmosis: Histoplasmosis is caused by exposure (typically through respiration) to fungal spores that are growing in the nitrogen rich droppings deposited by pigeons. It is essential that proper respiratory and vision protection be worn during inspections attic inspections.

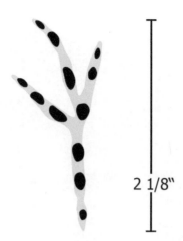

2 1/8"

Fig. 6. Starling track. Image by Dee Ebbeka.

Fig. 7. Droppings can appear brown when they are eating berries. Chapstick container used for scale.

Resources

Depenbusch, B. E., J. S. Drouillard, and C. D. Lee. 2011. Feed Depredation by European Starlings in a Kansas Feedlot. *Human-Wildlife Interactions* 5:1(Spring):58-65.

Elbroch, M. 2001. *Bird Tracks & Sign: A Guide to North American Species.* Mechanicsburg, PA: Stackpole Books.

Garrett, U. of Wildlife Services-Nebraska. Lecture.

Johnson, R. J., and J. F. Glahn. "Starlings." in *Prevention and Control of Wildlife Damage.* Editors, S. E. Hygnstrom, R. M. Timm, G. E. Larson. 1994. University of Nebraska-Lincoln. 2 vols.

Link, R. 2004. *Living with Wildlife in the Pacific Northwest.* Seattle, WA: Univ. of Washington Press.

McNeely, S. 2011. Vertebrate Pests in *Handbook of Pest Control: The Behavior, Life History, and Control of Household Pests* edited by A. Mallis et al. Mallis Handbook, LLC. 1119-1189 pp.

Sibley, D. A. 2000. *The Sibley Guide to Birds.* NY, NY: Alfred A. Knopf.

USGS Patuxent Wildlife Research Center. nd. European starling *Sturnus vulgaris.* http://www.mbr-pwrc.usgs.gov/Infocenter/i4930id.html, accessed 12/30/2011.

Wegner, G. 2008. European Starling. *Pest Management Professional,* (Aug):76.

Striped Skunks *(Mephitis mephitis)*

Biology

Size: 2.5 to 11.5 lbs (1.1 to 5.2 kg) and are 20 to 30 in (51 to 76 cm) in total length (body + tail) with a 7 to 15 in (177 to 381 mm) tail. Males are heavier than females.

Diet: Like raccoons, they are true omnivores. They will eat almost anything they can get in their mouth, but consume a great number of insects and other invertebrates, birds, and bird eggs. They are known to love grubs. They also will eat bird seed.

Habitat: They like to live along the edges of forests/fields near water. They particularly favor snags. They have adapted very well to suburban environments. Structures with enclosed spaces (e.g. enclosed decks, ground-level crawl spaces) are highly preferred for dens. Height of enclosed space is typically ≥ 3.94 in (10 cm).

Activity: Nocturnal/will den up when ground is frozen and can remain in a state of torpor for several weeks. Male activity continues till temperatures drop to 15°F (-9°C).

Procreation: Mating occurs between February and March with young being born 62 to 75 days later (May to June) and wean in 2 months. Skunks are polygamous. Litter sizes vary from 2 to 10 young. In my experience, the range is typically 3 to 5 young. The father does not stay and assist in raising the young. Young hunt with mother at 2 months.

Capabilities: Not good climbers. Some researchers claim skunks can spray up to 15 ft (4.6 m). Typically, they spray within 10 ft (3 m) in my experience. Sacs contain ~ 1 oz (0.03 ltrs) of fluid about enough for 5 to 6 sprays. Can travel at speeds up to 8 mph (12.8 km/h).

Symptoms

Fewer things are more known than the skunk's odor. Typically clients will complain about the odor, and it is their distaste for the smell that motivates them to call you. Understand however, that the odor can linger for days. Also the discharge site may not even be on the property. These odors will normally occur during mating season (Jan to Feb) when the female sprays a male she doesn't wish to mate with and in June, when the young skunks begin practicing.

Signs

Avg. Hole Size: 3 to 5 in (7.6 to 12.7 cm) in diameter (Fig. 1). Skulls are 1.5 to 2 in (38 to 50 mm) in width. Juvenile skunks will make even smaller holes, often 1 to 2 in (2.5 to 5 cm) in size under a shed wall. Common for skunks to inhabit ground holes dug by woodchucks.

Access: Skunks don't enter houses that have full concrete foundations. Houses with stone foundation, dirt floor, crawl spaces are vulnerable to the skunk's digging ways. Generally, the skunk will have 1 entrance that can be identified by the half circle depression below the building's wall and the ground. Obviously, if the building's walls stop 3 in (7.6 cm) above the ground, you may not be able to find the entrance. However, skunks will usually enter and exit in the most remote or secluded part of the structure. Always look for hair that may have adhered to the wood. If it is black and white you have found skunk hair. 99 % of the time the skunk's entry will be at ground level. They don't climb. I did have one job where the skunk climbed into the attic and fell down to the first floor in the gap between the chimney and the surrounding wall. If I didn't see it with my own eyes, I wouldn't have believed it. As it turned out the owner had

Fig. 1. Typical skunk digout under a crawl space.

Fig. 2. Skunks can become trapped in window wells greater than 4 in (10 cm) in depth.

Fig. 3. Skunk digging in yard.

piled up a lot of mattresses etc. in the garage. The skunk simply climbed the debris and crawled into the attic along the trusses, through the breezeway and into the attic.

Skunks prefer to dig their dens in enclosed spaces such as under concrete steps (they are hollow), porches which have a solid skirting, under sheds and in piles of debris. For the most part, they won't live under a structure that is open enough for you to directly crawl in unhindered. If too much light can get to them, they won't feel safe enough to live there.

Damage to Structures: Skunks don't damage buildings structurally. They just change the smell of the place. If a homeowner, whose house has a full poured concrete basement, swears that a skunk has entered their basement, check to see if they have window wells. Chances are a skunk has fallen into it and can't get out (Fig. 2). You also may not always see the skunk. If they can, they will actually dig a den hole in the window well, thus allowing you only to see a hole. So look carefully. If a skunk is trapped inside a garage, look for damage to items up to 1 ft (30 cm) high on the wall. In crawl spaces they will shred insulation if they can reach it i.e. within 2 ft (61 cm).

Damage to Lawn/Garden: Skunks will eat grubs and raccoons do too. When skunks are grubbing, you will find precise holes in the turf. Skunks will grub a lawn very systematically, 1 section at a time. On 1 job the skunks were digging around the heads of an automatic sprinkler system. Holes can be distinguished from squirrel damage by timing. Skunk damage occurs in spring and fall (throughout the summer when lawns are watered). Squirrel damage tends to occur in fall and throughout winter.

The holes will be a few inches apart and 1 to 2 in (2.5 to 5 cm) in depth and up to 4 in (10 cm) across. Others say the holes are 3 to 4 in (7.6 to 10 cm) cone-shaped diggings (Fig. 3). Squirrels move soil to 1 side.

Will feed on corn but damage is limited to the lower ears.

Damage to Livestock & Pets: Eggs. Will eat eggs which are eaten where found. Frequently makes small opening and pushes nose inside. Messier scene as embryo matures.

Bee Hives. Will attack bee hives. Large amount of damage suggests bears.

They will feed on pet food (Fig. 4) and fallen bird seed when available.

Tracks: The front foot is 1.6 to 2 in (4.1 to 5.2 cm) in length and 1 to 1.18 in (2.5 to 3 cm). Rear foot is 1.25 to 2 in (3.3 to 5.1 cm) in length and 15/16 to 1.18 (2.4 to 3 cm) in width. Five toes on all feet.

Scat: For practical purposes this sign is pretty weak. Chances are you won't find any and if you do it will look very much like a cat's except for the content. (Fig. 6). Feces are a great sign of a skunk being trapped in a building. It will frequently contain insect exoskeleton.

Hair: Black and white.

Sounds: Squealing often signals fighting between females fighting males eager to mate. They also click teeth, hiss, and growl.

Bite Marks: Distance between upper canines is $7/16$ to ½ in (1.1 to 1.3 cm).

Associated Animals: Skunks have few predators. But great horned owls and coyotes will feed on them.

Fig. 4. Skunk enjoying cat food.

Fig. 5a,b. Left print is the front foot, right print is the rear foot. Images by Kim A. Cabrera of Beartracker's Animal Tracks Den.

Health/Safety

Rabies: Skunks are key vectors for rabies in the Plains states. Subject to spill over rabies infection in other parts of the U.S.

Toxoplasmosis: Skunks can carry Toxoplasma gondii.

Odor: At close range, victims can have difficulty breathing and be blinded temporarily. Remnants of odor can last for weeks, and "reappear" when humidity increases. Odor should continue to decline. If it spikes sharply, it suggests the skunk is dead and the sac has broken open or a new discharge.

Fig. 6. Skunk scat. Photo by Tom Olander.

Resources

Azevedo, F.C.C., W. Gorsuch, S. Larivière, A. J. Wirsing, and D. L. Murray. 2006. Dietary breadth and overlap among five sympatric prairie carnivores. *Journal of Zoology.* 269:1;pp. 127-135.

Baldwin, R. A., A. E. Houston, M. L. Kennedy, S. L. Pin. 2004. An Assessment of Microhabitat Variables and Capture Success of Striped Skunks (*Mephitis mephitis*). *Journal of Mammalogy.* 85:6(Dec):1068-1076.

Dubey, J. P., N. Sundar, C. A. Nolden, M. D. Samuel, G. V. Velmurugan, L. A. Bandini, O. C. H. Kwok, B. Bodenstein and C. Su. 2007. Characterization of *Toxoplasma gondii* from Raccoons (*Procyon lotor*), Coyotes (*Canis latrans*), and Striped Skunks (*Mephitis mephitis*) in Wisconsin Identified Several Atypical Genotypes. *Journal of Parasitology.* 93:6(Dec):1524-1527.

Dustin, K., T. A. Messmer, M. R. Conover, and L. D. Dotson. 2010. *Skunks.* Wildlife Damage Management Series. Utah State University Cooperative Extension. (Dec):1-5.

Elbroch, M. 2003. *Mammal Tracks and Sign: A Guide to North American Species.* Mechanicsburg, PA: Stackpole Books.

Harding, J. 1979. *An Animal Damage Identification Guide for Massachusetts.* Amherst, MA: Cooperative Extension Service, University of Massachusetts, SP-113.

Huxoll, C. M., T. A. Messmer, and M. Conover. 2010. *Raccoons.* Wildlife Damage Management Series. Utah State University Cooperative Extension. (Dec):1-5.

Knight, J. E. "Skunks." in *Prevention and Control of Wildlife Damage.* Editors, S. E. Hygnstrom, R. M. Timm, G. E. Larson. 1994. University of Nebraska-Lincoln. 2 vols.

Lariviere, S., L. R. Walton, and F. Messier. 1999. Selection by Striped Skunks (*Mephitis mephitis*) of Farmsteads and Buildings as Denning Sites. *American Midland Naturalist.* 142:1(Jul):96-101.

Selko, L. F. 1938. Notes on the Den Ecology of the Striped Skunk in Iowa. *American Midland Naturalist.* 20:2(Sep):455-463.

Schwartz, C. and E. Schwartz. 1981. *The Wild Mammals of Missouri.* University of Missouri Press and Missouri Department of Conservation.

Voles

(*Microtus* spp.)

Meadow vole *Microtus pennsylvanicus* **MV**
Prairie vole *Microtus ochrogaster* **PrV**
Pine vole *Microtus pinetorum* **PiV**
The following voles will be called Pacific Northwest voles **PNV**
 Creeping vole *Microtus oregoni,* Gray-tailed vole *Microtus canicaudus,*
 Motane vole *Microtus montanus,* Townsend meadow vole *Microtus townsendii*

Biology

Size: MV: 1-1.5 oz. (22 to 66 g); 4.75 in (93 to 137 mm) + tail 1.5 in (30 to 62 mm).

PrV: 0.9 to 1.9 oz (25 to 55 g); 3.9 to 5.2 in (100 to 131 mm) + 1.1 to 1.7 in (28 to 43 mm).

PiV: 0.7 to 1.3 oz.(20 to 37 g); 3.2 to 4.8 in (82 to 122 mm) + 0.6 to 1.1 in (16 to 28 mm) tail.

Pacific Northwest Voles: Creeping vole—0.46 to 1.2 oz (13 to 33 g); 3.2 to 4.25 in (80 to 108 mm) + 1 to 1.6 (26 to 41 mm) tail. Gray-tailed vole—0.9 to 1.8 oz (25 to 52 g); 3.7 to 4.6 in (95 to 117 mm) + 1.25 to 1.7 in (32 to 44 mm) tail. Montane vole—0.9 to 2.3 oz (25 to 65 g); 4.4 to 5.4 in (112 to 137 mm)+ 1.6 to 2.4 in (41 to 60 mm) tail. Townsend's vole—2 to 3.6 oz (57 to 103 g); 5 in (104 to 145 mm) + 2.5 in (45 to 72 mm) tail.

Diet: MV consumes 0.58 kcal/day/gram. **MV** will cache food in the middle of field under snow. Look for trails extending from it.

PiV: Vegetation, some vegetable crops (potatoes and carrots), nuts, seeds and the roots of perennials. Vegetation, nuts, seeds and the roots of perennials.

Habitat: MV: Widest range of all voles in U.S. Prefers dense vegetation.;

PiV: Woodlands and grasslands. Have been known to live in swamps and around rocks.

PNV: Nest sites under objects like rocks and logs. In snow areas, nests on ground under snow.

Activity: All Nocturnal/year-round (Fig. 1). **MV** and **PrV** will reduce digging of burrows in areas with low predation. **PiV** Most activity is below ground. Will store food underground in volumes up to 1 gallon (3.8 ltrs).

Procreation: MV 3 to 5 young/litter.

Population densities vary dramatically across habitats. Alfalfa population density peaked at 638 voles/ha. bluegrass habitat was 156 voles/ha and tall grass was only 92 voles/ha.

PiV Mating occurs from Feb to Nov. Usually females have only 1 litter of 2 to 4 young born 24 days after mating. Young leave in 3 weeks and can reproduce in 8 weeks.

PNV in lower elevations mate from early spring to late fall. Litter size 1 to 13 with a gestation of 21 days. Population densities can vary wildly.

Capabilities: Voles, like mice, can enter a home almost anywhere there is a gap. Look for gaps where pipes enter building. Cracks along the foundation are very important to look at as well. Don't forget to investigate the soffit line. Voles will climb bushes and climb onto roofs to enter buildings. (I have trapped them inside houses).

Symptoms

Owners will complain of damaged grass and dying plants.

Signs

Avg. Hole Size: PiV 1.5 to 2 in (3.8 to 5 cm) in diameter. Skull width is 0.6 to 0.7 in (14.9 to 16.6 mm). Often found at the base of trees or other perennials. Photos are illustrative of other vole holes (Figs. 2 to 5).

Damage to Structures: Like other rodents voles will disturb insulation and chew wires. It is rare for voles to be in homes, but it can happen. They can also share a home with mice.

Damage to Lawn/Garden: All: Voles gnaw through bark of small trees or shoots up to about ¼ in (0.6 cm) in diameter. Bark gnawing will be as high as snow cover (Fig. 6).

MV: Will clip, cut, and gnaw tree trunks and branches. Problem can be severe in orchards. Bark gnawing usually done in winter. They also create runways through the grass which are routes 1.5 to 2 in (3.8 to 5 cm) wide

Fig. 1. This hole in the snow may be mice or voles. But it illustrates what voles would do.

Fig. 2. There is a penny at the left side of the hole.

Fig. 4. Meadow vole by a structure.

cut through the ground down to soil level (Fig. 7). They also have been known to pile grass and stripped twigs in their runways.

PiV They will eat the roots of various bushes. Look for dying plants. You may even see a trail through the grass that emanates from their den hole (Fig. 8), but these tend to be narrower than **MV** at 1.50 in (3.8 cm) and centered near trees. They also can eat grass as can be seen in the Spring after the snow melts like other vole species (Fig. 9).

Fig. 5. Hole used by meadow vole.

Fig. 3. Trail to hole under bushes.

Fig. 6. Vole damage to the bark of a fruit tree. Photo by Applied Mammal Research Institute.

PrV Trails are 1.5 in (38 mm) wide. Old, well used trails will expand to 2 in (5 cm). Some species will dig just below soil surface in a manner that mimics mole digging. Entrances to subsurface tunnels may have adjacent mounds (3 to 4 in; 7.5 to 10 cm wide).

Fig. 7. Vole run leading to tall grass.

Fig. 8. Trail of pine vole.

Damage to Pets & Livestock: Voles do not pose any real harms to animals except feeding on food and possible contamination of food sources.

Tracks: MV Typically not found. Width between front feet is 1.25 in (3.2 cm). **PrV** Typically not found, although trails in grass can be found.

Scat: All infrequently found. **MV** Sometimes found in the runways. They are tubular like mice $1/16$ in (1.6 mm) wide and ¼ in (6 mm) long. One is end fatter and blunter than the other. **PNV** feces slightly larger than house mouse scat found at feeding areas.

Hair: Rarely found.

Sounds: High-pitched clicking, wing flapping, and sounds of scratching as they climb walls.

Bite Marks: Gnawing on the trunks and roots of trees is usually less uniform than that of other rodents. Tooth marks can be at various angles, including small branches. Marks can range from light scratches to channels $1/10$ inch (0.3 cm) wide, $1/12$ inch (0.2 cm) deep, and ½ inch (1.3 cm) long (Fig. 11).

MV Gnaw marks will be irregular patches on tree trunks (usually the base) above ground surface. May appear as light scratches or deeper grooves. $1/8$ in (3 mm)

wide and $1/16$ in (1.6 mm) or more deep and $3/8$ in (9 mm) long. Trees less than ¼-in (6 mm) in diameter may be cut in a manner that looks like a small beaver did it.

PiV Bark will be gnawed below ground surface. Marks will be at all angles $1/8$ in (3 mm) wide, $1/16$ in (1.6 mm) or more deep and $3/8$ in (9 mm) long.

PNV $1/8$ in (3 mm) scrapes in the wood at different angles.

Fig. 9. Vole damage to grass revealed after snow melt.

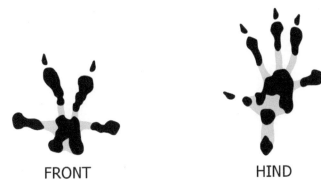

FRONT   HIND

Fig. 10. Tracks of the meadow vole. Image by Dee Ebbeka.

Fig. 11. Vole gnawing damage to plywood. Photo by Applied Mammal Research Institute.

Associated Animals: **MV** will exist in the same habitat with Prairie voles.

Health/Safety

Pneumocystis carinii: Cyst formations of the fungal parasite (*Pneumocystic carinii*) were found in some voles in southern California.

Resources

I would like to acknowledge that some information for this module was obtained from Gary Witmer.

Dolbeer, R. A., N. R. Holler, and D. W. Hawthorne. Identification and Assessment of Wildlife Damage: An Overview. *Prevention and Control of Wildlife Damage.* Editors, S. E. Hygnstrom, R. M. Timm, G. E. Larson. 1994. University of Nebraska-Lincoln. 2 vols.

Gates, J. E. and D. M. Gates. 1980. A Winter Food Cache of *Microtus pennsylvanicus. American Midland Naturalist.* 103:2 (April):407-408.

Getz, L. L., J. E. Hofmann, B. McGuire, and T. W. Dolan III. 2001. Twenty-Five Years of Population Fluctuations of *Microtus ochrogaster* and *M. pennsylvanicus* in Three Habitats in East-Central Illinois. *Journal of Mammalogy* 82(1) (Feb):22-34.

Harding, J. 1979. *An Animal Damage Identification Guide for Massachusetts.* Amherst, MA: Cooperative Extension Service, University of Massachusetts, SP-113.

Harper, S. J., and G. O. Batzli. 1996. Effects of Predators on Structure of the Burrows of Voles. *Journal of Mammalogy* 77(4)(Nov):1114-1121.

Krebs, C. J. 1977. Competition Between *Microtus pennsylvanicus* and *Microtus ochrogaster. American Midland Naturalist* 97:1(Jan):42-49.

Laakkonen, J., R.N. Fisher, and T. J. Case. 2001. Pneumocystosis in Wild Small Mammals from California. *Journal of Wildlife Diseases,* 37(2):408–412.

Link, R. 2004. *Living with Wildlife in the Pacific Northwest.* Seattle, WA: Univ. of Washington Press.

O'Brien, Jay O. "Voles." in *Prevention and Control of Wildlife Damage.* Editors, S. E. Hygnstrom, R. M. Timm, G. E. Larson. 1994. University of Nebraska-Lincoln. 2 vols.

Reid, F. A. 2006. *Mammals of North America.* Peterson Field Guides. 4th ed. NY, NY: Houghton Mifflin.

Smolen, M. J. 1981. *Microtus pinetorum. Mammalian Species,* No. 147(May 8):1-7.

White-Tailed Deer *(Odocoileus virginianus)*

Biology

Size: 100 to 200 lbs (45.4 to 90.7 kg). Height to shoulder 3 to 3.5 ft (90 to 105 cm). Males larger than females. Size increases with increasing latitude.

Diet: Herbivore browser (versus grazer). An adult male deer will eat 5 oz (143 g) of food per feeding (dry weight) and consume 2.2 to 3.1 lbs (1 to 1.4 kg) of food (dry weight) per day. Will eat corn, alfalfa, hay, pumpkins, apples, wheat (bearded and non-bearded), and a wide variety of ornamental plants.

Habitat: Forests broken by agricultural fields.

Activity: Crepuscular (early morning and late afternoon and evening)/year round. Males more active during the rut (Oct to Jan). Males may form bachelor groups, especially during spring and summer months. Groups break-up prior to pre-rut. Females will form matriarchal groups year round. Females group up during winter months and break up prior to parturition.

Procreation: Females give birth to 1 to 3 fawns (2 typical) during spring (May to June) 200 days after mating. Fawns lose spots at 5 months.

Fig. 1. White-tailed deer trail.

Capabilities: Capable of jumping over 6-ft (1.8 m)-high fences. Approximately 5% of all deer can jump 8-ft (2.4 m)-high fences but rarely do. Capable of horizontal leaps of 30 ft (9 m).

Symptoms

Clients will note extensive damage to their bushes. Illnesses such as Lyme disease and complaints of ticks may also be prevalent.

Signs

Avg. Hole Size: May crawl under fences with 1-ft (31 cm) gaps rather than jump them. Bedding areas consist of oblong-shaped flattened vegetation 3 to 4 ft (90 cm to 1.2 m) long and 2 to 3 ft (60-90 cm) wide. Deer hair almost always present. Beds of males usually larger than beds of females. When snow is present, deer often defecate in their beds or immediately adjacent to them.

Access: Check fences or look for trails (Fig. 1) to see where deer are entering the client's property. Trail width averages 5 to 5½ in (12.7 to 14 cm) width. Confirm through tracks, especially near fence crossings. When deer jump fences, they almost always take-off and land in the same spots. If the trail is heavily used, there will be damaged grass, exposed soil, etc., at the take-off and landing spots.

Damage to Structures: Typically don't damage buildings but have been known to crash through windows and enter open doors.

Damage to Lawn/Garden: Deer may damage gardens, row and agricultural crops (Fig. 2), and landscaping plants. Hungry deer will eat almost any vegetation to avoid starvation. For a list of plants damaged by deer visit (http://icwdm.org). Damage to woody plants through browsing starts at 2 ft (60 cm) and can be as high as 8 ft (2.4 m) when they stand on back legs to forage.

Trees/Shrubs. Tend to be damaged in the winter when other food sources become more limited. Browse branches up to ½-in (1.3 cm) in diameter (rarely thicker than 1 in (2.5 cm) in diameter.

Rubs. Bucks (typically dominant males >3.5 years old) may damage plants (Fig. 3) during the rut, when they rub the velvet off their antlers on plants at a high of about 4 ft (1.2 m). Rubbing occurs most intensely during velvet removal through mating season. Rubbing may start as early as September when bucks shed their velvet. While rubbing may facilitate the removal of velvet from antlers, rubbing is a territorial marking used to communicate with both males and females. Some research suggests that bucks select aromatic trees with smooth bark, less than 1 in (25 mm) in diameter and with the first branch about 3 ft (91 cm) above the ground. Damaged portion occurs between 1.5 to 3.5 ft (45 to 100 cm) on the tree. Others suggest typically in the 3 to 5 ft (91 to 152 cm) height region. Bark will appear shredded with some portions remaining on the tree. Smaller shavings and some larger pieces will be found on the ground around the tree.

Preferred rubbing trees vary by region: Ohio—green ash, plum, cherry, red maple (*Acer rubrum*), linden (*Tilia spp.*), and other small trees (0.6 to 1.0-inch (16 to 25 mm) diameter, about 6.0 in (15 cm) aboveground. Nebraska—black cherry, persimmon (*Diospyros virginiana*), Chinese chestnut, and butternut (*Juglans cinerea*). Georgia—hazel alder, eastern red cedar, loblolly pine (*Pinus taeda*), and sumac. The mean diameter of rubbed trees was about 1 in (25 mm).

Scraping. Though scraping has been observed in females before and during breeding season, typically done by bucks. Scrapes are 1 to 5 ft (30 to 150 cm) sections of ground torn up by the buck's hoofs and/or antlers. **Rub-urination** combining urine with secretions of the tarsal gland, often is associated with scraping behavior. Rub-urination is believed to communicate information about male condition and rank to both estrous females and other males.

Peeling. This refers to deer removing bark with their lower teeth. Motion is bottom to top with scrape narrowing at the top. Bark does not remain on the tree.

Damage to Pets & Livestock: Deer do not ordinarily cause physical harm to pets and livestock. Deer, however, do pose risks of disease transmission to pets (via ticks) and livestock (via diseases).

Tracks: Commonly found as deer are heavy enough to leave them unless ground very hard. Dew claws are usually only visible in soft substrates. Tracks (Fig. 4) typically

Fig. 2. Bean plant which bifurcated when its lead was snipped by a deer.

Fig. 3. Buck rub (right of walking stick).

Fig. 4. Deer track about 4 inches (10 cm) in length. Scale is in inches

2.5 in (6.4 cm) long for front feet and 3 in (7.6 cm) long for rear. Both males and females can leave dew claw marks. Also, it may be possible to determine sex and size of a deer by its tracks. Adult male tracks are usually larger and frequently have splayed toes.

Scat: Typically in piles scattered (Fig. 5a) where they walk. If you look closely at these round feces (pellet form), you will see a slight fold line and/or dimple in them. They tend to be black when fresh and lighten as they age. Research finds that deer may defecate about 25 times/day. They will defecate more in the winter and less in the summer. Rich or succulent foods will result in clumping of scat (Fig. 5b). Piles of lose scat average 4 to 6 in (10 to 15 cm) in diameter

Hair: Winter coat consists of hair with hollow shafts to aid in insulation and buoyancy in water.

Sounds: Generally quiet. Bawls when in distress. Snort when alarmed. Females grunt to signal young.

Bite Marks: Deer tear their food because they lack upper incisors. They have to break or rip off the twigs they consume, hence their browse sign (Fig. 6) is quite distinctive from that of rabbits, woodchucks, and animals with paired incisors.

Associated Animals: Deer are an important prey species for predators such as coyotes and mountain lions, and deer carrion is important for many scavenging species

Health/Safety

Vehicle Strikes: Deer strikes can bring physical harm to humans through motor vehicle accidents. Deer-vehicle collisions are difficult to estimate, but may exceed tens of thousands annually in areas with high deer and human densities.

Fig. 5a. Deer scat tends to be pelleted when eating fibrous foods (winter). Pellets tend to be < ½ in (1.27 cm) in length.

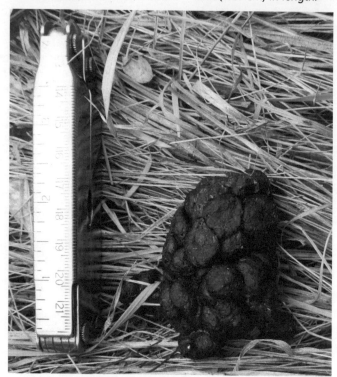

Fig. 5b. Deer scat clumps when eating moist foods.

Fig. 6. Left: stick browsed by a deer (note coarseness from ripping action). Right: stick cleanly snipped by a cottontail rabbit in classic 45°.

Ticks: Deer are also a significant host for ticks that can carry a variety of pathogens (e.g. Lyme disease) dangerous to humans.

Resources

I gratefully acknowledge the careful review provided by Aaron Hildreth and Tim Hiller. Some information in this module came from Dr. Jay Boulanger and M. Springer.

Craven, S.R. and S. E. Hygnstrom. "Deer." in *Prevention and Control of Wildlife Damage.* Editors, S. E. Hygnstrom, R. M. Timm, G. E. Larson. 1994. University of Nebraska-Lincoln. 2 vols.

Decker, D. J., G. R. Goff, J. W. Kelley, and P. D. Curtis. 1993. White-tailed deer: *Odocoileus virginianus.* New York's Wildlife Resources. Cornell University Extension. No. 7. 1-14.

Dolbeer, R. A., N. R. Holler, and D. W. Hawthorne. Identification and Assessment of Wildlife Damage: An Overview. *Prevention and Control of Wildlife Damage.* Editors, S. E. Hygnstrom, R. M. Timm, G. E. Larson. 1994. University of Nebraska-Lincoln. 2 vols.

Enature.com. Visited 10/1/2011.

Harding, J. 1979. *An Animal Damage Identification Guide for Massachusetts.* Amherst, MA: Cooperative Extension Service, University of Massachusetts, SP-113.

Hygnstrom, S.E., P. D. Skelton, S. J. Josiah, J. M. Gilsdorf, D. R. Virchow, J. A. Brandle, A. K. Jayaprakash, K. M. Eskridge, and K. C. VerCauteren. 2009. White-tailed Deer Browsing and Rubbing Preferences for Trees and Shrubs That Produce Non-timber Forest Products. *HortTechnology* 19:1(Jan-Mar):204-2011.

Link, R. 2004. *Living with Wildlife in the Pacific Northwest.* Seattle, WA: Univ. of Washington Press.

Sawyer, T.G., R. L. Marchinton, and W. Mac Lentz. 1990. Defecation rates of Female White-Tailed Deer in Georgia. *Wildlife Society Bulletin* 18:1(Spring):16-18.

Smith, W. P. 1991. *Odocoileus virginianus. Mammalian Species* No. 388, (Nov. 6):1-13.

Snyder, S.A. 1991. U.S. Federal Database.

VerCauteren, K. C., T. R. Vandeelen, M. J. Lavelle, and W. H. Hall. 2010. Assessment of Abilities of White-Tailed Deer to Jump Fences. *Journal of Wildlife Management* 74(6):1378-1381.

VerCauteren, K., M. J. Pipas, P. Peterson, and S. Beckerman. 2003. Stored-crop Loss Due to Deer Consumption. *Wildlife Society Bulletin* 31(2):578-582.

Verme, L. J., and D. E. Ulrey. 1984. Physiology and nutrition. Pages 91-118 in L. K. Halls, editor. *White-tailed deer ecology and management.* Stackpole Books, Harrisburg, PA.

Wisniewski, N. and V. Wisniewski. ND. How to Track Deer. E-how.com http://www.ehow.com/video_4417561_track-deer.html October 31, 2011.

Woodchucks   *(Marmota monax)*

Biology

Size: 6 to 10 lbs (2.7 to 4.5 kg) depending on sex and how much fat they have accumulated or lost. Length. 16.5 to 25 in (418-665 mm). (Fig. 1).

Diet: A variety of vegetation and grasses and will occasionally eat insects, such as June bugs, grasshoppers, and other creatures such as snails. In trees they will eat, leaves of hackberry (*Celtis occidentalis*), Norway maple (*Acer platanoides*), peach (*Prunus persica*) and red mulberry (*Morus rubra*). Among terrestrial plants, preferences include wild lettuce (*Lactuca scariola*), white clover (*Trifolium repens*), red clover (*T. pratense*), grasses (*Poa*), and sweet clover (*Melilotus alba*). Free water is sought only occasionally as their water needs are normally fulfilled by dew and water rich plants. Eating is heaviest in late spring and to summer. Feeding declines in late summer to hibernation.

Habitat: Hedgerows, inclines, watered gullies, human structures, and grassy areas. Den sites chosen with southern exposure and good drainage capable of holding form for tunnel construction.

Activity: Diurnal/True hibernators between Nov to Feb. Adults emerge from hibernation prior to yearlings and juveniles; males emerge prior to females. Emergence from hibernation tied to internal clock and external temperature. For south central Pennsylvania, emergence from hibernation is Jan 29 to Feb 13; in Maine emergence range is Feb 27 to Mar 12. Expect later dates for northern latitudes and earlier in southerly ones. Generally, woodchucks hibernate alone, but communal hibernation has been reported.

Procreation: Breeding occurs in early March to late April (depending on latitude) and 1 to 8 young are born (2 to 4 being typical) 32 days later. Young disperse in July. Females raise young alone.

Capabilities: Run up to 10 mph (16 Km/h). Can climb trees up to 12 ft (4 m) or more and swim. Excellent diggers.

Behavior: They build multiple burrows and move between them. Rarely travel more than ¼ to ½-mi (400 to 800 m) from burrow.

Symptoms

None; all will be sign. But don't forget that they can climb trees.

Signs

Avg. Hole Size: In the ground 10 in (25.4 cm; Fig. 2). Holes tend to be round whereas the holes of other animals can be oval. Size of skull at widest point 1.88 to 2.36 in (47 to 60 mm).

Access: Often they will dig along foundations, under sheds or under slabs. The main hole can be distin-

Fig. 1. Nebraska woodchuck.

Fig. 2. Woodchuck den under a trailer.

guished from skunk by the amount of soil plume on the outside (plume may be 4.5 ft (1.4 m) in diameter) as well as the larger diameter hole. Younger woodchucks will only dig 1 hole, but older woodchucks can have several hidden plunge holes that lack the dirt plume. Skunks will reuse an abandoned woodchuck den.

Damage to House: Typically, there will be none except for possible undermining of foundations and concrete prefab stairs. They have been known to chew through underground wires.

Damage to Lawn/Garden: Woodchucks can significantly impact vegetation within 16.4 ft (5 m) of their burrows.

Gardens. They will however, mow a garden like a lawnmower. The green beans (Fig. 3; plants in the photo were merely trimmed) in garden were so thoroughly ravaged that all the plants were evenly cut within 1 in (2.5 cm) of the ground. Look for trails between den and feeding areas (Fig. 4).

Plants known to be eaten by Woodchucks: *This plant information is by no means complete. It has been compiled by Wildlife Damage Control through contact with visitors to our web site,* http://icwdm.org. — Basil, Campanula persicifolia, Cilantro, Cosmos, Dahlias, Daisies (two reports), Echinacea, Egg Plant and Fruit, Hot Pepper plants but not fruit , Marigolds, Mums, Nasturtiums (one report said avoided one year ate the next) , Pansies, Parsley, Petunias (2 reports), Pumpkin vines, Queen Anne's Lace, Rosemary (laid on), Rudbekia fulgida, Strawberries, Violets, Zinnias.

Fig. 4. Woodchuck trail in grass.

Plants with Possible Resistance to Woodchucks: *We also want to warn readers that in times of desperation animals will eat food that they would otherwise wish to avoid.* — Bronze Fennel, Daffodils, Daylillies (2 reports that this plant is avoided), Dianthus (2 reports that this plant is avoided), Heather, Horehound, Lamb's Ear, Lemon Balm, Pumpkins, Squash, Sedum, Thymes.

Crops and Fruits. Alfalfa is preferred 10× more than grass. Will eat leaves of buckwheat sprouts. Will dine on the grains of oats and wheat. Corn usually eaten during milk phase. Ear is removed, partially eaten and stalk is trampled.

Trees. Woodchucks occasionally gnaw tree bark (Fig. 5).

Fig. 3. Beans clipped by a woodchuck.

Fig. 5. Woodchuck marking on an apple tree. Photo by Kevin Swihart of Purdue University.

length and 1 to 2.12 (2.5 to 5.4 cm) in width. Hind foot is 1.6 to 3.12 in (4.1 to 7.9 cm) in length and 1.36 to 2 in (3.5 to 5.1 cm) in width. The rear foot often oversteps and obscures the front. Only 4 toes versus raccoon's 5 (Figs. 6a,b). Trails avg 4 to 6 in (10 to 15 cm) in width.

Scat: Often not found as woodchucks bury them at the entrance or in cavities in their den. A better clue for discovering if a den hole is active is the presence of flies at the entrance.

Hair: Hair is grizzled gray in coloration. Rarely found.

Sounds: Whistle alarm call. Fear and/or anger is displayed by tooth chattering created by the grinding of cheek teeth. May emit muffled barks during handling. Squeals or growls can occur during fighting.

Bite Marks: Typical of rodent markings. Fruit trees are damaged by woodchuck scent marking (gnawing on main stem) and burrowing. Scent marking damage most common in the Spring. Toothmarks on bark not usually clear. Tooth mark size will approximate that of rabbit.

Associated Animals: One Connecticut-based study found that meadow voles (*Microtus pennsylvanicus*) and white-footed mice (*Peromyscus leucopus*) used areas within 6.6 ft (2 m) of woodchuck and theorized that burrows attract these species and the crop damage they cause. Craig Lewis (2007) stated he has seen a raccoon and woodchuck share a den.

Fig. 6a, b. (Left) Front track of woodchuck. (Right) Rear track of woodchuck. Images by Kim A. Cabrera of Beartracker's Animal Tracks Den.

Health/Safety

Attacks: Rare. Woodchucks will flee when given the opportunity. Bluff charges can occur.

Undermining Foundations: Woodchucks can dig to a depth of 6.6 ft (2 m) in sandy soil (less in gravely soil). Tunnels can range in length from 39 in to 42.7 ft (1 to 13+ m) and typically parallel the surface.

Rabies: Woodchucks have been known to contract rabies.

Hepatitis: Hepatitis virus common among mid-Atlantic woodchucks.

Ectoparasites: Woodchucks can carry fleas and ticks capable of transmitting tularemia and Rocky Mountain spotted fever respectively.

Resources

Thanks to Craig Lewis for the information he provided.

Bollengier, R. M. Jr. "Woodchucks." in *Prevention and Control of Wildlife Damage*. Editors, S. E. Hygnstrom, R. M. Timm, G. E. Larson. 1994. University of Nebraska-Lincoln. 2 vols.

Davis, D. E. 1977. Role of Ambient Temperature in Emergence of Woodchucks (*Marmota monax*) from Hibernation. *American Midland Naturalist*. 97:1(Jan):224-229.

Elbroch, M. 2003. *Mammal Tracks & Sign: A Guide to North American Species*. Mechanicsburg, PA: Stackpole Books.

Harding, J. 1979. *An Animal Damage Identification Guide for Massachusetts*. Amherst, MA: Cooperative Extension Service, University of Massachusetts, SP-113.

Kwiecinski, G. G. 1998. *Marmota monax. Mammalian Species*, No. 591, (Dec. 4):1-8.

Maher, C. R. 2006. Social Organization in Woodchucks (*Marmota monax*) and its Relationship to Growing Season. *Ethology*. 112:4(Apr):313-324.

McCarty, S. L., W. J. Fleming, D. J. Decker, and J. W. Kelley. 1987. Woodchuck: *Marmota monax*. New York's Wildlife Resources. Cornell University Extension. No. 13. 1-12.

Schwartz, C. and E. Schwartz. 1981. *The Wild Mammals of Missouri*. University of Missouri Press and Missouri Department of Conservation.

Swihart, R. K. 1991. Influence of *Marmota monax* on Vegetation in Hayfields. *Journal of Mammalogy*. 72:4(Nov):791-795.

Swihart, R. K. 1991. Modifying Scent-Marking Behavior to Reduce Woodchuck Damage to Fruit Trees. *Ecological Applications*. 1:1(Feb):98-103.

Swihart, R. K. and P. M. Picone. 1995. Use of Woodchuck Burrows by Small Mammals in Agricultural Habitats. *American Midland Naturalist*. 133:2(Apr):360-363.